Men, masculinities
and social welfare

UCL
PRESS

© Keith Pringle 1995

First published in 1995 by UCL Press

UCL Press Limited
University College London
Gower Street
London WC1E 6BT

The name of University College London (UCL) is a registered
trade mark used by UCL Press with the consent of the owner.

ISBNs:
1-85728-401-1 HB
1-85728-402-X PB

British Library Cataloguing-in-Publication Data
A CIP catalogue record for this book is available from the British Library.

Library of Congress Cataloging-in-Publication Data
Pringle, Keith, 1952–
    Men, masculinities and social welfare / Keith Pringle.
        p.   cm.
    Includes bibliographical references (p.   ) and index.
    ISBN 1-85728-401-1. — ISBN 1-85728-402-X (pbk.)
    1. Men.   2. Masculinity (Psychology)   3. Human services.   4. Men—
Psychology.   I. Title.
IN PROCESS
305.32—dc20   95-9566
                                                                      CIP

Typeset in Palatino.
Printed and bound by
Biddles Ltd., Guildford and King's Lynn, England.

To my mother and father

Contents

Preface

This study deliberately focuses on men who are welfare workers and men who are service users because they have remained shadowy figures in previous welfare literature.

It is not designed to be a handbook of practice for welfare workers who are men. Many issues need to be debated, many questions need to be asked about both men and welfare before anyone is in a position to write such a handbook on this subject.

However, the alternative is not inaction. We can act and seek to find our way at the same time. Consequently, my aim is to examine critically the concept of masculinities and the nature of social welfare services. From that critical analysis I hope I provide a framework within which men who are welfare workers and men who are service users can seek to challenge and transform the relations of power that structure forms of oppression inside and outside social welfare organizations. In this project, such men have both a particular responsibility and a particular role to play. For the power relations referred to above are associated with the ascendancy of certain forms of masculinity.

This study tries to provide a preliminary map of the different levels of activity at which men may seek to engage with that project of challenge and transformation. The levels extend from, at one end, each of us working to develop the range of our own masculinities to, at the other end, seeking societal change. We men who are involved with welfare, as workers or users or both, can and must collectively engage at those two levels and all points in between. We must do this, first of all, for the sake of people who are oppressed: children, women, men. We must also do it for our own sakes.

Acknowledgements

Many people have helped me to think through these issues over the years. For those I do not mention specifically I say thanks to you now.

Of those I do mention, I would like to acknowledge my colleagues at the University of Sunderland for assisting me to take time out for a research secondment, part of which was spent on this book. I have also been grateful to Justin Vaughan at UCL Press for staying with the project through various difficulties and for his guidance; also to Sheila Knight for her tolerance.

I have benefited greatly from conversations with Mark Liddle, Patrick Price, Trefor Lloyd, Malcolm Holt and June Turnbull in the United Kingdom; with Margareta Bäck-Wiklund and Sven-Axel Månsson from Sweden; and with Petra Gieseke and Elke Joennsen from Germany.

To the members of People Against Child Sexual Abuse (PACSA), I am so grateful for what they have taught me, and are still teaching me. Several friends are owed a lot: Marietta, Sharon, Diane, Marjorie, Douglas, Malcolm, Loura, Shahida, Jeanette, Dave and Berni. Of the humans, the people to whom I owe the most in relation to this book are those friends with whom I have travelled at different times in confronting the violences of men: Barbara, Edna, Liz and Shelagh. Of the non-humans, thanks to Daisy and Tigger who kept me company through many late nights and shared their love unconditionally.

Naturally, I alone bear responsibility for what is written in the pages that follow.

While this book was in production, I learnt about the tragic death of Franki Raffles, who played a central role in Edinburgh's Zero Tolerance Campaign. I will not be alone in remembering her energy, creativity, determination, sensitivity and warmth of personality.

Chapter 1
Men talking about masculinities

Introduction

The aim of this study is to consider the situation of men in the field of social welfare: men who work there and men who use the services it provides. My approach is explicitly anti-sexist and anti-oppressive. I hope this study will make a contribution to the process by which men can seek to work together to counter oppressions associated with dominant forms of masculinity as well as to develop ways by which men can express themselves and relate to other human beings more creatively.

My main geographical focus is on the United Kingdom, although many of the debates are common to what we might term the Western societies and some of the evidence we shall use comes from outside this country, and in particular from the United States.

Thematically, my focus is on "social welfare", which is admittedly a rather amorphous concept. By social welfare I refer to those systems of service provision whose ostensible aim is to promote social wellbeing and alleviate social distress. In practice that means statutory and voluntary agencies in fields such as social services/social work, health, community work, youth work, education, housing, social security, employment. Some of these fields are, of course, more central to issues of social welfare than others and therefore warrant more attention. However, they all feature at some point in this study as do agencies in other fields that can impinge on the social welfare of human beings such as the law and the police. It is my contention that men need to forge alliances across the welfare worker/service user divide, as well as within those categories, if their anti-oppressive activities in social welfare are to be successful. However, such alliances have limitations placed upon them

1

by the overarching nature of patriarchal relations and other forms of domination in which they must be forged.

Power and domination enter into all issues relating to being a man in our society and that includes the situation of a man writing about men and masculinities. So before we try to clarify the situation of men and social welfare, we first need to clarify some questions about the practice of this enterprise itself.

Praxis and the process of men writing about men

In recent years, there has been something of an explosion within Britain and the United States in the production of sociological texts by men writing about masculinity. Most of these studies have a strongly theoretical and methodological flavour. Relatively few of the academic publications by men have focused primarily on empirical or practice-oriented issues. This is certainly true, as we shall see, in the area of social welfare.

There are undoubtedly good reasons for this concentration on issues of methodology and of theory, and I certainly am not disparaging such efforts. For a start, as Hearn suggests (1992), "the very separation of the personal, the political, and the theoretical in malestream discourse is questionable". Moreover, many of these theoretical studies have challenged the gendered character of the "scientific outlook" prevalent in much other sociological enquiry (Morgan 1992). Anyway, given the relatively early stage of anti-sexist studies by men (compared to the longer tradition of feminist women writers), it has clearly been important to chart the conceptual maps by which such studies by men can be developed in the future.

However, it is also possible that the emphasis on theoretical and methodological considerations may betray an over-concentration on issues that are relatively abstract and "safe" in emotional terms: a potential emphasis on the theoretical at the expense of the political and the personal. Seidler (1991, 1994) has surveyed the connections between dominant forms of masculinity, rationalism, and Enlightenment traditions. It would, perhaps, be naïve to assume that men engaged in struggling against sexism (and writing about this struggle) have necessarily escaped that heritage. It is emotionally easier to deal with concepts than feelings.

Like all Western men seeking to counter sexism in their writing, I am drawing massively on the work and insights developed over decades and generations by women, some of whom would call themselves feminist and others would not. This indebtedness on the part of men writers and

2

practitioners extends to all aspects of the study of sexism. An example is already at hand in the topics I have mentioned so far: the challenges to malestream methodological discourse in social science research and the development of the concept of praxis have a considerable feminist history (Roberts 1981, Stanley & Wise 1983, Stanley 1990).

As a man struggling to write effectively in this area of study, I have to say that I admire the way so many feminist women commentators seamlessly combine the personal, the political and the theoretical in their academic output. Recently, some male academic commentators on sexism have attempted to introduce a more personal approach into their writing: for instance Middleton (1992), Morgan (1992), Christian (1994), Edwards (1994).

This is a very encouraging development, given that it seems to reflect a growing congruence between process and content. However, to myself, some of these attempts seem rather forced, almost as though the writer knows he ought to introduce more of the personal into his work but feels ill at ease about it. I am not suggesting that men writers cannot successfully match process with content. For instance, Jeff Hearn (1992) has written both movingly and effectively about one of the most uncomfortable facets of men's oppressive power, men's sexualities and men's violences. I am merely suggesting that it does seem hard for some writers who are men to manage the combination successfully; and that this is also a problem I face here.

This is a crucial issue and certainly not one of simply stylistic or superficial merit. As Hearn suggests (1992), "the personal is political is theoretical". However, Morgan (1992) is also right to stress that pursuing this dictum can be problematic: a careful balance has to be struck between the personal and the political so that one of them does not take undue precedence at the expense of the other. As he notes, both personal "confessions" and structural "alibis" constructed by men can obscure the true sources of gender oppression.

Because at the moment I myself find it difficult to weave very personal and autobiographical material into the political and theoretical, I have decided on the whole not to do so in this book: it would not convince me and so probably it would not convince anyone else. What I want to stress is that my difficulty here has much (but perhaps not all) to do with the way I have learnt to behave as a man. Perhaps in time I will be able to weave the personal, the political and the theoretical together more authentically than I can at the moment.

Let us now consider issues that are related to the personal, the political and the theoretical.

3

The personal

What I have said above does not mean that the personal bears no relation to this study. Far from it. The personal does overtly surface from time to time and where it feels authentic and useful to what I am saying I have retained it. Moreover, the personal may be largely silent here but its presence is constant. My personal experiences of being a man have informed my political awareness of the importance of masculinities in the shaping of our world; and of course my political awareness has gone on to inform my personal experiences.

Many of those experiences have occurred in the world of social welfare: I grew up in a family where my father was a social worker; I was a social worker for thirteen years myself; I have taught social work for four; I still practise a sort of social work.

The political

In terms of the political, my approach to social welfare draws very heavily on a model that regards oppression and ways of countering it as being the core of practice: anti-oppressive practice (AOP). The literature describing this model is now extensive: Thompson (1993) and Ahmad (1990) provide useful summaries. Social welfare systems often claim that their main objective is the relief of social distress. One of the major tenets of an AOP approach is a recognition that in fact those systems often reinforce social oppressions and the distress that flows from them. AOP seeks strategies whereby social welfare agencies can in reality address and challenge social oppressions. I should add that it is a model that now seems to be strongly challenged in Britain by current government policies; and by the government's intentions for the future of social welfare (Langan 1992, Clarke 1993).

The social oppressions that social welfare systems often claim they are seeking to counter include sexism. However, power differentials in Western societies operate along many other axes of which "race", class, sexual identity, age and disability are the most important (Thompson 1993). In terms of social welfare as a whole it would be oppressive to privilege any single one of these over the others. Moreover, it would actually be an impossibility since they constantly interact with, cut across, and compound one another in complex and contradictory ways (Ahmed 1994, Hudson et al. 1994). Not the least of these interactions is that which occurs around the concept of "masculinity" itself.

4

The limitations of many approaches that have been used in the past to understand the issues of gender and masculinity are already very well documented and rehearsed in the literature (Connell 1987, Clatterbaugh 1990, Segal 1990, Cornwall & Lindisfarne 1994): biological, evolutionary, psychoanalytic perspectives, sex-role and socialization theories. None of these approaches are able to account for the massive diversity of masculinities and femininities that occur across time and space. In line with the critiques cited above, our analysis is based on a perspective that clearly identifies gender as a social construction. The approach adopted here builds, like that of other pro-feminist commentators such as Hearn & Morgan, on the model of gender and power suggested by Connell (1987, 1995) who envisages a complex and dynamic construction of multiple masculinities and femininities contingent on a wide range of variables and dimensions of power. He draws upon a broad spectrum of sources to explain those complex processes of social construction, including: feminist perspectives, gay theory, the sociology of knowledge, discourse perspectives, classical and existential schools of psychoanalytic theory.

This seems an appropriate juncture at which to note the interdependence of the political and the theoretical. Consequently, we now move our focus slightly in the next section towards the theoretical.

The theoretical

As Morgan notes (1992) it is not simply a question of there being a "black masculinity" or a "gay masculinity"; for terms such as these can themselves mask a diversity of realities. He argues (as do Hearn & Collinson 1994) for a recognition of the power relationship between men as well as between men and women, a hierarchy of diverse masculinities, in line with Connell's concept of "hegemonic masculinities", "subordinate masculinities" and "marginalized masculinities" (Connell 1987, 1995). Thus, at any one time in any one place, numerous forms of masculinity will be contesting and interacting with one another:

> Rarely, if ever, will there be only one hegemonic masculinity operating in any one cultural setting. Rather, in different contexts, different hegemonic masculinities are imposed by emphasizing certain attributes, such as physical prowess or emotionality, over others. And, of course, different hegemonic masculinities produce different subordinate variants: as we know from the

feminist concern with women's "invisibility", powerlessness in one arena does not preclude having considerable influence elsewhere. (Cornwall & Lindisfarne 1994).

Some commentators (for instance Cornwall & Lindisfarne 1994) have further developed the "dislocation" of masculinity, drawing upon sources within anthropology. In particular they emphasize that not only is gender without essence but that "biology itself is a cultural construction and that the link between a sexed body and a gendered individual is not necessary but contingent".

Like Morgan (1992), I am torn between the need to acknowledge this plurality on the one hand and, on the other hand a concern lest it should distract us from getting to grips with what is a real and massive problem: namely the oppressions exercised by men. Morgan seems to strike the right balance on this matter:

> But overall I feel that the only fruitful line of development lies in the recognition of complexity and diversity while also recognizing that these complexities are variations on a deeply entrenched theme. (Morgan 1992)

Let me be clear about the ultimately practical goals of this study in relation to the field of social welfare: to advance the formulation of an agenda for men in developing creative social action to counter oppression; to do this for men who work in that field and for men who use the services of social welfare.

What is encouraging is that the theoretical perspective adopted by commentators such as Morgan and myself, emphasizing as it does the importance of contingency rather than fixity in the construction of masculinities, lends itself to an approach seeking real social change. As Cornwall & Lindisfarne (1994) note,

> Individuals embody many different subjectivities. Though hegemonic discourses of masculinity may suppress, they never totally censor contradictory subjectivities. In focusing on the subordinate variants of hegemonic masculinities, we challenge the authority of hegemonic formations.

In this passage, the influence of poststructuralist theorists such as Michel Foucault is obvious. In Chapter 7 we shall see that feminist reworkings of Foucault's approach to issues of power offer the prospect of creating change in apparently monolithic power structures, such as welfare agencies. We shall also find that the processes alluded to by Cornwall & Lindisfarne (1994) have relevance to other ways in which men can challenge forms of oppression associated with hegemonic masculinities.

One valuable source upon which I will draw are men who commentate upon masculinities using critical sociological perspectives such as those described above. A few of these commentators have applied these fruitful theoretical approaches to the specific field of social welfare. For instance, I have already made mention of Jeff Hearn's work on men's sexualities and their violences (Hearn 1992). Perhaps even more valuable in terms of social welfare practice has been his contribution on child abuse and men's violence (Hearn 1990). In this study I want to extend such critical approaches throughout the field of social welfare.

One of the contentions of this study is that to understand the processes by which men's violences are generated it is necessary to consider the nature not simply of masculinities in general, but specifically of heterosexual masculinities.

In particular we need to examine the way the latter are referenced by, and formed in reaction to, homosexual desire (Carrigan et al. 1985, Hearn in Hearn & Parkin 1987, Hearn 1992). Thus, the relationship of heterosexual and homosexual masculinities to the normative concept of hegemonic masculinity and the insights of gay theory regarding this process are another focus of our attention (Blatchford 1981, Plummer 1981, Carrigan et al. 1985, Metcalfe & Humphries 1985, Weeks 1985, 1989, Herek 1987, Edwards 1990, 1994, Humphries 1992, Connell 1995).

In this context, we may consider the processes by which hegemonic formations can be challenged, noted by Cornwall & Lindisfarne above. It may be that men involved with social welfare agencies can seek in their work with other men to bring into focus forms of heterosexual masculinity less aligned with hegemonic variants and characterized by qualities such as emotional openness, caring, a willingness to be dependent, nonviolent. Outside the field of social welfare, some commentators (for instance Christian 1994, Connell 1995) have begun empirical explorations of how such challenge of hegemonic forms may develop. In this study we sketch out how similar explorations may be initiated in the context of social welfare.

Perhaps the richest source of direct material is to be found in the work of feminist women writers. For the explicit study of men by women has a long history: it is the study of men by men that has a much shorter history. As Jalna Hanmer says (1990): "The Women's Liberation Movement began with a critique of men."

Moreover, there is a very extensive literature by feminist women writers devoted specifically to issues in social welfare. Much of it focuses primarily on the situation of women in social welfare but as David Morgan (1992) states: ". . . feminism is not, and never was, simply about women and their problems. Men, their thoughts and practices, are clearly implicated."

Given the amount and depth of this feminist analysis, is there any particular value in a man exploring issues that might just as well be explored by a woman? Why am I doing this? Those questions signpost a major debate that exists about the role of men in the project of interrogating masculinity and masculinities. It is a debate that we need to examine now before we can proceed any further since it calls into question the whole status of this study.

Why should a man write about men?

Many feminist commentators have questioned the status and existence of what has been called by some of its advocates "men's studies" (Brod 1987).

This debate has many aspects. For instance, Hanmer (1990) points out that one cannot simply regard "men's studies" (the study of masculinities) as the male equivalent of "women's studies" because the latter has always been far more than the "study of femininities". As we have already seen, feminism from the beginning offered a wide-ranging and in-depth critique of men and masculinities. Hanmer goes further and quite validly stresses that the Women's Movement has challenged the whole way that the world is understood and how it can be changed.

Concern has also been expressed about whether "men's studies" represents a "Johnny come lately" colonization by men of an academic growth area that had originally been discovered and then nurtured by women: men now see jobs, career advancement, and lucrative research grants as prizes to be had. In addition, there is also the possibility that (whether deliberately or not) the academic critique of masculinities by men might in a sense dilute and undermine the trenchant critiques that feminist writers have developed over the previous twenty-five years (Canaan & Griffin 1990, Hanmer 1990).

These criticisms have been particularly levelled against several American scholars. In Britain, both Jeff Hearn and David Morgan have tended to respond positively to the feminist critique. Along with feminist commentators, they have sought to find an alternative term to "men's studies", an alternative that will more appropriately define the role of men's critical engagement with the concept of masculinities. For instance, Canaan & Griffin (1990) suggest "anti-sexist perspectives". My own preference for a more suitable label would be the suggestion of Hearn (quoted in Morgan 1992): "the critique of men".

I share the suspicions of Canaan & Griffin (1990) and Hanmer (1990) regarding the colonizing tendencies of so-called "men's studies". A similar feminist critique has been applied to the situation where men professionals have colonized some "growth areas" in social welfare, not least the field of child sexual abuse (Armstrong 1991, Hudson 1992).

In the course of this study we will also encounter situations where men engaged in anti-sexist or anti-oppressive practice within the field of social welfare actually reinforce oppression. A similar phenomenon can occur in the academic study of gender and sexuality (Cornwall & Lindisfarne 1994).

I certainly question my own career and this enterprise in terms of the strictures of Canaan & Griffin (1990) and Hanmer (1990). Once again, I share David Morgan's self-doubts:

> There is another question lurking in the background, one that I have not asked directly yet partly because I am not sure whether I know the answer. This is simply, what can men say or write about men that has not already been said by women, or could not be said by them in the future? (Morgan 1992)

He puts forward several responses to these questions that go some way answering my doubts; but not all the way. For instance, he suggests that men can act as "ethnographic moles" (Morgan 1992), passing on information about subjects to which women do not have access such as all-men institutions, in which category he places common venues like work groups, drinking groups, toilets. He also says that men can open up facets of their more "inner" lives for examination.

While there is considerable truth in all this, I have some qualms about it. For instance, I acknowledge that Harry Christian's recent study about the making of anti-sexist men (Christian 1994) provides useful empirical data. It provides access to the way the men in his study interpreted their lives. On the other hand, in reading his study I was continually aware that I was hearing the voices of men defining the reality of the worlds around them. I have doubts about this approach when there is an absence of answering voices from the other people in those worlds, people whose perceptions of reality might be different. In the past those other voices, the voices of women and children, have traditionally been drowned out by the louder voices of men. In giving a voice to men, it is vital that we do not (perhaps inadvertently) once more drown out the voices of the former.

As we shall see in Chapter 4, studies in social welfare using a similar methodology of giving a voice to men, and men alone, can present the same problems. This is particularly the case when those men are drawn from some of the more dominant groups within society. Moreover, there are always potential problems about providing a critical approach to masculinity when a study is carried out by a man. I think Morgan acknowledges this difficulty when he warns (1992): ". . . men's attempts to study themselves must always, to some extent, be suspect since it is their power that feminism has challenged".

Morgan has another suggestion about what studies of men by men can uniquely contribute. He indicates (Morgan 1992) that men can explore power relations between men and then, in concert with feminist scholars, compare this material with what we know about the power relations between women and men. Once again, this seems a useful suggestion. I do wonder, however, whether there is any particular advantage in men (as opposed to women) studying the power relations between men. Given the problem of men studying themselves that we have already noted, it should be at least equally appropriate for women to carry out such studies – if, that is, feminist scholars feel that they want to devote their time and resources to this work.

My own rationale for what I do, and for what I am doing now, is drawn directly from Jalna Hanmer's summary of the situation:

> If men write self-serving apologia, do not recognize feminist scholarship, restrict their questions, use inadequate theoretical perspectives, try to split feminist academics and theory by accepting some and rejecting the rest, it will sharpen the critique of men and male class privilege. If occasionally research and writing on men contribute to our understanding of how men gain, maintain, and use power to subordinate women, then we have more positive material for women's studies and feminism. (Hanmer 1990)

It seems to me that men have a responsibility to counter the oppressions that are associated with forms of hegemonic masculinities. For, as Connell notes (1995), although many men in some respects may be disadvantaged by the operation of hegemonic masculinity, most men also benefit from the patterns of domination associated with it: through complicity with hegemonic masculinity, a great many men reap what he calls the patriarchal dividend. This study is a contribution to that project of resistance against complicity. We shall argue that there are a multitude of opportunities for men involved with social welfare to contribute to this resistance.

So my central motive is anti-oppressive. In the course of this anti-oppressive project, strategies by which men can develop for themselves more satisfying emotional lives will be suggested. Those strategies flow directly from men's attempts to challenge the oppressions perpetrated by men. However, while improvements in men's lives are to be welcomed, they are not my first priority. My first priority is to end those oppressions perpetuated by men or in the name of hegemonic masculinity.

Some commentators might not fully agree with my emphasis. For instance, there seems to be a difference between my position and the view of Seidler on the ultimate independence of what he calls "men's studies" from feminist agendas (Seidler 1994).

Of course, simply making a commitment to anti-oppressive practice, as I have done here, is no guarantee that I will maintain it in my writing. In this study we will see that, in men's social welfare practice with men, the possibility of collusion with oppression is always a serious threat and measures have to be taken to safeguard against it. In writing this, I also have to build in checks on what I am doing, even although safeguards will never be watertight.

There are some very simple strategies I can adopt to limit the risk of oppression in my writing. One is constantly to bear in mind the strictures of Hanmer (1990) and continually evaluate and re-evaluate what I am doing in the light of those strictures. Another strategy is to consult about this study with men who are genuinely trying to engage in anti-sexist and anti-oppressive practice and who I know from experience are not afraid to challenge my tendency to oppress. Finally, it is important for me to consult about the content of this book with women who adopt feminist perspectives and are willing to be consulted: women who I again know will not countenance oppression on my part.

Men and feminisms

At this point it is relevant to pick up on an important and valid topic mentioned above by Hanmer (1990), which often seems to be overlooked in critiques of men writing about masculinities. For she suggests that

11

men commentators sometimes seek to privilege specific parts of feminist agendas or to privilege one form of feminism over another.

While critical debate about different feminist perspectives is perfectly valid in men's writing, I have become aware of a sometimes rather uncritical dismissal of certain feminist approaches and I want to consider the reasons for this.

For instance, Seidler's rather negative approach to radical feminism sometimes appears to be based on an over-stereotypical representation of the "all men are rapists" kind (Seidler 1994). He feels that this allegedly radical feminist message often puts too much pressure on men in relationships with women. My concern about his approach here is twofold. First, it can lead to an analysis that may help some men avoid their responsibilities for the part they play in the breakdown of their relationships. Secondly, I do not believe his version of radical feminism does justice to either the sophistication or the insight of most writers who are influenced by that perspective, for instance Liz Kelly and her colleagues (Kelly 1987, 1988, 1991, 1992 , Kelly et al. 1991).

Seidler is not alone in his somewhat dismissive attitude towards some forms of feminism, particularly radical feminism. Another example is the recent work of Harry Christian (1994). He talks about "separatist feminists who see all men as undifferentiated enemies". He infers that some feminists are "radically anti-men" and believe that all men hate women. Christian never actually tells us who these alleged feminists are.

What follows is a quotation from Sheila Jeffreys (1990), a revolutionary feminist writer, discussing charges of essentialism against some American feminists including Andrea Dworkin and Mary Daly:

> It will be a surprise to anyone who has read the writings of these feminists that they believe in essential masculinity and femininity. In fact they constantly seek to understand the construction of gender and they desire the end of male supremacy. There would be little point in challenging male sexual violence if it was thought to be innate. The only point in challenging it is the belief that it can be changed.

More recently, Caroline Ramazanoglu and Janet Holland (1993) have mounted a similar defence of radical feminism, using the excellent radical feminist magazine *Trouble and Strife* as an example and commenting that "the force of the political logic of radical feminism has been to challenge essentialism in dominant ideas of sexuality . . . Many feminists have had to struggle against being labelled 'essentialist'."

It seems to me that all feminist perspectives have much to offer a project such as this. Moreover, all should be treated with due respect for their complexity and sophistication. A critical approach to the debates between them is valid and constructive and that is the approach I shall try to adopt.

AOP and hegemonic masculinities

I believe it is vital to be explicit about the fact that I am writing this study not only from a pro-feminist perspective but also within an anti-oppressive practice (AOP) framework. It is probably important that I should set AOP in context by briefly reviewing how it has developed and how it connects with a pro-feminist perspective.

As Mary Langan has recently reminded us (Langan 1993b), in Britain radical perspectives on social welfare that were well established in the literature of the 1970s tended to be almost exclusively class-focused. A broad anti-oppressive framework only began to develop much later and rather fitfully. By the end of the 1980s a considerable body of experience, theory and knowledge about gender relations had found its way into print, the product of assiduous efforts by feminist practitioners in the preceding years. Not surprisingly, this literature was almost all written by women who drew upon feminist approaches to social analysis (Hanmer & Statham 1988, Dominelli & McLeod 1989, Hallett 1989).

However, some useful contributions were already being made by a few men commentators committed to an anti-sexist and pro-feminist project, sometimes in collaboration with feminist writers (Hearn & Parkin 1987, Langan & Lee 1989, Hearn 1990). We can safely assume that this history tells us something about the structural resistances within the field of social welfare to addressing sexism.

Having said that, it has taken even longer for critical anti-racist perspectives to be recognized and given wider dissemination (Dominelli 1988, Ahmad 1990, Ahmed 1994): as recent debates in the Central Council for Education and Training in Social Work demonstrate, it is still a major struggle for them to be heard. Moreover, critical studies in social welfare primarily focusing upon heterosexism are still few and far between (Brown 1992).

Only now, in fact, are we beginning to see critical texts in any number that incorporate a broad anti-oppressive approach to the nature of social welfare (Hugman 1991, Langan & Day 1992, Clarke 1993, Thompson 1993). This is vital because it is impossible to consider one form of

13

oppression in society without at least taking into account the mediating impact of the others.

The perspective that informs our approach to oppression in this study is that of Connell (1987, 1995) who goes beyond a simple categorical model. He posits a much more sophisticated process by which all forms of domination shift and slide in a dynamic process of structural formation and reformation. Both Connell and AOP address forms of oppression such as racism, heterosexism, ageism, disabilism, classism and sexism: as such they are compatible. For our study, Connell provides a suitably sophisticated analysis of oppression within which we can frame our anti-oppressive practice. This is the basis of the approach that we adopt in the chapters that follow.

Outline of this study

The outline of the study to a large extent flows from the issues reviewed in this chapter. In Chapter 2 we consider the way patterns of domination associated with hegemonic masculinity permeate the structures of social welfare agencies and the implications of this for the staff working there.

Chapters 3 through to 6 review the situation of social welfare service users in relation to those same patterns of domination that operate within both society as a whole and social welfare organizations. The areas considered in this review of service users are broad and deliberately cover a wide range of experiences. However, given the huge size of the field of social welfare, they are certainly not intended to be comprehensive: child protection; child care and the family; adult care and Care in the Community; adult violence. In these chapters a portrait is built up of how practice interacts with the lives of service users at the ground level. In view of our anti-oppressive perspective, it is clearly important to give due weight to such a portrait.

In Chapters 7 and 8 we bring these two pictures, of agencies and users, together in sharp focus by concentrating on what happens in a couple of specific welfare practice areas: woman abuse; child sexual abuse. These two have been chosen partly because they illustrate with particular clarity the operation of structures associated with hegemonic masculinity inside and outside welfare organizations. In addition, they are both areas of welfare practice where strategies to challenge those structures have already been developed extensively. This is crucial for our study because in these two chapters we draw out the major themes, issues and problems of men engaging in this practice.

14

In Chapter 9 we draw together the material from the two preceding chapters specifically, and from the study generally, to outline a framework for men working with men across the whole spectrum of social welfare.

Chapter 2
Masculinities and social welfare organizations

The discourse of social welfare in the 1990s

In this chapter, I want to begin to focus on what anti-oppressive practice tells us about the place of men who work in the field of social welfare. However, first we need to reconsider in the light of that practice one specific aspect of the current discourse about welfare: how the roles of people who work in social welfare agencies and those who use social welfare services are defined.

In a study such as this, it is reasonable to consider men who work in social welfare separately from those who are on the receiving end of social welfare services, because the structural situation of the two categories will in some respects be different. However, I do not mean to imply that there is a total lack of conjunction between the experiences of men in those two categories. On the contrary, I shall later seek to show that there are considerable parallels between them.

Nor am I suggesting that there is a rigid division between the two categories in terms of who actually occupies them. At any time in their lives many people working in the field of social welfare may need, or be forced to have, services themselves. Moreover, the identity of each welfare worker (like anyone else) can be seen as a combination of shifting and overlapping identities, drawn from all our past and current life experiences. For instance, given the high levels of child sexual abuse in our society, it is inevitable that many welfare workers will themselves have been abused (Glaser & Frosh 1993); and as we will see later, we can also assume that a number of welfare workers will have been, and may well still be, abusers (Pringle 1993b). Certainly, few workers will have had wholly untroubled personal lives. Two thoughtful reflections on this issue have been provided by Shelagh Scott (1993) and Pat Cox (1993).

If we are going to study the two categories of those who provide and those who receive welfare services separately, we need to be careful about how we choose to label them. The development of anti-oppressive perspectives and the growing awareness among social welfare commentators about the relevance of ideas drawn from poststructuralism (Sands & Nuccio 1992, Rojek et al. 1988) have meant that we are more alert to the way meaning and "reality" can be defined by language; especially when that language is constructed by those with more power in our society.

Within one area of social welfare, social work, the term "service user" has come into common currency to describe those who receive services. It is important to realize that such terminology gives particular weight to one version of reality about social welfare. It is a version that reflects the ideology of the current British government, particularly with regard to "Community Care". That ideology has to be viewed critically.

For instance, there is one particular reservation about the terminology that deserves to be considered. "Users" seems to suggest a free exchange of services in which the latter go to the welfare agency to have their needs met. Such a picture ignores large areas of social welfare where services are imposed on users. Indeed, one could argue that with the retrenchment of the "welfare state" an increasing proportion of services reflect this (Langan 1993a). In the field of child care we have witnessed a steady move towards a focus on "dangerousness" and "protection" in terms of legislation and resource allocation (Parton & Parton 1989, Parton 1991, Saraga 1993). Similar comments might be made with reference to the statutory element within the field of mental health.

In the wider area of adult care, the free-exchange model often seems inappropriate despite the rhetoric about "customers" and "purchasers". For, as Langan notes (1993a), generally the "customer" will not buy the services: that will be done for them by a care manager after the latter has assessed the former's needs.

In the past, we had different words for users: for instance "clients". There were probably good reasons for abandoning such terminology since it was patronizing. What should have replaced it is open to question. There are terms current in some agencies that seem even further removed from reality than "service user", such as "consumer" and "customer".

Given this state of affairs, I propose to use the term "service user" because it seems to be the least offensive and least unreal of those currently available.

As for a term to describe people who work in welfare services, that too is problematic. Because there is such a spectrum of terminology across different services and there are the complications attendant upon the various structures of community care across the country, I have chosen the simplest option available to me: "welfare worker".

Men as welfare workers

There is now a very substantial body of literature that explores power relations within the staffing of social welfare organizations. Much of this material focuses primarily on the situation of women. Nevertheless, it is a valuable resource in analyzing the issues pertaining to men.

It is quite clear that gender dynamics have a powerful impact on the distribution pattern of men and women within welfare agencies. These patterns are marked with respect to both vertical and horizontal structures. Let us take vertical ones first.

Vertical segregation

A common pattern seems to exist generally across social welfare systems, although the situation does vary in degree between professions. For instance, Hugman (1991) reports that in nursing men account for about 3 to 10 per cent of the workforce, yet 33 per cent of the managerial posts. In local authority social services agencies, the pattern seems to be even more clear, although as Grimwood & Popplestone (1993) mention, poor data collection in this area is a problem. While women constitute 63 per cent of all local authority workers, they account for 87.2 per cent of social services staff (Hallett 1989). Langan (1992) reports Howes's findings from the late 1970s when data were more plentiful:

> . . . some 83 per cent of social work assistants and 64 per cent of social workers were women; at every other level from team leader/senior (49 per cent women), through area officer (29 per cent women), divisional area officer (17 per cent), men predominated.

Grimwood & Popplestone (1993) report the 1991 figures from Manpower Watch which suggest the situation has not improved:

Forty-four of the 116 Social Services Departments in England and Wales have no women at all in senior management . . . There are only thirty-three with more than one woman senior manager . . . From observation, we have noted that most of the top jobs in voluntary organisations are being taken over by men, probably because much higher salaries are now being offered.

The data reported by Langan (1992) confirm this trend:

Still, more than 90 per cent of directors are male and more than 70 per cent of area officers are men . . . [There is] an increasing feminization at the lower levels of the social services hierarchy: 74 per cent of social workers and 90 per cent of social work assistants are women.

Langan continues:

At the very lowest level of the social services hierarchy – care and domestic staff in homes and day centres, home helps, and other domiciliary care workers – women make up around 75 per cent of staff.

Of course, these gender dynamics are mediated and in some cases compounded by other power relations. For instance, with regard to the nursing profession, Hugman (1991) comments as follows:

Gender boundaries cross occupational boundaries, so that although heterosexual male nurses do not gain an equivalence with doctors, they have greater power both in relation to the doctors and to their female (and homosexual male) colleagues.

Similarly, issues of racism have a major impact on these patterns in terms of social work (Langan 1992):

Black people appear to be under-represented at every level of the social services hierarchy. Though no national statistics are available on the ethnic composition of the social services workforce, local surveys suggest that relatively few black workers are taken on, especially at higher levels . . . Statistics on minority ethnic entrants into relevant training courses confirm continuing racial bias.

We should add that the mass of clerical and administrative staff in welfare organizations are women, and Grimwood & Popplestone (1993) note that black people also tend to preponderate in the lowest levels here.

There are various explanations for the vertical gender bias we have described. Several studies of social work have indicated that women in the profession may have lower aspirations than their male counterparts (Popplestone 1980). Other studies (Taylor 1994) indicate that this apparent lack of ambition may have rather more concrete roots than simply socialization. Taylor surveyed social work students and found that there was no indication that the women had lower aspirations than the men. What she did find were:

> . . . striking differences in anticipated discrimination dependent on their gender, with 59 per cent of female students but only 4 per cent of male students expecting that their chances of promotion would be negatively affected by their gender . . . Just over three-quarters of students thought that "women are discriminated against by men on the basis of gender", was an explanation as to why fewer women than men are in management positions in social work departments . . . Whether the anticipated discrimination is unfounded or not is less relevant than that it exists for both male and female employees and the implications of this are cause for serious concern.

These perceptions, as well as real discriminations, which women may well encounter, perhaps explain the later lack of aspiration that studies have discovered with women who are practising. Taylor suggests that if this is the case, then sending female workers on management training courses, valuable although they are, may be less important than implementing strategies to tackle discriminatory practices.

Another recent study based on student training casts a striking anti-sexist light on the same issue. Moira Kirwan (1994) studied a set of Diploma in Social Work (Dip.S.W.) professional training courses in Scotland. She found several gender differences in favour of men. This was particularly marked in terms of the relatively large number of women occupying part-time lecturing posts and the relatively large proportion of men occupying full-time and promotable posts (Carter et al. 1992). Interestingly, there also seemed to be an over-concentration of men acting as student representatives on these courses. Kirwan suggests that such patterns are not conducive as models either for later anti-oppressive practice in the field or as encouragement to women in terms of their career horizons, especially when such sexism occurs in the context of a curriculum that allegedly stresses the value of anti-sexism.

In a similar vein, Henderson (1994) explicitly identifies the mirroring that can occur between oppressive practice endured by students on a Dip.S.W. course and the oppression that social work service users experience at the hands of welfare agencies: for instance, participation in decision-making without power, top–down empowerment as opposed to bottom–up (Beresford & Croft 1993). She suggests this can then have a detrimental impact on the way students treat service users when they qualify. We can easily envisage a three-way process of oppression whereby the differential, gendered experiences of women and men as social work students and as social workers not only mirror the different levels of oppression in the lives of service users but actually go on to compound that oppression by influencing the poor practice of those social workers.

Of course, concentration of female staff in part-time, non-promotable jobs compared to men colleagues is a feature not only of colleges but also of welfare agency hierarchies and is another reason for the preponderance of men at managerial levels. Moreover, when we consider why it is that women rather than men hold part-time posts, we see patterns that will be found again in the lives of service users when we later consider their situation.

Many feminist and pro-feminist commentators (Hallett 1989, Hugman 1991, Langan 1992, Grimwood & Popplestone 1993) clearly identify the main reasons for this pattern in relation to part-time work, although they may disagree about the relative weight given to different factors. One reason seems to be the social construction of women as primary family carers and the continually confirmed research finding that working women are still responsible for a disproportionate amount of work in the home (Hallett 1989, Segal 1990).

Furthermore, employers gear part-time employment to women's needs because they can pay them less than men: in general terms, women in full-time paid employment earn on average 77 per cent of men's pay while part-time women workers earn little over 50 per cent of that of men (Grimwood & Popplestone 1993).

And finally, these factors are amplified by the poor support given to parents in Britain in terms of alternative child care provision and maternity/paternity leave (Hallett 1989, Cannan 1992). Thus, occupational gender segregation in the welfare services has many of its roots in social trends that will equally impact on service users.

21

However, another factor in the over-representation of men in welfare management is more specific to that field. Grimwood & Popplestone (1993) identify a strong bias towards themes of control rather than care in the managerial ethos of social work management and they trace its development from the Seebohm Report of 1968, through the reorganization of personal social services (early 1970s), to the rule of the Audit Commission in the mid-1990s.

They also provide evidence (as does Eley 1989) that such values are more consonant with those held by male managers rather than female ones. They ruefully warn that the inexorable trend towards the dominance of budgetary control in Care in the Community policies may well exacerbate the situation. Clearly, a "chicken and egg" process may be in operation whereby women are less attracted to the ethos of management that then reinforces that unattractive ethos. Grimwood & Popplestone (1993) are aware of the irony that much of the latest management theory in industry actually stresses the need for care and validation of staff – but that this has not yet percolated down to welfare organizations.

With rather bitter irony Grimwood & Popplestone (1993) survey the fact that in the personal social services men control the most personal aspects of women's lives and manage a largely female staff working mainly with female service users:

> If men's prisons were managed by women, if men were expected to discuss their sex problems with women hospital consultants, if all chief inspectors were women, steps would quickly be taken to redress the balance.

Similar comments could be made about the health service. Already in 1991 Hugman (1991) was analyzing the growing managerialism in that field and events in the NHS since then are unlikely to have reversed the trend.

However, vertical segregation in favour of men is only half the story. The inequalities we have noted so far are the product of the interaction of those vertical patterns with equally pervasive horizontal segregations and it is to these we turn now.

Horizontal segregation

It is striking that in many fields of social welfare men are to be found working in much greater numbers in some areas of work. For example, in the nursing profession men are far more numerous in psychiatric work than in the general sector and relatively absent in the remedial therapy sector (Hugman 1991). In social services, Grimwood & Popplestone (1993) note that women workers preponderate in hospital social work, day nurseries, residential care (particularly for older people), occupational therapy, and home help services while Hugman (1991) locates more men as being employed in the areas of mental health and child care (particularly child protection). To these we may also add probation work (Dominelli 1991, Raynor et al. 1994).

Several points need to be made about this segregation and, again, "chicken and egg" processes are probably in operation. For instance, many of the areas in which men work are regarded as more skilled (and so better paid) than those in which women work (Grimwood & Popplestone 1993). Do more men apply for these jobs because of this? Are those jobs felt to be more highly skilled because men tend to occupy them? We should not discount any possibility. For instance, Hallett (1989) emphasizes the gendered nature of skills assessment and draws on research demonstrating that employers (often men) regard women as being suited for "domestic" work that is therefore "natural" to them rather than skilled work. Hallett (1989) and Jones (1989) have applied an awareness of this sexist thinking to the particular situation of home helps, pointing out the numerous, complex skills that this work entails. Hallett's scathing conclusion is:

> It is ironic and perhaps an important comment on contemporary society that those who visit homes to service washing machines are classed as skilled whereas those who come to "service" dependent people are not. The home helps and allied workers are not marginal or secondary workers in the social services department. They occupy a central position in the labour process. Yet their work is "unskilled". (Hallett 1989)

Similar processes can be discerned in other welfare professions. For instance, Grimwood & Popplestone (1993) note research demonstrating how female community workers are usually identified by managers and colleagues as being responsible for working with girls and women and that these activities are often regarded by men and management as marginal.

Of course, many of the posts in the areas where women preponderate also tend to be part-time or job-shared, thus linking with the factors we have already surveyed in relation to vertical segregation. Conversely, most managerial posts are not part-time, nor often open to job-share, which weights the situation again in favour of men, given what we have said above about the patriarchal relations that tend to characterize family care (Hugman 1991).

The link that Hallett makes between the general devaluing of women's domestic work and the devaluing of their work in the field of welfare is surely crucial and not simply because discriminatory employment practices may ghettoize them in the more domestic forms of welfare work. For Hallett's point is relevant to the whole concept of social welfare: whatever welfare work they predominate in may be devalued.

Hugman (1991) notes the historical origins of nursing in women's domestic activity and that it represents a professionalization of women's domestic role. Similarly, he notes that social work is also "concerned with the emotional, reproductive and domestic areas of life in its focus on the coping of families and individuals". He also characterizes it as "the scrutiny of women's domestic performance, controlling caring and caring through control". Grimwood & Popplestone (1993) trace in detail the transformation by which gendered charity and domestic work in the nineteenth century became gendered social work in the later twentieth century.

In this context, the social devaluing of much of social welfare can be seen as an extension of the pre-existing and parallel devaluation of women's labour in the home.

It is interesting, then, to see how men in these professions and semi-professions cope with this situation. For instance, let us take social work. We have already seen some of the ways in which men are accorded more prestige, for example by moving into management.

However, horizontal segregation also has a role to play. We noted that men tend to be found in greater numbers in some fields such as mental health and child protection. Now, of course, both of these areas tend to entail a greater element of "control" than other areas such as working with older people or people with learning difficulties (although, of course, control is not wholly absent from those specialisms). We might parallel this in nursing with the situation of psychiatric or paediatric care (Hugman 1991).

These fields of social work where men are in greater numbers have other characteristics in common as well. They are generally regarded as being the most skilled and prestigious in social work and current trends are accelerating this process rapidly. For instance, as Cochrane (1993a) notes, the implications of the 1989 Children Act in the long run may well be that child care workers will have to be given specialist training as a matter of course, replicating the situation that already exists in the field of mental health. Moreover, because of their higher status and alleged skills quotient, they also tend to be the ranks from which many managers are recruited.

Cochrane (1993a) also points out another important developing trend: the much greater status of "purchasers" over "providers" in the new world of Community Care. Langan (1993a) takes this scenario further and persuasively argues that a sharp bifurcation is occurring in terms of status and training: on the one hand, the prospect of high status, well trained care managers ("purchasers") and on the other, low status, relatively poorly trained "providers". Of course the latter to a large extent equate with precisely those areas of social welfare where women predominate and men are sparse.

In a sense this pattern is only an extension of what has gone before. In the past a *de facto* two-tier training system operated in social work with the CQSW (Certificate of Qualification in Social Work) largely for field workers and CSS (Certificate in Social Service) for residential and day care staff. The Diploma in Social Work was designed to remedy this split, although its success was debatable and its future seems uncertain.

Feminist and pro-feminist commentators persuasively argue that the process by which fields such as child protection, mental health and care management are accorded skill and status is also heavily gendered: in a sense the reverse of the way in which female-dominated areas tend to be de-skilled (Hugman 1991).

Virtuosity, managerialism and masculinity

Hugman (1991) examines the way welfare professions (or parts of them) claim what he terms "virtuoso status" and "virtuosity". He regards such claims as steps towards the goals of managerialism and professionalization. Drawing on the work of Jeff Hearn (1982), Hugman notes that virtuosity is often judged in terms of values associated with masculinity (such as instrumentality and technical knowledge) rather than values attributed to the feminine (such as emotional sensitivity): a preference that reflects the privileging of Enlightenment values in society generally, as Seidler (1991, 1994) has frequently emphasized.

If we match this perspective to what is currently happening in the field of social care, we find some striking correspondences. We have already noted the established and growing virtuosity associated with child protection and mental health in social work: areas where more men practitioners congregate. In addition, we have above witnessed a growing divide via Community Care between allegedly unskilled carers (whether inside families or outside) and the virtuosity of care managers who assess and/or purchase services (a category of worker which, by the way, straddles the increasingly dissolved boundary between health and social services). What is interesting is the massive emphasis placed on technique in all these valued areas. Let us take child protection and care management as two examples.

Technique in child protection

In Chapter 3 we focus on the field of child protection, so I do not want to pre-empt the discussion there. At this point, I merely mention that in recent years there has been a plethora of government guidance and professional literature on the myriad techniques and procedures to be followed in relation to child protection. In Chapter 3 we shall pursue in detail the implications of the following scathing conclusion drawn from one of the most methodologically thorough, and largest, research studies on child protection to date:

> . . . it seems that social work has bought another "lemon". In response to a moral panic it has obtained new resources, changed laws and agency procedures and introduced new technologies of intervention in order to secure the safety of a small number of children . . . The narrow "effectiveness" test of child protection stands up well, but the price which is paid considering the difficulties faced by many caregivers is excessive . . . Child protection has become a "Panoptical device", a means by which the private lives of those who struggle to bring up children in difficult conditions are made public and what is made public is more often than not a misrepresentation of what is required. That which does not conform to standard middle-class patriarchal child-rearing norms is represented as "at risk" of abuse, neglect or abuse. (Thorpe 1994)

As we noted briefly in Chapter 1, feminist writers (Armstrong 1991, Hudson 1992, Kelly 1993) have not been slow to point out that this burgeoning child abuse industry has largely been promoted by, and to the career benefit of, men professionals in the fields of health (psychiatry and paediatrics) and social work (child protection and mental health).

Technique in care management

This area encompasses a broad span of social welfare, absorbing major elements of health and social services provision. It is important to recognize that in theory the framework of Care in the Community has potential for developing in many different directions entailing both benefits and risks (Orme & Glastonbury 1993). Based on early experience of practice in some areas of the country and the gloss being placed on policy by the Department of Health, it is becoming apparent to some commentators the direction it will take (Hugman 1991, Cochrane 1993a, Langan 1992, 1993a).

This direction can be gauged by looking at one of the standard texts for welfare workers on Care in the Community (Orme & Glastonbury 1993). In this text, numerous references exist to budgeting and related activities, assessment, contracts and contracting, costs, consumers and consumerism, purchasing, monitoring, management, quality assurance, resources, workloads and workload management. Relatively few references are made to "race", empowerment, gender or discrimination. This is hardly surprising since the situation of black people warrants only one paragraph in the White Paper itself, *Caring for people* (HMSO 1989a). The act that resulted from the White Paper "virtually ignores the now widely acknowledged fact that the vast majority of carers are women, and fails to take account of demands for alternatives which do not exploit women" (Langan 1992).

In a later contribution to the debate, Langan (1993a) neatly sums up the situation for staffing:

> [Care managers'] responsibility is to assess needs and to plan and supervise the purchase and provision of appropriate care from a variety of agencies. The acquisition of managerial skills and qualifications could become a better guarantee of career advancement in social work than more conventional professional qualifications.

The emphasis in current Community Care policy seems, therefore, to be placed squarely on technique. The connection between this and what we have said above about virtuosity, managerialism and masculinity is obvious.

Conversely, as we have seen, the caring function within Community Care seems likely to be even further devalued in terms of both status and training. Earlier, we discussed how some aspects of social welfare had their origins in "women's work" and domestic care, with the result that there were historical reasons why these aspects were not accorded status. Community Care can be seen as reversing history and returning care back to the domestic world of women in families whence it came: and, of course, in the process that devaluation process is magnified.

New frontiers in therapy: family, systems and social constructionist therapies

The theme of virtuosity, managerialism and masculinity is also relevant to social welfare in other respects. In particular, if we look back over the last fifteen years at what have been regarded as some of the most "exciting" and technically prestigious models of therapy, a familiar pattern emerges.

In surveying the history of family therapy, Veronica Coulshed (who was herself a proponent) could say in her classic social work textbook:

> Although there has been dismay at calling these methods of practice "marital and family therapy" with connotations of clinical work and learning "tricks of the trade" . . . I shall refer to them as such, merely for convenience. (Coulshed 1991)

Certainly a massive therapeutic industry grew up around family therapy in the United States and Britain during the 1970s and 1980s: conferences, colloquia, journals, centres for specialized study, and numerous books describing the multifarious schools of therapeutic technique. And it was very much technique-oriented, having its origins in biology, ergonomics and communication theory.

Each school of family therapy tended to have its own leader or "guru"-figure and most of the original leaders were both white and men: for instance Bateson (1972), Erickson (Haley 1986), Haley (1976), Minuchin (1974), Watzlawick et al. (1974). Perhaps not coincidentally, in terms of what we have seen already, much of this early work in the field of social welfare came out of psychiatric or family and child care practice.

In the 1980s family therapy metamorphosed into the broader concept of systems therapy that again spawned its own academic and practice industry. The technological principles and ethos remained very much the same and indeed continued to be based on the work of many of the "founding fathers", particularly Bateson and Erickson. This is not to deny that some prominent figures were women (e.g. Palazzoli et al. 1978, Papp 1983) and that their contribution increased with time. The reasons for the transformation from family to systems therapy is a complex issue but critiques by feminist and anti-racist commentators were certainly a factor. By the late 1980s concerted efforts had been made to incorporate this anti-oppressive critique into systems therapy.

By then, systems therapy was again metamorphosing itself, this time into social constructionist therapy by drawing upon poststructuralist and linguistic theories. Perhaps not surprisingly, the theoreticians mainly utilized were men (Foucault, Derrida, Wittgenstein). And once again, the "market leaders" in the new therapeutic industry tended to be men: for example Michael White and David Epston (1990), Steve de Shazer (1991), Tom Andersen (1991), Gianfranco Cecchin (1987). In many ways, this latest "new frontier" in therapeutic methods takes technique to unsurpassed levels. It sometimes seems that its texts (for instance Steier 1991, McNamee & Gergen 1992, Shotter 1993) are almost unintelligible unless one has an expertise in philosophy, psychology, sociology, sociolinguistics, ethnomethodology, cybernetics, communication theory, anthropology, physics and history all at the same time.

In this social constructionist therapy, efforts are made to incorporate notions of empowerment of service users. Is it a paradox, or simply a contradiction, that an approach that says it espouses empowerment is in its process and content so apparently esoteric, arcane and exclusive? We shall return briefly to this model of therapy in Chapter 7 for further evaluation of it.

My aim in surveying these models, which have all in their time claimed so much for themselves as being breakthroughs in therapeutic practice, is to underline several features about them: their marked technological ethos; their domination by men; the manner in which they have generated huge academic and therapeutic industries that have afforded invaluable career passports to many men and some women. In all these respects, the models briefly reviewed bear a clear correspondence to the analyses of Hearn (1982) and Hugman (1991) about virtuosity, managerialism and masculinity.

This seems an appropriate point at which to recap on what has gone before. We have discussed the mechanisms by which both vertical and horizontal segregation occurs in the staffing of social welfare agencies to the general advantage of men and disadvantage of women. However, we have seen that this pattern is even more complex as it also involves power dynamics centred on issues of sexuality and "race" (Hugman 1991). Furthermore, other dimensions of power, such as age, disability and class also need to be incorporated. We have examined these patterns of domination as they operate in several high status and high profile fields of social welfare. Finally, we should note that these patterns reflect structures of oppression associated with hegemonic masculinity which pervade our society as a whole (Connell 1987, 1995).

Strategies for addressing these issues are not hard to find. Several commentators who write from a critical perspective have set out clear agendas for change (Hanmer & Statham 1988, Dominelli 1988, Dominelli & McLeod 1989, Ahmad 1990, Grimwood & Popplestone 1993). It seems pointless to replicate them in detail here. All of them seek a combination of structural reform with changes in organizational ethos and personal attitudes. We should note that these strategies can, and should, also be applied to professional and academic training for welfare workers since training reflects and reinforces oppressive structures and attitudes in welfare agencies.

What is important from our point of view is that men should play a full part in working towards these goals. It is important not only from a moral perspective: i.e. men have a responsibility to work against oppressive practices that have their roots in structures associated with hegemonic masculinity. It is also important because men, as men in organizations, may possess particular assets they can contribute to projects for change. For instance, their structural position may give them considerable leverage in pressing for structural change. That will be enhanced if they can network with other men for the same objective. This in fact constitutes men's second potential asset: the influence that men working anti-oppressively may have with other men.

In this picture we can see the link between personal change and structural change. Men working with other men in support groups to examine their feelings, attitudes and behaviour within the organization can contribute to collective action for structural adaptation. Conversely, structural change may foster an ethos in which personal awareness and behaviour can be addressed more productively.

This is stating the situation in simplistic terms, of course. For instance, provision has to be made in efforts for change to encompass all the dynamics of oppression we have mentioned, not simply those of gender. Let me give an example. In one agency where I worked, considerable lobbying by some women led eventually to management allowing time and resources for a woman's support group to be set up. This then became a forum for raising awareness among other women about issues of oppression and a base for development of strategies for structural change. Some time later, a similar process led to the establishment of a black support group, the women's group having acted as a precedent for management. It was only much later that a gay and lesbian support group became established.

The relationship between such movements for change in an organization is also not simple. In particular, there is always a danger that they will compete for resources rather than work together: indeed it may often be in the interests of management to promote such competition.

In the context of this study, it is especially important that men networking for anti-oppressive practice in an organization do not either "colonize" the efforts of women and other groups working for change or develop facilities for men by drawing resources away from the initiatives of other staff members. Otherwise what occurs is anti-oppressive action by men on behalf of men which in practice compounds oppression of, for instance, women or black people in the same organization. Unfortunately, this scenario is not uncommon. It is therefore vital that a men's network liaises closely with other networks, respects what they are doing, and supports them in whatever ways are acceptable to those other networks. In working for change in organizations, men can use not only networking and support groups but a whole range of strategies that we consider in more detail in Chapter 7.

At this point we will also mention in passing that service users can also network for change in agency structures and service provision. In many cases men users may be able to collaborate with men welfare workers sharing similar objectives (Beresford & Croft 1993). For, as we shall see shortly, what happens within an agency in terms of oppression is by no means unrelated to the forms of oppression outside in the rest of society.

These ways of proceeding that are open to men, as well as some of the problems that go along with them, have been dealt with relatively briefly here. That is deliberate. In the course of this study, we will see many of the same themes repeated in different situations. In the last three chapters we draw all these themes together and use them to construct a framework in which men involved with social welfare can engage in anti-oppressive practice. At this point we are simply setting the stage for those later considerations.

The issues we have addressed in this chapter are important. However, so far we have failed to mention one of the most crucial components in a critical analysis of masculinities and welfare agencies. Harlow et al. (1992) suggest that this component has often been completely ignored in feminist studies of gender and organizational life: "Far less attention has been directed towards what is in some ways the most obvious element of gender relations, namely sexuality in organizations." It is to this issue, which will be so crucial to the analysis of our study, that we now turn.

31

Organization sexuality

Hearn & Parkin (1987) trace in modern Western history the movement of patriarchy from private to public forms: "over the last century or more a huge transfer of power [has occurred] from the multitude of 'private' fathers to the 'collective' power of the state . . . and other organisations".

One vital aspect of this patriarchal transfer is what they term the "male sexual narrative" and they emphasize that sexuality is now an intrinsic part of organizational life. Harlow et al. (1992) acknowledge that an organization can construct sexuality, for instance by the value (or lack of value) it places on certain forms of sexuality. However, their interest focuses on the many occasions when sexuality constructs organizational life. This is what is called "organization sexuality" by Hearn & Parkin (1987) or "the sexuality of organization" by Burrell & Hearn (1989).

Part of the complexity around this issue is that sexuality is a feature of the private and the public domain, although in the latter there is often a reluctance to acknowledge its presence.

Social welfare organizations have a particular relation to these concerns for several reasons. First of all, in welfare work there is a particular blurring of the private and the public. Generally speaking, men dominate in both spheres and between the two the public has precedence over the private in terms of power. So in social welfare settings, especially, men have a double domination over women (Harlow et al. 1992). Parkin (1989) has applied this to residential settings where, as we have seen, female staff preponderate at basic grades. In these settings the dual agendas of the private and public can be manipulated and deliberately confused to mask the oppression that those in power (frequently men, of course) perpetrate. Secondly, social welfare tasks often have explicit or implicit connections with sexual matters (Harlow et al. 1992).

These same authors outline the way organization sexuality can oppress service users and colleagues who are gay or lesbian (Harlow et al. 1992, Brown 1992) and distort black sexuality and identity in welfare settings (Harlow et al. 1992).

Female students in the welfare services are at risk of abuse and harassment in welfare agency settings (Harlow et al. 1992) and this parallels their similar vulnerability in colleges (Carter & Jeffs 1992). Female staff in academic settings are also vulnerable (Ramazanoglu 1987).

Both female welfare staff and female service users are also at risk in this respect and so too may be male service users, especially when the power dynamics constitute what Connell (1995) terms "subordinate or marginalized masculinities": for instance, where male service users are children/young people or are disabled. We shall examine these themes, and others related to the oppression that flows from organization sexuality, in more depth when we look at the specific areas of child care and men's violence in later chapters.

At this stage I only want to make a few, vital points about organization sexuality. First of all, I am not arguing that all sexual oppression is exclusively perpetrated by men. Some women clearly do engage in violence or abuse positions of power and there is a growing literature that documents this (Segal 1990, Hanks & Saradjian 1991, A. Campbell 1993, Elliott 1993, Orme 1994). However, instances are infrequent compared to the amount of such oppression generated by men. Moreover, abuse by women needs to be analyzed in the context of the patriarchal relations that permeate our society: not to exonerate women's violence but in order to fully understand it (Kelly 1991).

My second point is to emphasize that organization sexuality operates across the board of social welfare settings. As we will see in Chapters 3 and 8, some settings have attracted more publicity than others in this respect. Residential care of children and of people with learning difficulties, along with nursery care, have been in the public eye in the last two or three years. There are specific reasons why such settings may well be the sites for particularly gross examples of abuse (Pringle 1994c). However, some other (less publicized) welfare settings are probably just as problematic: for instance, foster care (Pringle 1993a). Moreover, all welfare settings will be problematic for the reasons discussed above in relation to organization sexuality. Indeed, Harlow et al. (1992) mention some of these other settings. For instance, they discuss the relationship of field social workers with service users and the abusive relationships that can exist between psychotherapists and patients.

My third and final point about this topic is that the manifestations of organization sexuality are varied. Our discussion so far might indicate that it is confined to sexual abuse perpetrated on staff or service users. Common though that may well be, sexuality can construct existence in organizations in many other ways: ". . . through sexual meetings, sexual liaisons, sexual relationships, affairs, gossip, rumour, innuendo, myth, as well as sexual harassment" (Harlow et al. 1992). Some commentators (including myself) would regard many of the items in that list as constituting potential abuse in an organizational context (Kelly 1987).

However, defining what is abusive and achieving some consensus about it, is difficult. For instance, when does the fact of a male welfare manager having a relationship with one of his staff become abusive?

Right at the start? When the relationship becomes sexual, and how is that defined? When they continue working together? Only when one or both parties behaves inappropriately at work? Never? Are the issues different if the manager is a woman, or a gay man, or lesbian? These are very practical questions. After all, this type of short-term or long-term encounter can easily happen in any organization. It can happen even more easily in a social welfare agency where people are often working closely together dealing with intense emotional material.

Other, wider, variations on this theme are also brought into question when they are placed within the framework of organization sexuality. For instance, what about relationships that develop between male and female staff who are peers in social welfare agencies? I am not arguing that all such relationships have elements of abuse in them simply because they flourish in those contexts. I am suggesting that we do need to be aware that (as we have seen) each organization is to a greater or lesser extent a very real focus of power relations. For reasons outlined earlier, the power relations in a social welfare agency may be particularly focused by sexuality.

In this context, I would argue that, as a matter of personal responsibility, people who work in welfare settings should always examine the nature of their relationships in those settings with a critical eye. This is especially the case in areas of work where sexuality is a prominent theme (Pringle 1990, 1992).

All these issues are complex and messy. Certainly every agency should possess harassment policies and systems that are accessible, usable, clear, firm and sensitive to the many points we have raised. That is far easier to write than to achieve. It is important that men working in agencies are fully committed to such practices and work for their implementation. This is part of the task of seeking structural change in agencies, which we mentioned earlier. Harassment policies should extend beyond gender to encompass all forms of oppression, not least heterosexism and racism.

Equally, attention needs to be paid to relationships that develop between staff and service users within welfare agencies. It is reasonably apparent that any form of sexual relationship is unacceptable between welfare workers and service users. But here too questions arise as to how a "sexual relationship" is defined: a whole range of contacts between staff and service users may be potentially abusive.

Effective complaints procedures need to be worked towards and implemented for service users, taking into account many of the same considerations as applied to staff harassment policies. These procedures need to be readily accessible to all service users. This is a particularly important injunction because in the chapters that follow we shall see that welfare workers who abuse service users often target those for whom agencies make the least provision in terms of access for making complaints: people with serious disabilities, people who are very old, people who have profound learning difficulties or people who are very young.

In Chapter 8 we discuss in relation to child care how men who are welfare workers can limit the risks of abusing or being perceived to abuse service users. Many of the suggestions put forward in Chapter 8 to some extent may be applicable in other fields such as adult care. We shall see in Chapter 6 some evidence that abuse of adults using welfare services is considerable and many forms of this abuse are perpetrated largely by men.

Clearly, the issue of organization sexuality has broad and deep implications for the role of men working in welfare organizations. Despite (or perhaps because of) the size of the issue, it is interesting to note (Parkin 1989) that welfare workers, their managers, and service users frequently do not address sexuality in a formal way and so there tends to be a lack of rules, procedures, management guidelines and training on the issue.

Typically, such procedures develop only when the issue is forced on the agenda by managerial crises or public scandals. Even then, agencies struggle to find alternative discourses to allow them to avoid confronting the reality of sexuality in organizations. For instance, it seems welfare agencies and the Department of Health may have avoided facing up to the problem of men as sexual abuse perpetrators in welfare agencies (Pringle 1992, Ch. 8 below).

What is even more sinister is the way welfare agencies seek to manage, or even cover up, crises which would force the reality of organization sexuality into the open. Parkin (1989) details several examples where harassment of staff or abuse of service users has been repeatedly brought to the attention of managers of agencies, only for the issue to be dismissed or swept away until it became "unmanageable". Since then a couple of particularly spectacular examples of this have occurred in child care settings and we consider those in Chapters 3 and 8.

It is well known that "whistle-blowers" in organizations are rarely thanked and frequently eliminated, and this applies to social welfare agencies as well. Here we see another parallel with the oppressive relations that exist in society and which are reflected in organization sexuality. After all, "whistle-blowers" who disclose what may be happening in ordinary peoples' homes suffer the same fate. In relation to this, Grimwood & Popplestone (1993) refer to the experiences of Judith

Dawson in Nottingham and Marietta Higgs and Sue Richardson in Cleveland. Grimwood & Popplestone suggest, with reason, that gender was probably a factor in the treatment they received when they tried to open up the issue of sexual abuse in families.

Reviewing what we have said about organization sexuality, it is surely relevant that the management systems that allow abuses of power to go unchecked, and which in some cases actively collude in abuse, are themselves riven by oppressive (and especially patriarchal) relations.

Conclusion

This chapter has surveyed the picture of the role of men working within social welfare services as portrayed by feminist and pro-feminist commentators. It is a picture of deeply gendered structures and of entrenched patriarchal relations that have profound implications for people using the services as well as for those who work in them.

Moreover, oppression is experienced not only by people who are female: for example, being black or being homosexual often results in marginalization and discrimination. We have discovered a pattern of oppression in these settings that once again corresponds closely to Connell's analysis of power dynamics (1987, 1995).

The size of the problem in welfare agencies can seem overwhelming. I think the alternative and more productive view is to say that there are endless opportunities available to men to play a part in changing this state of affairs in welfare agencies. We have begun to outline a framework and some strategies for that change. Many men have already started to put similar strategies into practice. More men have not. Part of the challenge is to encourage other men to join in.

Although it can sometimes be a naïve view, there is much truth in the idea that if men re-examine the feelings and attitudes that generate their oppressive behaviours, they may develop ways of living that bring them more satisfaction. Hearn clearly points to this:

> Men's traditional male solidarity, bonding and class culture needs to be transcended by a solidarity of intimacy. Men's fear of each other, "nurtured" from the earliest encouragements of aggression, the terror of hurting others of the same gender and of being hurt, stands in the way, abstractly solidified into organisational structures, roles and hierarchies. (Hearn & Parkin 1987)

Men may explore these personal features of their lives in the same support groups in which they devise strategies for structural change for welfare agencies – or they may do it elsewhere. Either way we are reminded that the personal is political and vice versa.

I think we are also reminded in the last quotation that it is particular features of particular masculinities that seem to be especially problematic. Some commentators have suggested that the problematic issues identified by Hearn relate more specifically to heterosexual forms of masculinity (Herek 1987). This is yet another issue that will re-occur throughout our study. It is brought home to us again by Hearn who says:

> Organisation sexuality is for men characteristically a mixture of homosociability, latent homosexuality, homophobia and heterosexual phallocentrism given structured form. Thus, men's sexuality towards women has to be seen in the context of, in relation to, and even as the result of men's sexuality with each other. Accordingly, an understanding of supposedly "normal" straight male heterosexuality, in organisations at least, necessitates a consideration of the relevance of homosexuality and homosexual desire amongst men, both as a constituent part of that "heterosexuality" and as something often feared. (Hearn & Parkin 1987)

He goes on to explain that many of men's relations with women may be projections of men's desperate need to prove their heterosexual masculinity including violence, objectification, falling in love and organizational oppressions.

Clearly, these are issues that are central in all work with men by men, inside and outside agencies, whether they are dealt with explicitly or implicitly. Moreover, we will encounter these themes repeatedly in this study.

We have seen one side of the picture in this chapter: the agencies and organizational frameworks. We need to turn now to the other side: the range of services provided by those agencies and the people who "use" them. That range of services is extremely diverse, too diverse to cover in a book of this size. Consequently we look in some detail at four wide areas of social welfare practice.

Child protection we consider separately from child and family care, not because, in an ideal world, they should be separate but because that separation is the framework that policies and procedures create in most welfare agencies (Parton & Parton 1989, Thorpe 1994). Adult care and adult violence, the two other areas covered, are both extremely broad, and so inevitably we focus on some issues that are more relevant to us than others.

Diverse though these areas are, it will come as no surprise to find that the oppressive life experiences of service users, and the response of agencies to them, are structured by power relations very similar to the ones we have studied here.

Chapter 3
Child protection

Introduction

The context within which men receive services from social welfare systems is as deeply patterned by power relations as the context within which men deliver those services. However, in the last chapter we noted the complexity of this pattern: some forms of masculinity benefited in terms of power more than others; and there were other structures of oppression that reinforced or cut across those of gender. In this chapter and the following three where we review the role of men as service users we discover a similar complexity.

In our preceding survey of welfare hierarchies, a reasonably clear demarcation was discernible in terms of the roles occupied by women and men. At first sight this pattern seems to be completely mirrored in the distribution of women and men as service users. It may appear that men and boys tend to receive or "use" welfare services where those services are oriented to "control" rather than "care": for instance, child protection, criminal justice. By contrast, women as users may appear to be most involved with welfare services in the context of "caring" functions: as carers of children or carers of dependent adults; and as dependent adults themselves.

This picture is broadly accurate but it disguises many other patterns that do not conform to the stereotype. To an extent this arises from the complexity of power relations, gendered and otherwise, that we have already witnessed. However, it is also due to the fact that the dichotomy between care and control that we have posited is itself over-simplistic.

The irony is that current child protection approaches and procedures seek to impose such a false dichotomy on social welfare practice, since they focus on the alleged identification of "dangerous" families and individuals, separate from issues of general child care. The inadequacies, and indeed failure, of this approach have been pointed out by several commentators (Parton & Parton 1989, Thorpe 1994).

Men and boys who abuse

Gender issues are a major factor in the genesis of much child abuse. This is most dramatically marked in the case of sexual abuse. The literature on prevalence in the field of sexual abuse is now massive but controversy still exists, particularly about the alleged under-reporting of sexual abuse by women (Peterson et al. 1993). Finkelhor (1984, 1991, Finkelhor et al. 1986, 1988) continues to provide a reliable commentary on these debates. Since 1984 the most methodologically sophisticated prevalence surveys in the United States and the United Kingdom have repeatedly indicated that about 90 per cent of child sexual abuse is perpetrated by males (Finkelhor 1984, Finkelhor et al. 1990, Kelly et al. 1991).

In other areas of child abuse, the gender factor is less pronounced. Christine Parton (1990) acknowledges that women seem to constitute about 30+ per cent of physical abusers and 50+ per cent of emotional abusers. However, she also makes two further important points. First, we have to view those statistics in the context of the massive imbalance between the amount of time children actually spend in the company of women on the one hand and with men on the other hand. If we take this into account, the proportion of physical and emotional abuse for which men are directly responsible seems far more significant than it does otherwise. Secondly, she reminds us that we have to consider the pressures on women who abuse arising from the sexism in their own relationships and from wider societal structures: in saying this, she seeks not to condone women's violence but to explain it.

We should also note that a recent study (Andrews 1994) suggests that men's direct role in the physical abuse of children is considerably greater than has hitherto been acknowledged.

O'Hara (1993), Mullender & Morley (1994) and Saunders (1994) deepen the feminist analysis by reviewing the extensive evidence that links men who abuse their partners with men who physically and/or sexually abuse their children.

Hearn (1990) broadens the analysis by linking child abuse to much wider issues about men's power in "normal" contexts, ranging through fatherhood, employment practices, teacher authority, heterosexual inter-course and the nature of capitalism. Part of his analysis indicates the need to break down what is essentially a false dichotomy between "child protection" and "child care", a move that has been echoed by other com-mentators more recently (Parton 1991, Thorpe 1994).

So men and their actions often do have a role to play, directly or indi-rectly, in a large proportion of child abuse cases. It is not surprising then that men often come into contact with the welfare services via child protection procedures.

Who is given responsibility for child abuse?

However, at this point the picture starts to become more complex again. For even although it is true that one of the major channels by which men come in contact with welfare services is via child protection, it is remark-able how far those services actually ignore the importance of gender issues. Indeed, it is striking how often they fail to fully engage with men (either conceptually or in reality) even when the man is the perpetrator of violence against the child (MacLeod & Saraga 1991, Saraga 1993, Milner 1993).

The written law, most particularly the Children Act 1989 (HMSO 1989b), official child abuse enquiries (most spectacularly the Cleveland Enquiry (HMSO 1988a) and the Warner Report (HMSO 1992)) and official guidance (*Working together* (HMSO 1989c), *Protecting children* (HMSO 1988b)) stead-fastly and perversely fail to either distinguish between abusing and non-abusing parents or to note the gender imbalance among perpetrators particularly in relation to child sexual abuse. This is a remarkable fact given the data that are readily available about these issues.

As studies such as Hooper (1992) and Milner (1993) indicate, actual practice is often even more questionable than official guidance in the way that mothers become the focus in child protection cases where the father is the perpetrator. As Milner notes (1993), "parenting" in the official guidance is generally translated in practice as "mothering": it is a phenomenon that we will later see again in relation to the "community care" of adults.

If this practice focus on mothers presaged a desire to support them in a positive and empowering fashion, that at least would be constructive, even if it ignored important structural issues (MacLeod & Saraga 1991). Yet as Milner (1993) demonstrates, the focus on the woman is often negative and destructive to both herself and the child.

The reasons that Milner (1993) identifies for what she describes as the "disappearing act" of fathers in child protection work are interesting. First, she notes a major structural reason: the different societal expectations about mothers and fathers regarding parenting. Mothers are seen as responsible for the wellbeing of their children and so as being responsible when they suffer harm: she supports this hypothesis with case examples.

Another reason identified by Milner (1993) is the simple fact that welfare professionals prefer to avoid the angry response that confronting a father about his violence will often entail. She points out that assaults on welfare personnel are a very real problem and an even more widespread source of fear among workers. It is easier, and safer, to deflect attention on to allegedly "colluding" mothers and "abusing families".

Practical issues also play a part: for instance, the fact that meetings and case conferences are often scheduled for the benefit of professionals rather than parents, particularly fathers if they are working full-time. However, Milner (1993) points out that such arrangements may mask a reluctance by professionals to welcome parents, especially fathers, to case conferences.

Milner's (1993) final point about men is that welfare workers seem uncertain about how to engage them. O'Brien (1990) has usefully reviewed the data on this topic, which demonstrate that, in the context of marital, family or individual problems, men are far less likely than women to present themselves for help. The reasons she provides are partly those we have already noted: for instance the way appointments for therapy are timed, the way agencies may collude with men by regarding the mother as the "real" parent.

However, some of the other reasons put forward by O'Brien include men's unease in dealing with emotions and the threat to their sense of self in having to admit weakness in public (by acknowledging problems at home and, presumably in child protection cases, the violence they may have perpetrated). She notes that some evidence suggests men may feel more at ease in this kind of a situation when a man worker is present. This might indicate that some men would engage more easily if a male worker was involved. We would suggest that co-working between women and men welfare workers might in some cases be beneficial. As we will see in Chapters 7 and 8, there are other reasons why co-working between women and men may be advantageous when engaging with abusive men. Of course, successful co-working requires considerable care, co-ordination and planning especially if an anti-sexist "message" is going to be given to abusive men via the co-working relationship. Moreover, having two workers involved in a case is expensive: and in fact a third should often also be available to give separate support to non-abusing mothers who, as we saw, tend to be scrutinized rather than supported (Hooper 1992, Smith 1994).

Many relevant welfare agencies, and in particular social services departments, are over-stretched at present even without providing services such as are recommended here. Resources need to be found to make these recommendations a potential fact rather than a fantasy. We are reminded that anti-oppressive practice must include work for change by men inside agencies to adapt their structures and the structures within which the agencies themselves operate if more resources are to be made available. In Chapters 7 and 8 we look at strategies to assist men workers and users to achieve structural changes that will influence the scope for anti-oppressive policies and practices.

In those chapters we will also see that changes must be worked for by men at all levels: change in themselves; individual work with men; groupwork with men; policy and practice change in agencies; campaigns for local and community awareness about issues; campaigns to change oppressive attitudes at a societal level. One cannot make changes at one level without being aware of the connections below and above which anchor oppressive practice. Of course, each person cannot work for change at all levels. But there should be some awareness, co-ordination and networking wherever possible regarding change at those different levels. The issues that we have just identified regarding the linkage between direct work with men in child protection cases and changes in agency resourcing are a good example of the need for a multi-level approach.

Returning to what Milner (1993) and O'Brien (1990) say about fathers and welfare agencies, we can see that their observations regarding men's lack of emotional engagement and fear of authority are quite close to some of the feelings identified by Hearn (1992) (quoted in Ch. 2) as ones that men need to abandon in favour of a more open emotional approach to life. In Chapter 2 we associated this with the nature of heterosexual masculinities. It follows that in individual and group work with men, one issue to address must be those heterosexual masculinities. In Chapters 7 and 8 we consider further this specific topic and the general question of how men can challenge patriarchal and other patterns of oppression.

To summarize: child protection is one of the main areas in which men do come to the attention of welfare services; however, that attention is often cursory and far less intensive than men's responsibility for abuse warrants. Instead, the focus on women frequently becomes the major concern of child protection. Men users may be reluctant to make themselves "vulnerable" and welfare workers may regard trying to engage them as more trouble than it is worth when a relatively compliant woman is available to focus upon. Women's societal role as chief caregiver deflects attention away from fathers which is, of course, extremely convenient for a society like ours dominated by patriarchal relations.

We might note the paradox that it is women's assigned caring role in society that directly leads to their involvement in the controlling functions of social welfare as service users here. This is the first, but not last, example of how the caring and controlling aspects of welfare are related in complex and contradictory ways.

Masculinities, femininities and child abuse

So far in this chapter we have talked about "men" and "women" in general terms. However, once again we must recognize that some men and some women are more likely to be involved in child protection cases than others. In a review of foster and residential care, David Berridge (1994) comments that some social and economic stresses hinder positive relationships in families. He notes that:

> . . . for children between the ages of five and nine years, there is a one in ten chance of entry to local authority care or accommodation where all of the following factors apply: if he or she comes from a lone parent household, is of mixed ethnic origin, the household head receives income support, there are four or more children, living in a private rented home with more than one person per room. Where all the above factors do not apply (and children are White), the likelihood of entry is one in 7,000 – a dramatic difference.

There are two points to make about these figures. First, although not all children come into care for child protection reasons, these data suggest that some categories of mothers and fathers may see more of welfare workers in connection with child protection than others. These categories include some black parents, some lone parents, some parents in poverty: and to an extent there will be an interrelationship between these categories. The corollary is that white, middle-class, heterosexual couples may well have less contact with welfare personnel in the child protection context. Clearly, issues of class and "race" once again seem to cut across or run parallel to issues of gender in a complex and dynamic pattern.

This hypothesis is supported when one considers the use of "at risk" checklists in child protection work and the clear bias within these checklists against the groups identified above (Parton & Parton 1989).

Mention of the checklists leads on to the second point about Berridge's (1994) comparison. For he talks as though the over-representation of some groups in the care population is purely a function of social problems and economic stress. Of course, such stress may be a factor. However, in recent years we have become more aware of the sexism and racism that operates in our social welfare systems and which may cause unwarranted over-representation of certain sectors of the population in care. Such oppressive practices are particularly clear in relation to the focus on separating out "dangerous families" from the mass of the population within child protection procedures (Dingwall 1989, Parton & Parton 1989, Frost & Stein 1989, C. Parton 1990, Channer & Parton 1990, Carlen & Wardhaugh 1991, Barn 1993).

It is true that some of the more crude uses of an "at risk" checklist have been abandoned. Nevertheless, oppressive assumptions regarding social and economic profiles remain in a more subtle and unspoken form in major official guidance such as *Protecting children* (HMSO 1988b). This important practice document demonstrates little sensitivity to issues of gender, "race", class or culture and has been effectively deconstructed to this effect by McBeath & Webb (1990–91).

So, if child protection is a major conduit for men as fathers into social welfare systems then those men may be far more likely to be poor and/or black than well-resourced and/or white. Such a distribution is probably unjust in relation to all categories of child abuse but particularly so in the case of sexual abuse where prevalence studies have repeatedly demonstrated that the occurrence is unrelated to social class or to being black or white (Kidd & Pringle 1988, Channer & Parton 1990, Glaser & Frosh 1993).

Moreover, in the field of sexual abuse gay men and lesbian women may be focused upon more than is warranted by the evidence. One of the myths around sexual abuse of children is the image of the predatory gay man. An important fact to recognize is that the sexual abuse of children does not seem to bear any particular relationship to homosexuality. We now know that many boys are sexually abused before they are 18: perhaps 1 in 6 (Finkelhor et al. 1990) or 1 in 4 (Kelly et al. 1991). Moreover, the majority of abusers of boys are indeed men: Finkelhor et al. (1990) suggest about 83 per cent. However, most research indicates that many of these men are identified, and identify themselves, as heterosexual: the same applies to men who commit male on male adult rape (McMullen 1990).

One caveat should be entered at this point: these judgements are based on current data. It is true that we do need more research on all these issues, particularly male rape and the relationship of sexuality to sexual abuse. Nevertheless this is the picture that we have at present and there is no reason to think it will change.

These sexual abuse prevalence data also have to be used with care in relation to the size of the problem that they portray. For the statistics do depend on what definition of sexual abuse is being used when respondents are questioned. The definitions used in producing the data above were broad ones, although I personally think they are perfectly valid. The important point is that even with a much narrower definition, the size of the problem is still huge. For instance, even when exhibitionism, abuse attempts that were successfully resisted and "less serious" forms of abuse by peers are excluded from Kelly et al.'s study (1991), the prevalence figure for females is about 1 in 5 and for males is about 1 in 14. As Dawn Fisher (1994) concludes from a recent review of prevalence data: "Despite the variations in the different studies, all reveal that sexual abuse is a serious problem, affecting a significant proportion of the population."

The situation regarding lesbian women and sexual abuse is even more clear-cut than is the situation regarding gay men since the vast majority of abuse of girls and young women is committed by males: probably 98–99 per cent (Finkelhor et al. 1990, Kelly et al. 1991). In saying this, I am not seeking to place lesbian women on a pedestal as Pam Carter seems to suggest (Carter 1993). Of course it is true that some lesbian women do engage within their own relationships in sexual practices that other lesbian women might well regard as abusive. For instance, Sheila Jeffreys (1990) and Liz Kelly (1991) seek to place lesbian sadomasochism in the context of oppressive patriarchal discourses regarding sexuality. The only point I am making is simply that from a statistical point of view it is clear that lesbian women have very little to do with perpetrating child sexual abuse.

This relative non-association of sexual abuse with gay or lesbian people is in stark contrast not only to media images but also to heterosexist welfare agency policies on fostering and adoption (Pringle 1991, Rickford 1992, Taylor 1993) and proposed government adoption legislation (HMSO 1993) which has a very narrow view indeed of "real families".

Our overall conclusion is that the system for protection of children seems to be weighted against certain sorts of parents: those who are poor, black, alone (particularly female and alone), homosexual. It seems to be weighted in favour of others: white, middle class, heterosexual couples. In recognizing this fact, we are not, of course, suggesting that parents in the former categories never abuse their children.

This weighting occurs for two reasons. First, social workers come into contact with the former categories of family far more often than they do with the latter for a variety of factors that we consider later, so there is a different degree of surveillance anyway. Secondly, as we have seen, the criteria for assessing "risk", as represented in *Protecting children* (HMSO 1988b), are loaded towards certain forms of family; these criteria may sometimes be misleading in terms of physical abuse. With regard to sexual abuse, they are virtually irrelevant, for in Chapter 8 we shall see that committing sexual abuse seems to bear little or no relation to social deprivation, individual stress or family configuration.

In view of the discussion so far in this chapter, it is clear that Connell's concept of power dynamics relating to "hegemonic masculinity" (1987) is as relevant to the situation of service users here as it was to welfare workers in the last chapter. While the evidence in relation to child abuse demonstrates that men who are poor and/or black and/or gay can indeed abuse children, it also shows that such men tend to be scrutinized more rigorously than their white, middle class, heterosexual counterparts.

However, we have to place that statement in the context of our finding earlier in this chapter: in the field of child protection men are, overall, scrutinized less intensively than their responsibility for abuse might warrant compared to women.

Young people and children in the care system

There is yet another area within the child protection system that we have so far failed to consider and that throws up additional complexities. We have focused on service users who are parents. However, what about service users who are children in the care system and other parts of the welfare services? How far do patriarchal relations govern the experience of young people in care, many of whom (but by no means all) may be there as a result of having been abused or neglected at home?

Who is in the care system?

Much writing on the care system has focused on the preponderance of boys in that system. There has been a tendency among social scientists to overlook the plight of young women in care. Simply in numerical terms this is the case: for the number of young women in care is around four fifths of the figure for young men (Carlen & Wardhaugh 1991). Moreover, feminist commentators (Gelsthorpe 1990, Carlen & Wardhaugh 1991) have begun to document the manifold ways in which young women are disciplined and regulated by that system in a very gendered manner.

Similarly gendered are the reasons for young women entering the care system in the first place. For if the care system is becoming increasingly a mechanism for social control, that mechanism is particularly focused on the situation of women. For instance, Frost & Stein (1989) emphasize that delinquency in young women is seen by courts as not only wrong but also "abnormal". We should note that "delinquency" is not the only behaviour that is interpreted in a gendered way. Pitts (1990) points out that a young woman's sexuality is far more likely to lead to judgements about "moral danger" than is a young man's. In fact, "promiscuity" (which has become a gendered term in itself) can draw a young woman, as opposed to a young man, into the care system:

> Once . . . [young women] come to the attention of the authorities as a result of, say, aggressiveness, rowdiness, truancy or "promiscuity", they are then likely to be seen as being very gender-deviant indeed, and ripe for assessment and categorization as "cases for care". These assessments are constituted not only within conventional constructions of female sexuality and femininity, but also within individualized typifications drawn from class and racist stereotypes. (Carlen & Wardhaugh 1991)

This quotation serves to remind us again that not only gender but also other power dimensions such as "race" and class contribute to complex patterns of oppression. As we have already seen, the population within the care system is often black and/or poor.

We also need to make a link between the experiences of young people in care and the oppressive relations arising from that organization sexuality within the structures of welfare agencies that we surveyed in Chapter 2. For those relations often result in the oppression of users as well as staff. It is to this topic that we now turn.

Oppression and abuse of young people in the care system

Young people in the care system are highly vulnerable to oppression partly because of the power differential that exists between them and staff in terms of age and hierarchical position; and partly because so many of the young people already have extremely low self-esteem due to their prior life experiences (Pringle 1990, 1993a, Stein 1993). Moreover some young people are especially targeted by abusers because they lack power in additional ways: perhaps because they are so young that they are without language or because of physical and/or learning difficulties. We should note, however, that the powerlessness of the latter children may often be due to an absence of proper resources for communication and safety provided to them by agencies (Kennedy & Kelly 1992).

There are now numerous studies, mainly from the United States, detailing the large extent of extremely serious abuse by staff on young people in a wide variety of care settings: for instance, children's homes, foster homes, boarding schools, day care, ordinary schools (Pringle 1993a, 1993b, Stein 1993, Benedict et al. 1994). We will review this data in more detail in Chapter 8.

In addition, we are aware of the day-in/day-out "routine" degradations that many young people endure in care settings, often documented by user groups or those writing on their behalf (Jones et al. 1988, National Association of Young People In Care 1990).

In recent years we have been deluged by official and semi-official guidance aimed at ensuring the interests of children in the care system, all laying down the same kind of injunctions to counter abuse there. The fact that these reports go on being produced after further "scandals" in the care system occur, is one of the best pieces of evidence regarding their overall ineffectiveness. No doubt they have made some impact in some places on some forms of ill-treatment. However, the scandals continue.

Most of those major care scandals centre on the sexual assault of young people within the system. One important question that we must ask in this study is why official recommendations do not seem to make the care system a markedly safer place, given that the reports are invariably written by the most distinguished members of what we might call the social welfare "establishment".

In Chapter 8 we will ask that question in relation to child sexual abuse and make some alternative suggestions about how to reduce abuse in the care system. Suffice it to say at this point that our analysis will place much emphasis on issues of gender which the official reports, significantly, never do.

So, the care system can be oppressive in two respects: first, as a mechanism for policing families that lie outside narrow "traditional" norms, norms that happen to correspond quite closely to the contours of hegemonic masculinity as analyzed by Connell (1987, 1995); and secondly, the way it damages many of the young people whom it is designed to protect.

This is not to deny that some children require protection from one or both of their parents (more usually their fathers). They most certainly do. Nor does the care system always fail children. For some children do benefit from the care of the state. There is good practice going on, often in the face of terrible resource problems and lack of adequate management support.

However, it is still true that far more children than we have dared to admit in the past have been, and are being, additionally traumatized by what happens to them "in care", and in welfare systems generally.

Summary

We can summarize the situation of young people in the care system. Young men predominate in this system and there are probably disproportionate numbers of poor and black children among these boys. Moreover, a very significant minority of the care population is female and for them "care" often serves a particularly controlling function. For quite a number of children of both genders, the "care" system (and indeed the welfare system more generally) is not merely a controlling experience: it can be a punitive and abusive one.

Conclusion

The protection of children is a major sector within the social welfare services of the United Kingdom. We have seen that men and boys loom large as service users of this system, albeit often as involuntary ones. We find them as adults who exercise power over children inappropriately in a variety of ways (not least sexual) or who may indirectly contribute to their partners' physical and emotional abuse of children. We also find them as the majority of children in the care system.

One of the major functions of the child protection system is the state's regulation of families, which is valid insofar as child abuse has to be stopped; but that may sometimes be invalid in the way the system is structured by forms of domination associated with hegemonic masculinity. This structuring has increased with the focus of child protection on isolating "dangerousness" (Parton & Parton 1989).

As regards targets of change for men seeking to work anti-oppressively, the field of child protection throws up many possibilities. First is the lack of emphasis placed on men users in child protection assessments and "treatment". Men workers may have a particular role to play in working with men users here, especially as it seems the latter may engage more readily with the former.

Lack of engagement with fathers in child protection cases may partly be a function of their resistance. There is probably only a limited amount that can be done about this resistance itself, and we have suggested some ways of dealing with it: use of men workers, possibly co-working with female colleagues; more sensitivity and flexibility of workers about the timing of appointments. However, the impression drawn from the evidence in this chapter is that the main problem may not be the depth of men's resistance: what may be more important is the ease with which welfare workers and their agencies collude with any signs of resistance demonstrated by men.

In many ways it is convenient for agencies and individual workers not to pursue men too closely. Assessing mothers fits in more easily with societal (and personal) stereotypes and may consume fewer agency resources. Those are not good enough reasons for colluding with the resistance of fathers to involvement. So the issue may be not so much about devising new strategies for engaging fathers in child protection work, as about workers and agencies being more determined in what they are already doing. This will entail expending more effort and perhaps being more flexible about when work is done with families. Margins for more effort and flexibility are scarce in agencies, such as social services departments, where resources are already far too overstretched.

This point takes us back to the necessity of men workers expending much of their energy initially working on, and with, their agencies to make more space and time available. Work with agencies is also necessary to adapt those structures, examined in Chapter 2, which result in sexist practice: structures that extend from the top to the bottom of organizations. As we advance through this study, we will be continually reminded that change within agencies is not an optional extra in terms of men's anti-sexist and anti-oppressive practice. It is an essential component of that practice and men committed to this perspective in agencies must work together to create change at all levels in organizations.

One of the objectives of agency change is to enable men workers to have the space to work with users in ways consonant with an anti-oppressive perspective. Nor should men in agencies simply be working to change structures, policies and practice in relation to men users. For instance, this chapter has highlighted that mothers, especially as non-abusing parents, do need attention from welfare agencies: but in the form of support to help their children rather than the burden of scrutiny that they often now carry. In Chapter 7, we look in more detail at strategies by which men can work together in agencies to counter those oppressive practices that were so prominent in Chapter 2 and that have also been apparent in this chapter.

A second target of change for workers who are men is the cluster of policies and procedures that skew risk assessments. Men can play an important role in working for change inside their agencies at different levels. For instance, alongside female colleagues (if the latter feel this is appropriate) they can network to persuade their agency to reconsider the use of *Protecting children* (HMSO 1988b) as a tool in child protection assessments, especially sexual abuse ones.

A third target is the oppression that the care system inflicts on many young people within it. We shall consider how to deal with one of the most serious forms of this oppression, sexual assault, in Chapter 8.

In this chapter we have reviewed the patterns of domination that structure child protection systems in Britain. Similar patterns of oppression shape the wider issue of child and family care, and this issue is the focus of our attention in the next chapter.

Chapter 4

Child care and families

Introduction

We have already noted some ways in which the sharp dichotomy between child care and child protection is difficult to sustain. For instance, we observed the way in which the role of carer that is often socially assigned to a woman can catapult her into becoming the focus of very controlling child protection procedures.

We also witnessed how a system allegedly designed to provide alternative care for young people can serve to control and regulate their lives and the lives of their families via child protection procedures. We saw how, for too many children, the care system can become the site of further abuse. Finally, we have mentioned that some of the leading British researchers in this field (Parton & Parton 1989, Thorpe 1994) have concluded that separating out protection from care, using such concepts as "dangerousness", ensures in practice neither sufficient safety nor adequate support services for the general wellbeing of our children.

Bearing in mind that in some respects the dichotomy of care and control can be problematic, let us consider the issue of child care as it is addressed in government regulations, official guidance, and the literature about practice. Where do males fit in to what we know about child care?

This is a major issue in relation to social welfare and social policy that also reveals many of the fault lines in the problematic subject of men and the caring professions. In this chapter we consider the powerful forces that in recent years have sought to reinforce the idea that men are crucial for the wellbeing of families. We then take up the challenge of that movement and ask what is the value of men to families.

53

Back to basics or back to the bunker?

In terms of government rhetoric about "traditional family values" and "back to basics", men are seen as having a major role in families and in child care. Moreover, the government has gone well beyond rhetoric in trying to support the importance of men in families and these actions have been well reviewed by Mary Langan (1992): unmarried fathers are encouraged to claim parental rights and responsibilities via the Children Act 1989; unmarried women using artificial insemination are at risk of their anonymous sperm donor claiming parental rights. There is also the emphasis in the Children Act on continuing parental responsibility as something shared between mother and father which, as Langan says, "reveals underlying assumptions and evasions about motherhood, fatherhood and the white nuclear family which have important consequences for women and their children" (Langan 1992).

She also suggests that when the Children Act repeatedly refers to the family as the best place for the child, an ethnocentric nuclear ideal is clearly assumed. Her suggestion has since been confirmed by the explicit preference expressed by the government for two-parent heterosexual families in the White Paper on adoption which also struck a blow against the trend towards "same race" placements (HMSO 1993).

The state's promotion of the role of fathers in families has to be set in the context of current social and political concerns. For a start, the traditional nuclear family is increasingly a less common form of social organization. Williams (1992a) sums up the findings of the Family Policy Studies Centre: increased cohabitation, increased divorce, increased childbearing outside marriage, increases in one-parent families and reconstituted families, ethnic and sexual variations in household forms, an ageing of the population with an increase in households with only one or two people, an increase in female employment and dual-earner families. Her conclusion drawn from these data follows: "It is clear that the traditional male bread-winner, nuclear family . . . accounts for only one of a diverse range of living arrangements in which people may find themselves over their lifetimes" (Williams 1992a).

So the importance attached by the government to "the traditional family" seems to be inversely correlated with its actual existence: and the growing absence of men as a feature in households is one manifestation of the dissolution of the idea of the traditional family. As Jane Millar (1994) points out, on present estimates it may be that as few as half of all children in Britain by the year 2000 will have spent all their lives in a conventional two-parent family with both their natural parents.

In numerous public statements, members of the government have attributed various social ills to the absence of fathers in families. In 1994 the government slightly toned down its moralistic rhetoric partly because of public reaction following a series of scandals in which politicians were alleged to have been acting in far from "traditional family" ways.

Nevertheless, as Sophie Laws (1994) admirably demonstrates, government pressure is still very much on lone parents. She also notes that in terms of media coverage by the press,

> There's that popular touch of racism in it too, when it is reported that the proportion of lone parent families is higher amongst Afro-Caribbeans, while the fact that the figures are lower amongst Asian people than in the white population is given less prominence.

Within a feminist perspective she neatly summarizes the government's intentions as perceived in the Child Support Act:

> The Government want to revive the traditional bargain, where women with children are expected to put up with anything in return for being supported by a man rather than the state, and men are expected to financially support their children and their children's mother/s. Childcare and domestic work exchanged for the woman's and children's keep. Feminists have always analyzed this deal as exploitation of the woman, and everyone knows that there has always been a lot of cheating even within that bargain. We also know that massive levels of long-term unemployment remove it as an option for many people. (Laws 1994)

Jane Millar (1994) has also demonstrated how the government marries ideological considerations with financial expediency in the work of the Child Support Agency. This is symptomatic of the overall attack on lone parenthood: a return to a past with a supposedly rosy glow; withdrawal of the role of the state in the family; reduction of government expenditure; social control of marginalized groups such as the poor, black people, women, lesbian and gay people; and, as we shall see, a scapegoat for social ills actually arising from structural problems exacerbated or created by public policies.

Such a combination of elements is to be found in many government social policies: including, significantly, those relating to child protection surveyed in the previous chapter. Once again, we encounter the impossibility of understanding issues of child protection and child care in isolation from one another.

Laws goes on to demonstrate that, despite the furore created by men's groups, the Child Support Act is very much part of the process of promoting men's role in families:

> Most heterosexual women certainly feel that men should fulfil their responsibilities to their children. However, there is a very long distance between the ideal of fully shared responsibility for care and support of children and the Child Support Act's attempt to enforce the deal where men have to pay and women have to be dependent on them. (Laws 1994)

However, she shows that it is not only the lack of choice that alienates many women from the Act. For in practice it is of little or no financial help to many of them. At the same time, she cites some initial evidence that suggests many women are afraid that the Agency's actions will lead to ex-partners interfering in their lives more than hitherto with the result that thousands of them seem to be withdrawing from income support (see also Millar 1994).

The government's promotion of men as fathers is, in fact, part of a much broader movement on both sides of the Atlantic and it is important to appreciate that wider context.

Right-wing ideologies and the riots of the 1980s

In Britain, this trend has been supported by some academic commentators working within right-wing "think-tanks". For instance Dennis & Erdos (1992) and Dennis (1993) draw on the underclass theories of the American academic, Charles Murray (1990). Social disruption is explained by reference to the "underclass" which is explicitly linked to issues of gender. In particular these authors focus on the growth of illegitimacy and the absence of unemployed fathers in poor families.

In a critique of Murray's position, Cochrane (1993b) notes that Murray has shown a correlation between illegitimacy, crime, unemployment and poverty but not proven the causal links. For instance, it is unclear why Murray assumes that illegitimacy is the causal factor. Cochrane suggests that logically it might well be structural poverty that is the main causal issue, with illegitimacy and crime being two responses to it. Certainly, the linkages will be more complex than the Right's version suggests.

Dennis & Erdos (1992) were writing in the wake of the 1991 riots, when groups of largely young men went on the rampage in three or four urban centres of Britain including Tyneside, Cardiff and Oxford (B. Campbell 1993). They identify mothers' capacity for economic independence as one key factor in the growing absence of men from families, with consequent family and social breakdown. Campbell shrewdly points out that the New Right did not see the riots as "a masculine response to an economic crisis – it saw instead the failure of the mothers to manage the men". The parallel here with women's "responsibility" in child protection cases that we discussed in the previous chapter is too clear to require further comment.

From a right-wing point of view, of course, Dennis & Erdos (1992) present a comforting analysis because it diverts attention from two far more plausible but also more inconvenient contributory factors in the social upheavals of 1991: economic deprivation and the structures of domination associated with hegemonic masculinity.

Campbell emphasizes that men's emotional and practical absence from the family long pre-dates unemployment, illegitimacy and indeed their physical absence. She notes that Murray never asks the critical question "which has vexed mothers for a millennium: what is it about cultures of masculinity that means men will not cooperate with women and take care of their children?" (B. Campbell 1993)

Moreover, she argues that the young men of the Meadowell Estate in North Shields who rioted were not "starved of role models . . . they were saturated with them. That was the problem with no name that set the estates on fire in 1991." (B. Campbell 1993)

She adds:

> The lads were surrounded by a macho propaganda more potent in its penetration of young men's hearts and minds than at any other time in history – they were soaked in globally transmitted images and ideologies of butch and brutal solutions to life's difficulties . . . they, like journalists and judges, consumed as well as created those images and ideologies.

Campbell movingly portrays the efforts of the women on the estates in trying to maintain some form of social sanity via community initiatives. She does not discount the economic hardship of the people there. The crucial point is the different ways that the men and women dealt with the anguish arising from that deprivation:

... there is an economic emergency in many neighbourhoods where the difference between what women and men do with their troubles and with their anger shapes their strategies of survival and solidarity on the one hand, danger and destruction on the other. (B. Campbell 1993)

Campbell's message seems to be that masculinity does not need bolstering: it needs changing. We are reminded of earlier discussions in this study about the central importance of helping men to address attitudes and behaviours that we have associated with hegemonic and heterosexual masculinities.

What is certain is that the ideologies propagated by Dennis & Erdos (1992) and indeed by the government, which seek to promote fathering at the expense of some women's extremely tenuous independence are likely to exacerbate social problems while ignoring the real issues: social deprivation and the nature of masculinities.

The men's rights movement

The promotion of fatherhood as being a necessity for children is also an explicit aim of a pressure group in the United Kingdom known as "Families Need Fathers". Such a group is symptomatic of the growth in the United States and the United Kingdom of what Richard Clatterbaugh calls the "men's rights movement" (1990). He summarizes the movement as encompassing:

both men and women, some of whom were once associated with various profeminist groups but became disenchanted with the feminist movement. These men and women believe that the women's movement wrongly blames men for the oppression of women and that such blame is counterproductive to ending sexism. They also deny that men live privileged lives . . . They also argue that feminism seriously misconstrues male and female reality and has instituted an agenda that only makes things worse for men. (Clatterbaugh 1990)

One of the most striking contributions to this perspective has come from Wayne Farrell (1994) who regards himself as a former pro-feminist turned "men's liberationist". Farrell's work is an ingenious compendium of selective facts that flies in the face of the massive weight of evidence, much of which is presented in this study.

The work of Robert Bly

Support for the idea of the essential need for fathers in families has also come from sources allegedly more sympathetic to feminist critiques of patriarchy, in particular from the work of Robert Bly (Clatterbaugh 1990; Bly 1991) which, significantly, Farrell (1994) also commends.

Bly's work has become very popular and influential in both the United States and the United Kingdom, offering as it does an account of why men are the way they are and a hope of them living better by gaining new strength through contact with their deeper selves (Clatterbaugh 1990). In Bly's view, it is only men who can initiate boys into manhood by helping them to get in touch with the primitive part of themselves including that vital fierceness that is the (allegedly) true source of men's creativity and energy: femininity overwhelms men and prevents them knowing their fathers. Bly has drawn some trenchant responses from within the feminist movement, including from bell hooks (1992):

> . . . we need a men's movement that is part of revolutionary feminist movement. If the masses of men in our society have not unlearned their sexism, have not abdicated male privilege, then it should be obvious that a men's movement led only by men with only males participating runs the risk of mirroring in a different form much that is already oppressive in patriarchal culture. Much of what Bly and his followers offer as an affirmation of a different masculinity is only a nineteenth-century notion of the benevolent patriarch.

The agenda suggested by hooks is clearly far closer to the men's anti-oppressive practice project that is being advocated in this study than Bly's search for the "wild man" (1991) or Farrell's defence of men as victims of feminism (1994).

I am not suggesting for a minute that current government policies are driven directly by an awareness of Robert Bly or Wayne Farrell. But the former have to be seen as part of a general social trend to reassert the importance of men in families which embraces the latter, and which permeates the media.

Moreover, like Bly and Farrell, what is particularly striking about the British government's pro-father policies is that they fly in the face of some important social evidence about the relation of men to families. So we must now turn to the question of assessing whether families need fathers.

Do families need fathers?

Men's violence in families

Men's violences are dealt with at length in separate chapters. Consequently, this chapter focuses on other aspects of men's relation to families. However, when we make judgements about what men bring to families, obviously violence has to be part of that equation.

In Chapter 5 we will review in detail the evidence and debates about men's propensity for sexual, physical and emotional violence against adults who are their partners. At this point all we need to note is that it is generally agreed men's violence to the people with whom they live is a major problem even if there is more controversy about the context of that violence.

In terms of men's violence to children, we have already reviewed some of the most relevant evidence in Chapter 3. However, we have to be slightly careful in applying this to families. We now know that sexual abuse of children is extremely common in our society: perhaps a fifth or even a third of the population has experienced some form of unwanted sexual experience before attaining adulthood (Finkelhor et al. 1990, Kelly et al. 1991). This is appalling and represents one of the greatest problems that we as a society face. We also know that men seem to be responsible for about 90 per cent of this abuse. How far does it happen within the immediate family?

There is a degree of difficulty in answering that question, partly because the data are not always consistent. We do know that most sexual abuse is committed by people acquainted with the child or young person. However, they may be uncles, grandfathers, extended family members or trusted adults outside the immediate family including, as we saw in the previous chapter, welfare professionals. Perpetrators may also be other children or young people related to, or acquaintances of, the child they abuse (Glasgow et al. 1994, O'Callaghan & Print 1994).

In a recent British prevalence study (Kelly et al. 1991), the proportion of sexual abuse perpetrated by actual parents was relatively small. On the other hand, there are methodological reasons for thinking that this study may have underestimated abuse by them (see Hooper 1992). Clearly, more research is vital on this matter.

Can men parent?

In surveying sociological perspectives on gender divisions within the family as it exists, Richard Barker (1994) has noted that the analyses of both functionalist and Marxist models focus on the relegation of women to a supportive home-based role while men act as the "breadwinners". Only in the last twenty years has a feminist set of theories specifically explored and challenged these assumptions.

Barker also points out that in previous centuries British fathers had an "imperial legal right" over their children *vis-à-vis* mothers and that in most disputed cases courts would grant custody to fathers.

Thus, the perception that women were central to families and that "mothering" was crucial for children has been a relatively recent invention over the last century and a half. It was reinforced by the childrearing ideology of Bowlby and the social policies of the post-1945 welfare state. Within this post-war model, a man's major contribution to the family would be as a wage earner in a full-employment economy (Williams 1989, Barker 1994).

In reviewing the development of the concept of fatherhood in the period between the 1950s and the late 1980s, Lynne Segal (1990) concludes: "Wherever we look, it seems hard to deny that there has been a remarkable shift in public opinion towards the idea that men should be, and are, more involved in child care."

However, she also emphasizes that there is a major gap between this change in outlook and an actual change in practical behaviour. As Fiona Williams (1992a) comments: ". . . in spite of an increase in women's paid employment, women still carry the major responsibilities for household tasks and emotional and physical care".

Although some commentators suggest that the employment practices that men have to cope with are responsible for that lack of change in domestic responsibilities, Segal (1990) is sceptical about this view as a full explanation of the situation. She cites evidence to show that men usually take on the more pleasurable aspects of child care, leaving the remainder to women; and that unemployed men often do less domestic work than men in employment, even when their partners have full-time jobs. She then adds that some commentators "would argue that men have no real wish to change, that they are happy, as a sex, to exploit women by leaving the labour of loving and caring to them". Men choose to leave matters as they are.

Segal does not totally give up hope of meaningful domestic change on the part of men, and in reviewing a series of studies on the issue, concludes:

> . . . when women can command a higher income, when men have already achieved higher levels of personal self-satisfaction and independence (usually when they are older), when there is a more supportive social milieu, or when there are fewer children and household demands are less onerous – in these rare circumstances, men are more likely to accept a primary commitment to home and childcare. (Segal 1990)

Clearly, this is still quite a pessimistic conclusion. She also notes that a few men do fully share in house and child care, including some male lone parents. In reviewing the literature on this, Segal emphasizes that clearly there is no paternal incapacity to "mother" [sic]. In fact, she points out that in one study of reversed-role parenting with full-time fathers it seemed to make little difference to the children, female or male, which parent parented.

Segal appears to be saying that there is no reason to think that men are incapable of taking a major role in child and house care but that to a very great extent they do not; and that this may largely be a matter of choice on their part rather than the product of circumstance.

Men as lone parents

A recent and important study of lone fathers in the North East of England by Richard Barker (1994) looks in more detail at many of the issues raised by Segal and seems in some ways to provide a more optimistic picture. Since this material is central to the concerns of our study and because in its sophistication Barker's work supersedes the relatively small amount of previous British research on this topic, we shall consider it in detail now.

Segal's positive judgement about the capacity of men to nurture and to manage a household is borne out by Barker. In relation to a checklist of common childhood problems, the vast majority of children in his survey were seen to present none of those problems to a serious degree. Barker

(1994) himself expresses some surprise at this, given that most of the children had experienced forms of prior trauma, whether the death of a mother or break-up of their parents' marriage.

There is, however, a major methodological problem with the study that is relevant to this issue and to other conclusions that Barker (1994) seeks to draw, for the study relies totally on the reports of the men themselves (Pringle 1994b). One wonders whether the children, or indeed the divorced men's ex-partners, would have rated the situation differently. Barker in this instance seems to discount any problem arising from the men's self-reporting.

The other indication from Barker's study that the men's parenting of the children might have been successful was the marked lack of involvement by welfare professionals in these families on account of childhood problems (1994). This finding is thrown into striking contrast when we recall that in Chapter 3 we saw that belonging to a lone parent family was, statistically, a major risk factor in terms of children being placed in care. However, this contrast may be less striking than it appears, for several reasons.

First of all, about 90 per cent of lone parents are female (Barker 1994). Being male as a lone parent seems to bring advantages:

> Of one-parent families headed by men 70 per cent have earnings as their main source of income in contrast with 44.6 per cent headed by women . . . Greater earning power enables men to purchase day care and other forms of help such as housekeepers . . . (Hanmer & Statham 1988)

As Hanmer & Statham (1988) note, poverty, housing problems, poor health and transport difficulties are interconnecting barriers to enhanced life opportunities for many families of lone parents who are women, and being female is a most significant structural variable in that oppressive equation (Laws 1994).

Moreover, one striking feature in Barker's study (1994) is the extent to which many of the men did have external assistance with child care, often from female relatives or acquaintances. The picture was similar in relation to housework.

In addition, another structural factor is relevant to Barker's findings (1994). For all his sample of men were white and able-bodied. This too may well have had an impact on their experiences as lone parents. For instance, we know that all the factors disadvantaging female lone parents mentioned above tend to be compounded by the effects of racism when lone parents are black (Hanmer & Statham 1988, Bryan 1992).

From Barker's own data (1994) it seems there may well have been additional reasons for lack of intervention by welfare professionals in his sample of families. He notes that, apart from some initial contact with court welfare officers when custody was being decided, social work intervention was very limited indeed and some of the lone fathers actually "felt that social welfare agencies were failing in their duties by not ensuring that everything was satisfactory in new lone father households". Similarly,

> . . . there was a surprising lack of involvement by health visitors in the lives of the lone fathers and their children. Whether this was the result of mismanagement, a respect for patriarchal rights to authority and privacy, difficulties in (female) health visitors relating to (male) parents, or some other cause, is unclear. It does appear however that at least a sizeable minority of lone fathers felt they would have benefited from some professional being available to give them advice and validation in their parenting roles, health visitors would have been ideally placed to have adopted such roles, and some lone fathers were surprised that they had not. (Barker 1994)

Surveying the overall pattern of involvement by state and voluntary agencies in his sample of families, Barker (1994) concludes:

> The impression is that such individuals and institutions were slow to invade the privacy of lone father households, in fact, at times, slower than many lone fathers felt was legitimate. It was not the case that "fit fatherhood" was being nurtured or monitored . . .

This is in direct contrast with what is happening to mothers, as Hanmer & Statham (1988) make clear when discussing child care assessments. From the point of antenatal care onwards motherhood is increasingly scrutinized by the full spectrum of social welfare agencies to assess a woman's "fitness" for the role. This, of course, can be linked to the responsibilities attributed to mothers in cases of child protection by social welfare agencies and to the guilt heaped upon them by politicians and the media for most social ills.

It is open to debate as to why social welfare professionals may display differential approaches to female and male lone parents. Clearly, the impact of gender in terms of both the welfare workers and the users needs to be considered. We may be encountering here a key problem about the delivery of welfare services in relation to men. It is a problem that we saw Judith Milner (1993) identify in the previous chapter with regard to child protection investigations: welfare professionals do not seem to know how to deal with men.

As Hanmer & Statham (1988) put it, "There is no corresponding 'fit father' role for social workers to use in their assessment and planning." So gendered are the social welfare services internally (see Chapter 2) and externally in relation to child care, that dealing with men poses a major challenge. Barker (1994), too, appreciates this:

> . . . the process of giving consideration to the issues involved in creating, in appropriate circumstances, "male centred practice" which takes gender and masculinity seriously, has only just begun.

Clearly, in outlining this need and that for support services, these commentators are identifying further objectives for men's practice as workers within social welfare. We should note, however, that there is scope for men who are lone parents, as well as men who are welfare workers, to push for these developments. One of the themes of this study is that anti-oppressive activity by men in the field of social welfare should be a concern for men as both workers and users, in some cases acting in alliance with one another.

Turning back now to the specific issue of men as lone parents and what their experience tells us about men as carers, we should note that Barker's (1994) data conflict with Hanmer & Statham (1988) who state: ". . . social services are more responsive to requests for assistance from one-parent families headed by men". In fact, the experience of Barker's sample seems to be that most men carers are no better at dealing with welfare bureaucracies than are women carers.

We have to remember that Barker's study (1994) is relatively small: 35 men in the sample. So we must be careful not to draw too broad a conclusion from it. Bearing in mind that caveat, we can say that many men who are lone parents may avoid the close regulation by welfare personnel that female lone parents frequently endure. Moreover, in terms of economic resources and perhaps also in terms of support from female relatives and friends, men who are lone parents may often enjoy benefits not accruing to women who are by themselves.

These factors have important practical and structural value and we cannot underestimate the degree to which they may relieve the pressure on some men struggling with lone parenthood. In saying this, I am not denying that men who are lone parents sometimes face immense difficulties; nor am I suggesting that men who are lone parents are necessarily inferior to women as nurturers.

However, I think we do have to recognize that, by virtue of the patriarchal relations that structure our society, the experiences of men and women as lone parents are often different and that these gendered experiences are usually detrimental to women. Moreover, within the category of men, some will tend to be less structurally advantaged than others: for instance, black men. For those reasons we must be cautious about being too optimistic regarding the conclusions that can be drawn from Barker's study (1994) about men's success in adopting the major domestic role.

Moreover, we need to reiterate that Barker (1994) is almost wholly reliant on the men's self-reports, and this is a major methodological problem with regard to many of his other conclusions. From the perspective of standpoint theory (Swigonski 1994), giving men "a voice" in research is not the same as giving it to women or children because of considerations of power in terms of gender and age.

I am not arguing that the men in Barker's study (1994) should be silent. I am arguing that it is problematic to give them a voice without also having the benefit of hearing the voices of their children and ex-partners who will probably have less structural power than they do. That is especially the case when men are commenting upon the experiences of their children and ex-partners and not merely of themselves.

Without the additional voices of the women and children, we can neither test the validity of the men's judgements nor add depth to our understanding of why events happened as they did: our understanding remains one-dimensional and flat.

For instance, in his study, how does Barker address the question of child sexual abuse that we have seen is a major social issue and one highly relevant to any study of men? In fact it is scarcely dealt with because as he tells us (Barker 1994), "there was no indication in any of the families studied that child sexual abuse was occurring, or had occurred". The unanswered questions remain, of course: who did he ask? who is telling us this? Once again, Barker seems dependent on the men's reports for this information.

We need to bear this methodological point in mind when we assess Barker's major finding about the development of men as parents (1994). For he identifies some fathers, whom he calls "pioneers", who are moving away in their behaviour from the old patriarchal mould.

He develops this argument by first noting that the vast majority of the men in his sample (both patriarchs and pioneers) were more involved with their children than they had been prior to becoming lone fathers and the same applied to household management. From this Barker draws the following conclusion:

> . . . this research illustrates that in certain circumstances "men can mother", that fathers can take primary responsibility for tasks and activities that are traditionally seen to lie within the feminine domain. In taking on such responsibilities lone fathers did not feel either particularly diminished in their sense of masculinity or assert that they were behaving in "ideologically sound anti-sexist practices" – they did not appear to see themselves as "Old Women" or "New Men". (Barker 1994)

What marks out pioneers from patriarchs in this process according to Barker is that:

> . . . gender pioneers had orientations to masculinities which prioritised child care and parenting as being important for men as well as for women, and they tended to be generally more child-centred in the ways in which they generated a sense of meaning and purpose in their lives. As parents, they were generally inclined not to regret the additional responsibilities of lone fatherhood, and tended to perceive that they had become "softer" in their relations with their children as a result of being lone fathers. (Barker 1994)

According to Barker (1994), this pioneering orientation to child care and fathering "marked a form of discontinuity from past parenting influences".

This is an important conclusion, for it bears out again that men can nurture very adequately if they choose to do so. More crucially, it also seems to indicate that such nurturing occurs in practice more often than Segal (1990) assumed. Furthermore, this shift seems to reflect an adaptation of heterosexual masculinity in terms of issues such as dependency, openness and emotional range (Herek 1987, Hearn & Parkin 1987).

However, before accepting this fully we need to note some inconsistencies in the data about the patriarch/pioneer dichotomy. For instance, Barker (1994) acknowledges that the distinction between the two categories of pioneers and patriarchs has little relevance to the issue of which men received assistance with child care from relatives and friends. Pioneers also had considerable assistance.

Similarly, we are told that pioneers actually tended to have more unfriendly contacts with ex-partners than did patriarchs. Barker (1994) explains this apparent anomaly by suggesting that ex-partners might pose more of a threat to the parenting commitment of the pioneers than to the patriarchs. Not only does this seem a rather tortuous explanation, but it also betrays a less than pioneering spirit on the part of pioneers. A much simpler explanation for this anomaly and others might be that the pioneer/patriarch dichotomy is flawed.

In fairness to Barker (1994), he himself acknowledges that the dichotomy cannot be sustained coherently across all the results of the study. He defines this as a legitimate complexity within his results and draws on a poststructuralist perspective to explain it: there are competing masculinities within each man struggling to resolve that competition in the context of a patriarchal society. This may be a valid explanation and certainly the theoretical approach towards masculinity that he adopts is similar to the one we accept in this study.

However, an alternative explanation is also possible for the inconsistencies in his data. By relying so exclusively on the men's own discourses, Barker (1994) has failed to contextualize them with alternative discourses such as those of the children and ex-partners. It may be that it is in the men's discourses about what happened that there are inconsistencies and not in their actual behaviour. Of course, those alternative discourses of the women and children would not necessarily tell us "the truth". However, they might, taken in conjunction with the pioneers' own versions of reality, have provided a picture of the pioneers that is more consistent: consistent perhaps in being more patriarchal than they appear in Barker's survey based on their own reports. We will never know if this is the case.

There is no doubt that Barker's research (1994) is an important study that provides much information about an under-researched issue of vital concern to our project. It certainly supports the view that many men have moved on in their ideas about child care since the 1950s. It also confirms Segal's view (1990) that men can take on the major nurturing and caring role in a family, although its methodological weaknesses limit the power of that confirmation. For the same reason, we can be even less sure of Barker's claim that his pioneers represented a discontinuity from past parenting influences. In these circumstances, it seems more prudent to maintain Segal's original view of the matter: many men like the idea of being more responsible for child and home care; many men could probably do it if they wanted to do so; few men actually fulfil the promise to the same extent as women.

Men and money

Given this state of affairs, what do men currently bring to children and a family? One answer is reasonably clear in view of our previous discussion about what it is that many lone female parents lack: money and resources.

The relative poverty of many female lone parents is well attested (Williams 1989, Cochrane 1993b). Their difficulties derive from a combination of low, means-tested income support instruments and confinement to low-wage, full-time or part-time employment. These factors are often compounded by social isolation and then in turn by consequent ill-health (Cannan 1992).

We have encountered many of these features already in this study. For instance, in Chapter 2 we saw how, for women working within welfare services (and outside), the labour market operates to their disadvantage. This is clearly another example of the way patriarchal relations within the world of welfare workers mirrors the situation of users. Moreover, as we noted at the beginning of Chapter 2 welfare workers can also be users and vice versa: a financially hard-pressed lone parent can be a care assistant in a residential setting or a clerk/typist in a hospital. Earlier in this chapter we also saw that the Child Support Agency is generally more successful in clawing back money to the state rather than improving the lot of lone parents on low incomes (Millar 1994).

The other factor that prevents many women escaping from this treadmill is the lack in Britain of mass, good-quality, low-cost publicly funded child care (Cannan 1992, Cochrane 1993b). Indeed, Millar (1994) concludes that lack "of child care is the largest single barrier to employment for lone mothers".

There is now a considerable literature available on the nature of day care (Hennessy et al. 1992, Cannan 1992). The provision of child care in Britain is a confusing patchwork of private and public services. In effect, most day care, especially for the poorest sectors of the population, is undertaken informally by friends and relatives. Its quality is, of course, variable and anyway it depends on a network being available and/or good cheap transport. As for the rest of the provision, Cannan (1992) provides a bleak summary:

> The consequences for children of British attitudes to family services is that what public daycare remains takes the most deprived and disturbed children. By contrast, professional and middle class parents may pay for their children to attend private

nurseries. There is thus a widening class and ethnic differential between the two types of provision . . . [a] large proportion of children attend childminders: this is regulated, but of variable quality, and characterized by a high turnover; it is inherently unstable. So too are the day nursery system and the private nanny system because the pay, training and status of nursery nurses are low . . . Playgroups have been heavily promoted by both the major political parties, but quality is variable, staff have low levels of training, and the hours are not suitable for working mothers.

Apart from demonstrating the extremely limited opportunities open to lone parents from this provision, the passage quoted has two notable features. First, the terms of employment described by Cannan for the almost wholly female staff in day care correspond precisely to those we described in Chapter 2.

Secondly, when Cannan (1992) refers in her first sentence to British attitudes to family services, she partly means the tendency to target state provision on "dangerous families". Thus, public provision now largely takes the form of family centres. There is a diversity in the focus of different centres but as Cannan indicates, a major role is the "monitoring" and, sometimes, "treatment" of "vulnerable" families referred by social services and/or the health service. Lone parents make up a sizeable proportion of the parents in family centres. As for heterosexual couples, Cannan notes:

Men tend not to use family centres to the degree that women do . . . to some extent they come to centres' "masculine" activities like youth clubs, unemployed clubs, DIY clubs, etc. There is a grey area where men's needs are neglected, yet where men are not held responsible for family life as women are – for it is the women who are encouraged to attend. (Cannan 1992)

Thus, we see again that the care and control functions of the welfare system overlap and interact. This pattern for the use of public day care mirrors the contours of the child protection system described in Chapter 3: in fact, to all intents and purposes most of public day care has become an adjunct of that system.

In 1994 the government made some financial assistance available to mothers in paid employment for child care costs. However, as Sophie Laws points out (Laws 1994), this assistance is far smaller than the actual cost of child care. Moreover, it is of no benefit to mothers without paid employment. Of course, proportionately fewer lone mothers are in paid work than married mothers for precisely the reasons we have just outlined, such as lack of available day care. Which brings us back to our point of departure: the economic vulnerability of female lone parents.

In surveying the mechanisms by which lone parents are trapped in an economic vice, we have to keep constantly in mind that all this is compounded for women who are black due to the multiple and multiplying effects of racism on life opportunities (Cochrane 1993b).

Given this desperate context, it is understandable that being with a man can have important financial and social advantages for women. As regards social advantages, we need to recognize that under these economic pressures social isolation and loneliness are major problems, especially with young children to care for. Of course, being with a man does not guarantee that these social needs will be met. Moreover, women can help other women as friends or as lovers. However, in some situations women return to men in (almost) the worst circumstances possible (a theme we pursue in Ch. 6). As Laws (1994) notes:

> These economic factors are very familiar to those who work with women escaping domestic violence. It's no mystery why women go back – there are huge economic and social forces pushing them.

So one element that men can provide for a family is the possibility of more resources. However, it is a possibility that is not fulfilled for many women with male partners. Cochrane (1993b) gives a useful summary of the research in recent years that demonstrates the economic disadvantage that women often endure within heterosexual relationships, and not necessarily always in poor families. The basic problem is twofold here.

First, because women tend to be highly disadvantaged in terms of overall power within families, the distribution of resources made within the family is frequently in favour of the man. Secondly, due to maternal expectations placed upon the mother by others and, perhaps, by herself women will often deprive themselves in favour of children and their partner if resources are limited.

For these reasons, and also because women tend to be more realistic about managing poverty than men, Cochrane (1993b) points out that some women feel in a more economically sound position after the breakup of a relationship than when they lived with a man. He is careful, however, not to generalize and for instance draws attention to cultural variations in these experiences.

We can now summarize the financial contribution of men to families. For households containing women with children and without partners, poverty is more likely than is the case for households with men. However, given the employment and labour market situation in the UK a man is clearly no guarantee of a reasonable income. Moreover, for the reasons discussed above, many women might well find themselves (and their children) economically oppressed when living with men.

Do children need fathers?

One of the central beliefs of the pressure group "Families Need Fathers" (which was mentioned earlier in this chapter) is that children suffer without the involvement of their biological fathers, either by their presence in families or where parents are separated by joint custody. They regard paternal access to children as vital even when there has been violence to female partners or children in the past, arguing that such violence would usually have been a response to provocation from the female partner (Segal 1990). We offer a critique of this last point in the next chapter.

For the time being we address the issue of parental contact and joint custody. Several arguments can be put forward that suggest that parental contact in cases where there has been a history of family violence needs to be handled very carefully indeed.

First, where paternal violence has taken the form of sexual abuse to the children, particular caution is required regarding contact. We know clearly that perpetrators tend to be persistent and ingenious in continuing their activities (Wyre & Swift 1987, Glaser & Frosh 1993). Many abusers are quite capable of abusing children even in highly supervised situations (Pringle 1994c, Hunt 1994). Decisions about the extent and nature of parental contact will also depend upon how far professionals believe it is possible to "treat" sexual abusers.

Where previous violence took the form of harm to partners or physical assaults on children, considerable caution is also warranted. Research (O'Hara 1993, Saunders 1994) suggests the following: there may be a considerable risk that a man who batters his partner will also have physically or sexually abused the children; the risk of a woman who has been beaten doing the same to the children is considerably lower; men can often use contact with children after separation as a conduit for continuing emotional abuse of their ex-partner; men who abused their partners are much more likely to enter into another abusive relationship than are

72

partners who have been abused; there are doubts about the efficacy of treatment for men who physically abuse women. Both O'Hara (in Britain) and Saunders (in the United States) recommend caution in granting contact or residence/custody to such fathers. (See also Hooper 1994 for a judicious review of these issues.)

Turning to the more general issue of how far children need fathers, Erica De'Ath (1989) points out that the degree of trauma that children endure at the dissolution of a marriage depends not so much on the separation or loss itself as on factors like: the domestic atmosphere preceding the dissolution; the way the parents conduct the dissolution and manage contact thereafter.

Angela Phillips (1993) finds conflicting data on how well children develop when brought up by fathers rather than by mothers. She concludes that:

> ... while it is clearly an advantage for a growing child to have a close relationship with an adult of the same gender, that is not as important in the long run as a relationship with a parent who loves them and isn't afraid to show it. Gender identity is important but it can be got from any man who takes the trouble to take a real interest. (Phillips 1993)

This judgement is borne out by a series of studies (not considered by Phillips (1990)) that have sought to determine the impact on children of being brought up in lesbian households. For it is important to emphasize that the pressures to reassert fatherhood are not only sexist. As we noted earlier, they can also often be racist. Moreover, as we have seen in the case of the White Paper on adoption (HMSO 1993) AND the myths about homosexuality and sexual abuse, those pressures are deeply heterosexist.

The research on lesbian households needs to be extended, particularly in terms of longitudinal studies. Nevertheless, considerable research has now been carried out and on the whole points in one direction (Golombok et al. 1983, Patterson 1992): children in lesbian and gay households seem to develop emotionally and physically just as well as children in heterosexual households.

Another perspective that places particular value on men in families is found in the work of Nancy Chodorow (1978) and Eichenbaum & Orbach (1982). Fusing approaches drawn from feminism and object relations psychology, this approach suggests that men's need to dominate others and to denigrate women arises from the exclusive nurturing relationship that exists between male children and their mothers (Segal 1990). The direct implication of such an analysis is that if men were more involved in nurturing boys and if that nurturing took an appropriate form, then it might lead over generations to less sexism on the part of individual men.

Some commentators have linked Chodorow's thesis (1978) more specifically to the development of men who commit sexual abuse (Finkelhor 1991, Glaser & Frosh 1993). They would regard her model as part of a larger framework, including structural factors as well, which explains the socialization of men who abuse. They also argue that the greater inclusion of men in child care could play a positive part in changing the socialization of men, possibly resulting in less sexual abuse being perpetrated by them.

There are considerable problems with Chodorow's hypothesis (1978) both in terms of the generation of sexism and sexual abuse. As Glaser & Frosh (1993) note, its focus on the mother–child bond tends to ignore structural, patriarchal factors. Nor does it explain how some men appear to avoid, or at least have widely different responses to, the mechanism that Chodorow posits. Another intractable problem deriving from its psychoanalytic origins is, of course, that it is more or less impossible to prove or disprove. Moreover, her approach could also be interpreted as another way to place responsibility on women for the ills of the world. We have already seen versions of this tendency and learnt to be suspicious of them in other contexts.

For all these reasons, a more sophisticated model of gender relations seems to be required. Connell's work (1987, 1995) incorporates some insights from both classical and existential psychoanalysis but positions them in a far broader framework centring on the structures of labour, power and cathexis. In Chapter 8 we consider that framework in more detail, particularly in relation to men's sexual violences.

So, do children need fathers? First of all, we have to say that we desperately want more research in this area. We particularly require more information about the experience of children in different family configurations and cultural settings. It is dangerous to generalize about the family context when it is open to the social politics of "race", disability, sexuality and class.

At present, the conclusion of this review seems to be that there is no evidence that children need to have fathers, as such, either inside the household or out. The particular concern expressed in the literature has been about boys without fathers, but nothing suggests that the latter are an absolute necessity. Phillip's summation seems balanced and accurate:

While boys need to learn about the male world, they can manage without a resident male, provided that their mother can provide a safe enough base from which they can explore. It is a great help if the mother has some emotional back-up but that doesn't have to come from a man. (Phillips 1993)

Conclusion

And what about our initial question: do families need fathers? Let us summarize what we have seen. On the one hand, we know men seem to be responsible for the bulk of family violence and that a large, very significant minority of women and children endure physical and/or sexual assault there (see also Chs 3 and 6). On the other hand, we have found that many men say they want to, and could, play a much larger role in child and household care, but we know that most of them choose not to do so.

We have seen the difficulties that many female parents without men partners face in terms of benefits, low part-time and full-time pay, housing, and lack of child care support. We know a large proportion are subjected to social regulation by the social welfare agencies, including family centres, and are held responsible for many social ills by the government and media. Statistically, there appears to be some clustering of single-parenthood, crime and social deprivation, but the latter is more likely to be the key variable rather than an absence of fathers. We noted that all these features of lone motherhood can be compounded by other social oppressions such as being black in a white society.

Having a man in the family seems to mean that the family may be less vulnerable to poverty in terms of benefits and income but there is no guarantee that the woman and the children will themselves necessarily gain any advantage from this. Women may (or may not) also gain social support from the presence of a man. However, this may also be available from other women.

Although it may be useful for boys to have masculine role models in the family, there is no guarantee that they will be positive ones. Moreover, boys can usually find role models outside the immediate family. There is evidence that children of both genders fare just as well emotionally and developmentally in families without men.

The overall evidence seems to suggest that families do not need fathers. That is not at all the same as saying that men should not be in families. Obviously many men are valuable to families in terms of money and/or social support and/or child care and/or in helping boys to develop. The question is not really whether men should or should not be in families. The question is what kind of man, what kind of masculinity, has most to offer to other human beings, including women and children.

On several occasions in this chapter we have seen articulated the need to develop qualities in men that are not associated with dominant forms of heterosexual masculinity: nurturance, emotional literacy, non-violence, openness to emotional closeness and dependency on others. We have seen this kind of masculinity related to parenting, offering support to partners, and helping to develop similar qualities in the next generation of children. In many ways the question is how can we promote these qualities in men? And as far as this study is concerned, how might they be promoted by men working in the social welfare system?

As we have said there are many opportunities to assist men with these issues in social welfare settings, either as individuals or groups. Some are particularly relevant to the issues in this chapter, for instance work with men by men in family centres, looking at parenting skills in the context not only of what it means to be a man but also of patriarchal relations. In addition, this would entail working with these men in ways that would help them choose not to abuse their position in families (see Ch. 8).

Men working in a similar setting or in social work/health community services might be able to look at the issue of lone fathers, finding out what supports would be useful to them and working with them to develop such supports. Much the same issues as those mentioned in the last paragraph could be addressed, again either individually or in a group with lone fathers. These kinds of projects can be carried out by networking in welfare agencies with other men or with women if that is appropriate. The same caveats apply here as they did in Chapter 2: services for men should not be developed at the expense of those to other users, and men workers should not colonize anti-oppressive work already being done by women.

Moreover, there is another side to this question of men and families. Of course, men involved with social welfare, as either workers or users, should develop services to assist men to play a constructive rather than a destructive part in families. However, men welfare workers also have a responsibility within an anti-oppressive framework to use all the strategies and techniques available to them in their agencies to push for changes in the structures governing the way lone mothers are treated.

We have seen that employment, income support and child care policies all conspire to act against them. Change can be worked towards at many levels: networking to try to persuade the agency to support public campaigns; gathering research to support the case for change; seeking movement at the local level; individual work; advocating with the various agencies. Obviously men engaged in working for change in this area would need to liaise closely with female colleagues and/or users who may well have been working in this direction for a considerable time.

The reason I place such emphasis on this issue of resources for lone mothers is not simply because it would improve the wellbeing of women and children, although that would be enough justification in itself. It is also because, without these changes, it is so hard for women to leave men whose behaviour, whose masculinity, is destructive to them and/or their children. This is the other side of the coin to helping men choose to behave more positively. If men choose not to behave positively, then the structures must exist whereby women and children can easily escape those situations. It might even be that if men knew women and children had a real and effective option of leaving, they would choose to change their behaviour more readily (Pringle 1994a).

Chapter 5
Adult violence

The following quotation is not from a radical activist outside the mainstream but from a professor of clinical psychology and a senior health service practitioner:

> A cursory look at history shows the enormity of suffering caused by male violence; in the wars, rapes, tortures and beatings that men have perpetrated on their fellow men, women and children. Indeed, male violence may even outrank disease and famine as the major source of human suffering. There is much evidence that many forms of adult pathology relate to a history of abuse, especially at the hand of men. If one wanted to instigate one mental illness prevention programme, then targeting male violence would possibly be the single most significant one. (P. Gilbert 1994)

Feminist/pro-feminist activists and writers operating further from the mainstream of academic social sciences than Gilbert have been making the same connections about the extent and depth of men's violences for many years (for example Susan Brownmiller 1975). Moreover, they are developing them further now:

> As more and more is uncovered about the extent and nature of male violence against women, the notion of an ongoing sex war is again clearly relevant. One way we have tried to make sense of this is to expand the concept of a continuum of sexual violence to include situations of social disorder and conventionally defined war. (McCollum et al. 1994)

What immediately prompted this comment by three activists/writers (McCollum et al. 1994) was their reaction to the use of rape and sexual assault as a deliberate strategy of war in the former Yugoslavia.

In this study, we have already examined part of the evidence relating to men's violences. We saw that child abuse was a massive social problem and that its occurrence was heavily gendered, particularly in its sexual form.

We now turn our attention to men's violences in relation to adulthood: violence that is perpetrated by adults on adults. How far is adult violence a gendered phenomenon? To the extent that it is, how do other forms of oppression impact upon it? How do social welfare agencies relate to men's violences and are there also patterns of oppression within that relationship?

How far is violence gendered?

Let us consider violence as direct physical aggression between two or more people. Elizabeth Stanko notes (1987, 1990) that most criminological research has focused on violence by strangers outside the home. And official crime statistics do indicate that to a considerable extent interpersonal violence occurs outside the home and that most of this violence is perpetrated by men on men (Stanko 1987, Archer 1994). This violence largely takes the form of crimes such as physical assault and robbery.

Men's violence to other men

This official man-on-man violence appears to be mediated by dimensions of power that we have encountered many times before in this study. Looking at American and British data, Stanko (1987) identifies the following groups of men as being most at risk: "Young, single, black, Hispanic or Asian poor men who live in urban areas have the highest likelihood of being victims of interpersonal violence." Moreover, many of these characteristics (young, single, poor, urban) also apply to many male victimizers in the official data so that Stanko can describe this violence as having the appearance of "exchanged" blows rather than predatory crime.

Crime by women largely exists in terms of relatively less violent offences such as theft, handling stolen goods, fraud and forgery and drugs offences (Abbott & Wallace 1990); even in these categories men predominate but the gender margins are somewhat less than is the case for violent crime.

In terms of explaining why violent crime should have such a gendered profile we will at this stage make two points. First, there is some evidence (Fagan et al. 1983, Maiuro et al. 1988; Levinson 1989) that men who perpetrate violence against women in close relationships may possess similar features to, and may in some cases actually be the same as, men who are violent outside the home. Consequently what we learn later in this chapter about men who sexually and/or physically assault their partners may in some cases be directly relevant to the form of violent crime described in this section, too.

Secondly, a particularly fruitful way of looking at men's violence both outside and inside the home has been suggested by the work of the social psychologist Anne Campbell (1993, Campbell & Muncer 1994) and we will consider her views in some depth in relation to violence outside the home.

For Campbell (A. Campbell 1993, Campbell & Muncer 1994) the crucial difference between men and women is not about whether they have feelings of anger: evidence inside and outside psychology laboratories tends to show that both genders have a capacity for such feelings. The real difference, she suggests, is the way men and women understand violence.

She takes robbery as an archetypal gendered criminal activity (A. Campbell 1993, Campbell & Muncer 1994) and demonstrates that men's preponderance as offenders cannot be explained in terms of physical strength, motives, opportunity or several other suggested reasons. Instead, drawing upon research studies by herself and others, she emphasizes that there seems to be a very significant correlation between being a man and holding a relatively instrumental view of violence, in contrast to women. By "instrumental" Campbell means violence that has as its objective social and/or material rewards including coercive power, social control, normative approval, self-esteem, the management of identity and "a variety of other social and material reinforcers such as the acquisition of territory, money, and peer approval". In making this interpretation, Campbell incorporates ideas and evidence linked to a variety of psychological models including behavioural and social learning. In passing, we may note how close this description is to features of what we have called heterosexual and hegemonic forms of masculinity that seem central to so many of the problematic issues addressed in this study.

By contrast, Campbell (A. Campbell 1993, Campbell & Muncer 1994) depicts female violence as tending to possess a much more expressive character. Again, drawing upon a range of psychological models (this time focused on intrapsychic mechanisms), Campbell interprets "expressive" violence as being about the discharge of anger in itself, rather than about social or material reward. As an example of the proposed difference between men's and women's violence, Campbell focuses on the issue of control. For many men much violence tends to be about the assertion of control in one way or another. For many women control is also a major issue in the manifestation of their violence but in a totally different manner: they fear the loss of their own self-control that their violence often represents.

There are clearly dangers if one adopts this approach too simplistically (which on the whole Campbell (A. Campbell 1993, Campbell & Muncer 1994) herself does not). For instance, a generalization can easily become a stereotype and ignore the heterogeneity of both men's and women's social situations and behaviours. In particular, we must be careful not to think in terms of simplistic clichés about women being "sad" (or perhaps worse "mad") and men being "bad". Having said all this, Campbell's approach does help us at a social psychological level to make sense of a striking and alarming feature of our world: the much greater extent to which many men compared to women do violence to other human beings and to the environment.

We are still left with some major questions. For instance, why do men rather than women have this instrumental approach? Why do they more than women tend to see the exercise of coercive power and control as social rewards? Why do some men demonstrate these attitudes more than others?

Campbell (A. Campbell 1993, Campbell & Muncer 1994) does start to provide clues to answer those questions: "It is likely that gendered differences in social representations of aggression may be traced to contemporary structural factors and to the socialization experiences of boys and girls." She recognizes the different levels at which socialization occurs, most of which we have already dealt with in earlier chapters: the structure of work hierarchies; social preparation for parental roles; models presented to children by parents; the sexism that permeates our society. However, Campbell, using data from a series of recent social psychology studies pays attention to one particular avenue of socialization:

Developmentally, the aggression of boys and girls is not differentially sanctioned by mothers . . . The critical differences between the sexes seem to lie in their peer group experiences . . . Boys' peer groups are larger, more public and organized hierarchically . . . Language is used as a means of achieving status within the group, as is physical aggression in the early years . . . Aggression

81

> is a particularly potent means of evoking a response from male peers . . . Girls, on the other hand, typically have one or two best friends, construct their friendships more privately and avoid direct confrontation as a means of settling disputes . . . Language is a means of establishing bonds and cementing friendship through self-disclosure rather than a combative device . . . Girls learn that aggression is both ineffective as a means of inter-personal influence and a threat to the harmony of relationships. (Campbell & Muncer 1994)

This material is important for several reasons. First, it provides empiri-cal evidence that the "common sense" emphasis on the role of mothers in socializing their children has been to some extent unwarranted. It contrasts with considerable evidence that witnessing abusive behaviour by fathers can have a considerable impact on sons in terms of future behaviour (Fagan et al. 1983, Saunders 1994).

Secondly, it directs our attention to both peers and groups as impor-tant arenas for intervention when we consider ways in which men can work within the social welfare system to counter sexism. In so doing, it also reminds us of Hearn's suggestion (Hearn & Parkin 1987), which we reported at the end of Chapter 2, that what happens between men and boys is often critical in shaping what also happens between them and women: deep-seated uncertainties about sexuality can result in "proofs" of manhood via such behaviours as violence and objectification. Some heterosexual masculinities have to be understood partly as reactions to homosexual desires between men.

Campbell's emphasis on peer pressure (Campbell & Muncer 1994) still requires us to understand why groups of males and females should tend to be so different in process and content. That question returns us to the general issue of the structural processes identified by feminist and pro-feminist writers in Chapter 1; and that have recurred throughout this study.

Campbell also offers some explanation as to why there seem to be dif-ferent extents to which different men will use violence. To a degree, her approach bears a similarity to the more complex conceptualizations of masculinity constructed by writers such as Connell (1987, 1995), Morgan (1992) and Hearn (1992) that were reviewed in Chapter 1:

> Social representations of aggression (and indeed a variety of other social phenomena) provide the cognitive glue that holds together social structural variables on the one hand and indi-vidual action on the other. (Campbell & Muncer 1994)

Campbell (A. Campbell 1993, Campbell & Muncer 1994) believes that men tend to resort to violence only when power is absent in their lives or when they feel that the power they do hold is threatened. Consequently, she tends to focus on men otherwise disempowered within society. While it does have some value, Campbell's analysis is problematic for a variety of reasons.

First, her conception of power seems over-simplistic: it appears, like money, to be something one has in one's pocket or does not. Post-modernist and poststructural analysis has challenged this view and suggested that the concept of power is a far more complex phenomenon, not least when considering issues of gender (Hekman 1990, Sawicki 1991, Ramazanoglu 1993).

Secondly, Campbell seems to ignore the fact that some powerful people and some institutions might regard violence as a legitimate way of aggrandizing power without any element of threat or defensiveness being present.

Thirdly, Campbell seems to be thinking largely about physical violence. As we will see later, some feminist writers (for instance, Kirkwood 1993) have recently been reconceptualizing the importance and serious-ness of men's emotional violence to women in relationships. We need to think again about whether physical violence is always something that men resort to when no other options are left. In some relationships, men may gain more satisfaction from emotional rather than physical violence and choose to use it in preference. Transferring this idea to violence out-side the home, how do we decide, for instance, that the emotional abuse visited upon female and male employees by some managers is less "violent" than if they were using physical violence? Certainly, in terms of the effect on human beings, it is not clear that emotional violence is necessarily less traumatic.

Finally, Campbell's analysis does not seem to consider the possibility that some men who are abusive may use violence, in whatever form, not as a last resort but because, in itself, it provides gratification to them; and that this phenomenon is by no means related to issues of powerless-ness. For instance, we have seen in Chapter 2 that sexual violence in the workplace can be related to the concept of "organization sexuality", which is very much concerned with hierarchical power. Similarly, child sexual abuse bears no relation to social class (Chs 3 and 8 here).

So, Campbell's (A. Campbell 1993, Campbell & Muncer 1994) for-mulation about why some men are more violent than others may be useful but has severe limitations. We need a more sophisticated concep-tualization about men and power, particularly in relation to sexuality, than Campbell provides. We have already suggested that Connell's analysis (1987, 1995) represents the basis of such a conceptualization (see Ch. 8 in this volume), especially as it allows us to think about the relation of different masculinities (including heterosexual and homosexual) to one another within the normative frame of hegemonic masculinity.

Campbell may have considered how issues of social class interact with those of gender in terms of violent crime. However, she pays less attention to other structural variables impacting upon the degree of power an individual or group may possess. It is to these that we now turn.

Black men and violent crime

It is important to recognize that the gendering of crime statistics relating to violence is also mediated by considerations of "race" and racism. This mediation occurs in two ways. The first relates to the situation of black men as victims of crime in Britain. Brake & Hale (1992), examining the official data, suggest that in Britain rapes, robbery and assault are predominantly intra-racial. However, the problem of racial attacks is striking. They quote research to the effect that a young black male (i.e. 12 to 15 years) is 22 times more likely to have a violent crime committed against him than an elderly white woman (i.e. over 65) and 7 times more likely to have something stolen from him. Moreover, Brake & Hale (1992) continue:

> Locality, class, race, and gender are central in serious crime happening to a person . . . Asians and Afro-Caribbeans are likely to be assaulted more than whites (Asians twice as much as whites), and while we have statistics where white victims are "mugged" by black assailants (a small part of robbery figures), we have no figures for street robbery, rape or racial assaults on black people by whites. We know about black people as victims, but not about white people as perpetrators of crimes against black people.

Gilroy (1987) suggests that the official crime statistics ignore the mass of racist attacks on black people and that, in fact, the police in urban areas are highly selective in their surveillance of black people. That point naturally leads us to the second issue where gender and "race" considerations come together: the subject of violent crime committed by black men.

As the quotation from Brake & Hale (1992) implied, we hear a lot in the media about crime perpetrated by black men. Some commentators, however, emphasize that this image partly represents the creation of a police and state discourse around black criminality (Gilroy 1987, 1992).

Cashmore & McLaughlin (1991) provide a detailed and persuasive analysis of the way the police in the 1980s have manipulated the presentation of crime issues and media reporting to enhance the idea of a law and order crisis, of which the image of black criminality was one major element. They suggest that this "crisis" has enabled the police to enhance their political influence, assisted the police to gain a professional status, given them greater control over their own destiny and increased their physical powers.

All this does not negate the fact that in recent years some sections of the black male population have been over-represented in crime figures, particularly members of the Afro-Caribbean communities. Jefferson (1991) provides a careful analysis of these statistics and demonstrates that the patterns within them are complex. To an extent they do represent higher levels of offending that Jefferson attributes partly to factors of social disadvantage. He also focuses on a vicious circle set up between Afro-Caribbean young men and the police in the face of harassment by the latter.

Moreover, there is ample evidence of the relatively harsh treatment meted out to black (largely Afro-Caribbean) men in the courts (Brake & Hale 1992). To some extent, this may represent the tendency for Afro-Caribbean men to be socially disadvantaged due to the oppressive structures of our society. However, there is also ample evidence of direct discrimination against black men in the courts (Landau & Nathan 1983, Walker 1988).

Women and crime

There are other major difficulties with the overall picture of violent crime portrayed by the official crime statistics. Many of these difficulties relate to the experiences of women. First of all, the picture hides a number of striking facts that exist within the official statistics. For instance, although female crimes of violence are much lower than male ones in official statistics, these figures show that women do commit some violent crime. In 1986, women accounted for 7.7 per cent of violent acts against the person in terms of indictable convictions in England and Wales.

Yet in the criminological literature as a whole there is relatively little consideration given to how the criminal justice system processes women and how much sexism impacts upon that system. Of course, valuable research has been carried out mainly by feminist scholars and practitioners.

85

Raynor et al. (1994) have summarized some of this feminist work, which clearly demonstrates that patriarchal assumptions are central to the criminal justice system:

> We know that women are likely to be given probation early in their criminal careers because of a welfare orientation in social inquiry reports and sentencing, but that subsequent offending leads to a harsher response. Often the response of the probation service to the needs of women is deficient to the point of compounding this process. Community-based sentences are often structured towards the needs of male offenders . . . Group projects particularly often exclude women because of understandable decisions not to increase the oppression of women by placing them in male-dominated groups. (Raynor et al. 1994)

Despite the important work of this growing number of feminist criminologists over the last twenty years, mainstream criminology has remained to a large extent uninfluenced by their efforts (Scraton 1990). This suggests an academic sexism that tends not only to ignore the overall situation of women in crime statistics but also particularly ignores their participation in crimes that women are "not supposed" to commit; and the circumstances in which they commit them.

Moreover, the situation of black women seems to have largely been forgotten even by feminist writers, although, as Marcia Rice points out (1990) the former make up at least 20 per cent of the prison population, as opposed to 5 per cent of the general population.

Chigwada (1991) attributes much of black women's over-representation in the prison population to the same discriminatory police and court activities as we noted above in relation to black men. She also summarizes particular reasons why Afro-Caribbean women are more likely to come into contact with the police than white women, including: general prejudice about their alleged criminality; being stopped for passport checks; police targeting them as suffering from mental disorder under Section 136 of the 1983 Mental Health Act.

Clearly, in the example of the neglect of black women by academic discourses, we have another instance of the way interpretation of social data is subject to the prevailing power dynamics within our society. Versions of social reality may be created that correspond with the requirements of power relations associated with "hegemonic masculinity"; and sometimes in relation to the needs of dominant groups of women, i.e. white and middle class.

Such processes may occur in other ways as well. So far we have considered problems arising from aspects of the official data that are neglected or otherwise manipulated. However, further major problems occur that are associated with what is not in official crime statistics. As Abbott & Wallace (1990) comment, we know nothing from these data about the mass of unsolved crime nor indeed about unreported crime. Unreported offences sometimes represent a significant segment of cases in specific areas of crime. In some instances, consideration of non-reported crime dramatically changes the picture. We will focus on one important example: man-on-man rape and sexual assault.

Sexual violence by men on men

What is not clear from official statistics is the considerable extent to which man-on-man rape seems to occur (McMullen 1990). Nor do the statistics indicate (as a growing number of studies reported by McMullen do) that such rape is frequently perpetrated by men who identify themselves as heterosexual: this applies to assaults on gay and straight men.

Often, these attacks may have as their main objective the humiliation and degradation of the other man by someone whose self-identity is aggressively heterosexual. In paralleling the work on war and women quoted above, we may recall that rape of men by men is also a ritual sometimes employed in war, by which the male victors symbolize their domination over the male vanquished. Similarly, the men using the *travestis* in Brazil for sex appear to regard the sexual act with other men as reinforcing their machismo as long as they retain the role of penetrating in the act rather than being penetrated (Cornwall 1994).

By "reducing" the man who is penetrated to a symbolic woman, the penetrator affirms his own masculinity and/or denies the masculinity of the other: in Western patriarchal societies, of course, the ultimate image of degradation for most men who identify themselves as heterosexual.

These examples highlight the deep paradoxes of some heterosexual masculinities. For instance, men may confirm their heterosexual credentials by having sex with other men. The critical factor, of course, in such a process is that the sex is inflicted within an unequal power relationship, whether by virtue of war, sexual assault or financial contract.

Returning to the issue of male rape in this country, we can now see that lack of data on this crime in official statistics constructs a picture of men's violence that not only fails to recognize a form of oppression towards men (including those who are gay) by men but also ignores some uncomfortable aspects and ambiguities relating to heterosexuality.

These ambiguities refer us directly again to Jeff Hearn's point (Carrigan et al. 1985, Hearn & Parkin 1987, Hearn 1992) that we must consider homosexual desire between men, and the desperate reactions against it, if we are to understand the operation of some dominant heterosexual masculinities. Nothing more clearly illustrates Hearn's point about the centrality of these issues to men's violences than the circumstances of male rape.

The fact that this form of men's violence has been so hidden, socially and statistically, in itself is deeply revealing of its importance. In Chapter 8 we shall see that the therapeutic response to it has been, and still is, equally muted.

Later in this chapter I want to consider another massive form of violent crime that official statistics tend to hide: men's violence to women. However, before I move on to that important topic, we should consider the way power relations associated with hegemonic masculinity structure the response of welfare agencies to the forms of violence that we have so far reviewed in this chapter.

Welfare agencies' responses to men's public violence

In this chapter we have already touched on many of the main issues particularly in relation to policing, the courts and the law. Dominelli notes the importance of gender in this respect:

> . . . although crime is clearly illegal, it is mediated by the prevailing definitions of masculinity and femininity, or masculinist ideology. In men a certain amount of law-breaking is necessary for character formation; in women it becomes a sign of their monstrosity indicating that they reside in a social nether world . . . Women who act out of stereotype are more severely punished in the courts, getting longer and/or more harsh sentences for similar offences and number of previous convictions than men. (Dominelli 1991)

In terms of the police and the courts, power dimensions of "race", gender, class and age are particularly important in determining the fate of individuals. Where there is a conjunction of two or three of these together the results are especially oppressive: drawing largely upon

Chigwada (1991), we considered the highly problematic situation of black women in the criminal justice system.

Of course, it is debatable how far one could legitimately characterize either the police or the courts as being engaged in social welfare, particularly as regards adult offenders. What is of more concern, perhaps, is the role played in this discriminatory scenario by agencies that have traditionally been regarded as partially or largely welfare-oriented – agencies such as health and probation.

The probation service has always contained different elements that are in creative tension and sometimes, though not necessarily, in conflict: welfare, justice and crime prevention (Raynor et al. 1994). So the confusions that we have noted in previous chapters around the concepts of "control" and "care" in social welfare agencies, have always been explicit in the probation service and perhaps for that reason they have possibly been more successfully managed.

The probation service plays a rather gendered part in the processing of men and women through the criminal justice system. We can see this in the writing of social inquiry reports and in the "treatment" of offenders where many community-based facilities are male-dominated (Raynor et al. 1994). Similar comments can be made about the experience of black people in terms of report recommendations and of community resources. For instance, Raynor et al. (1994) note that of 1,500 groupwork programmes surveyed in 1991, only three had exclusively black membership. Moreover, they note that black women risk a double jeopardy in their dealings with the service.

Raynor et al. (1994) call for a full anti-racist programme throughout the service, drawing and building upon the work of Bandana Ahmad (1990). Similarly, they outline the key elements of an anti-sexist approach. Such policies must encompass the very shape of the service, for as Dominelli (1991) points out there are few black officers. This fact is echoed by Raynor et al. (1994) who also note that both black people and women are under-represented in managerial grades. The structure of the probation service as a result conforms to that model of "organization sexuality" discussed in Chapter 2, with all this entails.

That is not to deny there are some pioneering projects within the service positively addressing sexism and racism. For instance, Murphy (1993) and Bensted et al. (1994) are accounts of excellent practice. However, as Raynor et al. (1994) note, it is a picture of piecemeal innovations, many of them (although not all) largely dependent upon practitioner initiatives. This is borne out, for instance, by the fact that an up-to-date volume on groupwork with offenders (Brown & Caddick 1993) contains only one example of work with men where gender is a central issue (Cowburn 1993) and that is in relation to woman and child sexual assault.

The health service tends to be seen as primarily fulfilling a caring function. Its role in relation to offenders reveals that such a view is simplistic. Dominelli (1991) mentions the use of psychotropic drugs to make women prisoners more passive and, by implication, more feminine. However, the complex involvement of health personnel and agencies in criminal justice goes well beyond this example.

For instance, in a study of emergency police referrals to an urban psychiatric hospital in a catchment area with a large Afro-Caribbean population, slightly more black women were prescribed psychotropic drugs than even white women. Black men seem to have had the highest prescription rate of all (90 per cent). White men had a far lower rate than anyone else (63 per cent) (Chigwada 1991).

In the same study (Chigwada 1991), twice as many of the black people referred by the police were diagnosed as schizophrenic. This finding is consonant with the general over-representation of Afro-Caribbean people receiving a diagnosis of schizophrenia (Fernando 1989, Littlewood & Lipsedge 1989) and there is some evidence (Dallos & Boswell 1993) that such diagnoses may involve cultural stereotyping by medical staff.

Chigwada (1991) reports that various studies have confirmed an excess of compulsory and police-referred psychiatric admissions from the African-Caribbean population.

Although at first sight such a medical avenue might seem more caring than a custodial route, we need to remember several facts. First, under Section 136 of the Mental Health Act the powers of medical staff are extensive. Moreover, resistance to having one's rights overridden can easily lead to diagnoses of "disturbed behaviour" and, consequently, prolonged hospitalization (Chigwada 1991).

Nor can we divorce all this from the form that the welfare agency takes. As we saw in Chapter 2, the health service is a rather hierarchic and gendered structure where the "sexuality of organization" is well able to flourish with, once again, the possible dynamics that can result. We might note in particular that the key personnel in terms of decisions about sanity and medication are the psychiatrists who are predominantly men. Black people are represented among psychiatrists. However, considerable research (Fernando 1989) suggests that many black psychiatrists largely adopt white perceptions of mental illness.

Conclusion

In the operation of both the courts and the health service with regard to criminal justice, we see replicated almost precisely the same contours of domination as we found in the care system (Ch. 3), particularly focused around issues of gender and "race".

There are many opportunities, highlighted in the material above, for men in welfare agencies seeking to challenge such patterns of oppression. Clearly, the police and the law are difficult to influence. However, workers in other agencies can work on two levels: at a local level building links with these authorities and seeking to improve local practice and change local structures; at a higher level, networking in one's own agency and other agencies to seek to have pressure put on the criminal justice system. Clearly, both these tasks can benefit by the adoption of such strategies as gathering information to build up a case supporting change. Once again, this is a task that service users can also undertake, possibly in collaboration with welfare workers. In Chapter 7 we will see how strategies such as these seem to have succeeded in changing some police practices in relation to woman abuse.

Similar strategies are applicable to the health service in terms of both workers outside and inside that agency.

In the probation service, the situation is slightly easier because there is perhaps at least some recognition that a problem exists. Nevertheless, we saw that there is still a long way to go as regards issues such as staffing, management and provision of a range of anti-oppressive services to users.

We now turn to a different, and massive, area of adult violence where gender is obviously a major issue: men's violence to women. However, we will see that here too patterns of oppression are diverse: issues of "race", class and sexuality intersect in complex and shifting configurations with the theme of gender.

Men's violences to women

Given the massive degree of men's violences to women, the relative absence of attention that has been paid to them in sociological and criminological studies can be seen as an example of both a skewed interpretation of the official data and also an omission within these data.

How large is the problem?

With regard to the interpretation of data, some evidence about men's violences to women does exist within official statistics. For instance, Archer (1994) details research by Dobash & Dobash (1984) wherein they examined police records in Scotland. This research demonstrated that over 90 per cent of violent offenders were male and in nearly 40 per cent of these cases the victim was female: in turn, of those 1,136 assaults, 841 were against family members, predominantly wives. Similarly, in a review of research, Foreman & Dallos (1993) note that "violence perpetrated by men on their partners within the family accounts for nearly a quarter of all reported violence and over 70 per cent of violence in the home".

So some official data do underline that women are the objects of men's violence and they even begin to tell us that quite a lot of violence occurs in the family. Nevertheless, official data still indicate that the majority of violent crime is directed at men. Moreover, as Stanko (1987, 1990) has frequently demonstrated, criminologists using these data have been keen to suggest that there is a mismatch between the fear of violent crime that women exhibit and the amount of violence that they experience.

Stanko seeks to explain women's fear by a number of related factors, a central one being the "true" levels of violence to women:

> . . . women's fear of crime may alert us to the unrecorded instances of threatening and violent behaviour by males and thus give us far more information about the structure of gender and violence in a gender-stratified society . . . The gap between women's fear of crime and the objective, official estimates of women's experiences of interpersonal violence is not an anomaly for feminists working in the area of violence to women. Even casual analysis of official data on interpersonal violence underscores what women working in rape crisis centres and refuges for battered women have heard so often: physical and sexual violence are common experiences for many women. (Stanko 1987)

She then quotes data from a prevalence study completed in 1983 in San Francisco: there was a 26 per cent probability that a woman would be the victim of a completed rape at some time in her life and a 46 per cent probability that she would experience a completed or attempted rape in her lifetime (Stanko 1987). These figures are comparable with later British data. For instance: a third of women will experience a form of domestic violence in their lifetime (Mooney 1993); 40 per cent of women are estimated to have experienced rape or sexual assault (Glasgow Women's Support Project 1990); just over 20 per cent of women are raped by their husband or partner (Mooney 1993).

Of course, these kinds of data are not uncontested. Debates about levels of date or acquaintance rape are an example of this contestation (Koss & Cook 1994, N. Gilbert 1994). In 1987 an American survey by Koss and colleagues estimated that 27 per cent of women in a college sample recalled an incident since they were 14 years old that met the legal definition of rape, including attempted rape (a definition considerably wider than that in operation in Britain) (Koss & Cook 1994).

Neil Gilbert (1994) questions these statistics on several grounds: how can there be a wide gap between official and unofficial statistics? How does one define such rape and who defines it? We do not need to enter the detail of the debate here, except to say that it seems Koss & Cook (1994) (who are feminist researchers) have much the better of the argument methodologically. The main reason I mention this debate is to illustrate the degree of resistance that feminist analyzes almost always meet both in terms of academic discourse and practical implementation. That is why I began this chapter by quoting Paul Gilbert (1994): mainstream academics and practitioners are now starting to endorse insights that some feminist commentators were formulating 20 years ago. As we saw in Chapter 2, welfare organizations and education institutions are subject to power relations that are just as oppressive as anywhere else: and these power relations have frequently resisted feminist interpretations of gender relations.

What makes the results of Koss's survey (Koss & Cook 1994) (and those that have replicated its results) particularly convincing is that, as far as sexual violence is concerned, parallel surveys have been carried out asking men about their own attitudes to the use of force in sex with women. Some of the most methodologically sound men's surveys have produced interesting results. For instance, Pollard (1994) reports on one survey carried out in 1983 where men gave self-reports about their behaviour towards women in sexual encounters: "Among the subjects 30 per cent indicated some likelihood of rape and a further 30 per cent indicated some likelihood of force."

Pollard (1994) reviews a range of such studies and this is his conclusion: "The frequencies vary quite considerably, but no studies reveal a very low proportion of reported aggression and some reveal very high frequencies." Moreover, as he points out, it is very likely that self-reporting produces an underestimate of men willing to use force.

Further evidence confirms the value of prevalence surveys as opposed to official statistics in revealing actual rates of violence against women. Brake & Hale (1992) report on local crime surveys carried out in 1986 by several Labour-controlled local authorities in London. One of these surveys (Islington) uncovered about 1,200 cases of sexual assault, of which only 21 per cent were reported to the police and only 9 per cent were recorded in the official crime statistics. Women who were council tenants were three times more likely to be sexually assaulted than were owner-occupiers, which demonstrates how class may interact with gender. Finally, the survey indicated that young females were 18 times more likely to be assaulted than those over 45. Brake & Hale (1992) comment that "these local surveys suggested that the fear that young women had concerning sexual assault was quite justified".

If the prevalence rates for physical and sexual assaults on women inside the home and outside (largely by people known to them) are of the magnitude represented in the prevalence surveys detailed here, rather than in official crime surveys, then what we are seeing is a social problem comparable in its immensity to that of child sexual abuse identified in Chapter 3. Such a realization naturally leads us to consider why so many men are abusing women and in what ways, if any, they are different from other men.

In the case of sexual assault on women, many useful studies in the field of social psychology have been carried out that may assist us to answer these questions.

Why do men sexually assault women?

The social psychology data has been usefully reviewed recently by Paul Pollard (1994). I will draw heavily upon his analysis. He points out that enforced intercourse by someone who is emotionally close to a woman produces traumatic effects no less serious than stranger rape and continues:

> Given this, the very high frequencies of largely unreported non stranger rape indicate an alarming number of criminals and victims who are not brought to the attention of the criminal justice system. Convicted offenders are thus an atypical sample of rapists . . . stranger rapists are too highly represented and . . . persons convicted of sex offences against adults usually have convictions for other offences as well . . . By contrast, the "typical" rapist

is an acquaintance, probably an intimate, of the victim, does not have a criminal background, and has not been reported to the police. (Pollard 1994)

Pollard (1994) then reviews research that explodes many myths about men's sexual violence. For instance, research on the whole does not indicate that rape proclivity has anything to do with lack of heterosocial skills, i.e. an inability to make relationships with women and lack of sexual fulfilment. Moreover, it seems that more heterosocially skilled males use their ability to increase their frequency of verbal sexual coercion of women. Consequently, it may be that the common therapeutic practice of giving convicted rapists social skills training will actually add verbal coercion to their repertoire of coercive sexual behaviours. Similarly, Pollard also explodes the myth that rape offenders are "mentally unstable".

Research suggests that particular attitudes are probably much more important than personality types, although some antisocial tendency may be necessary to translate rape-supportive attitudes into behaviour, particularly a degree of gender hostility. Pollard (1994) indicates that those attitudes include: rape myths (for example "she was asking for it"); a tendency to victim blame; support for interpersonal violence. Pollard notes that research also shows such attitudes are widely shared in society, particularly by men, reinforcing the idea of rape-supportive cultures. Pollard notes in passing that this analysis was posited much earlier by feminist writers such as Brownmiller (1975).

Pollard mentions that several studies have suggested strong links between the attitudes isolated above and both non-sexual and sexual aggression towards female partners: in practice, this is reflected in the fact that reports of marital rape are often accompanied by reports of other forms of woman abuse (O'Hara 1993, Ch. 5 in this volume).

It also seems that having a peer group with similar attitudes is a factor in the generation of violence. However, Pollard (1994) regards this and the personal attitudes detailed above as providing a background for rape proclivity. In the foreground are factors such as having a high frequency of social interactions and a hostility towards women. The sum total of his analysis is as follows:

> . . . in general the male population cannot be divided into those who may, or may not, sexually aggress. However, although all males probably have some proclivity to sexual aggression, particularly at lower levels, the "macho" male, whose sense of self

worth is bolstered by the pursuit of dominance and exploitation of the opposite sex, is particularly likely to translate his basic misogyny into sexual violence. (Pollard 1994)

This evidence from detailed social psychology studies once again reminds us of the issue of dominant forms of heterosexual masculinity and the process of their formation (Connell 1987, 1995): the importance attached to peer groups and rape-supportive cultures by Pollard (1994) reaffirms the need to consider what goes on between men in understanding the generation of men's violences towards both men and women (Hearn 1992, Kimmel 1994).

As a supplement to Pollard's analysis, we may note two other sets of observations drawn from social psychology research that he makes about trying to halt men's violence (Pollard 1994).

First, he indicates that increasing men's sense of empathy with the person abused may inhibit assaultive behaviours. Unfortunately, the effect of these inhibitors on men in general seems to be very tenuous. For instance, he quotes one study of undergraduate men who were found to show equal arousal to rape and consenting depictions when the rape victim was said to be involuntarily aroused, when the participant had been angered by a female, or when the participant had consumed alcohol.

Secondly, Pollard (1994) cites research indicating that most sexual assaults on women express both a man's desire for sex and his desire to dominate. This is supported by studies that highlight the tendency of many men to link sex with power more than do most women (Briere et al. 1994). Pollard comments:

> . . . for certain types of male in particular, and arguably for many males in general, even consenting sexual relations are expressions of power and dominance and mediate both personal and peer group perceptions of fulfilment of their masculine role . . . The general exploitative view of obtaining consenting intercourse will thus easily translate into a specifically aggressive approach to obtaining enforced intercourse. (Pollard 1994)

That raises an important question: at what point does normal heterosexual behaviour become oppressive? This is not to say that all heterosexual sex is abusive. What it implies is that drawing the line between oppressive and non-oppressive heterosexual behaviour on the part of men may not always be clear-cut. And if that is the case, then it again confirms a need to examine the formation of dominant heterosexual masculinities if we are to understand the generation of men's sexual violences.

Pollard's own conclusion regarding what we know from psychological material about the reasons for men's sexual violence to women is so crucial to our own study on several counts that I will quote it at length:

> It is clear that most rapes are committed by "psychologically normal" males, whose aggression may be both tacitly condoned by their immediate peer group, and more indirectly condoned by attitudes that are prevalent in society generally. I think it follows from this that, although interventions with convicted rapists, who may often have severe psychological problems, may be primarily the province of clinical psychologists, this is not the case for interventions aimed at reducing sexual aggression generally. Given the strong relation between rape-supportive attitudes and rape proclivity, a starting point would be for studies of informational interventions that may change attitudes, although later work would need to ensure that improved attitudes were eventually reflected in less aggression. (Pollard 1994)

I have dwelt on this material drawn from mainstream psychology for several reasons. First, I think it is important to acknowledge that this data is now telling us in quantitative and empirical form much of what feminist writers were starting to say as early as the 1970s basing their analyses on the experiences of women.

Secondly, this material confirms that in understanding men's sexual violences we need to go beyond the important issue of relations between men and women. Partly this is because we are more aware now that men too can be abused by men. However, it is also because we cannot explain the creation of men's sexual violences in general unless we examine what occurs between men as they grow up and as they interact on a day-to-day basis with other men. And this includes how we react to one another's sexuality, with all the uncertainties and apparent certainties that entails.

We are not denying that women, along with children, are the prime targets of men's violences: that is clearly the conclusion to be drawn from the evidence in this chapter and Chapter 3. But if men want to stop other men and themselves from doing violence to women, children and other men, then we have to consider ourselves not only individually but also collectively.

My third reason for dwelling on the material above is that it gives us important pointers about men's social welfare practice in terms of challenging power relations associated with hegemonic masculinities. Given the above comments, men need individually and collectively to consider their masculinity in the light of what we have discovered about dominant heterosexual masculinities. This work can be undertaken with different levels of intensity depending upon the nature of the engagement between men and men, and the focus of that engagement. However, because the issue of men's sexual violence is clearly a massive problem within our society, it should enter into all social welfare work with men in some shape or form. The very fact of men engaging in looking together at what makes them men is itself part of the process and content of reshaping masculinities.

We should note that welfare workers who are men need to reconsider what forms of masculinity they wish to express in their own lives just as much as do men who are service users. In some circumstances men workers and men users may be able to carry out this self-reflective work together to a greater or lesser extent: in one-to-one settings or group-work or in wider networks.

The social psychology material reviewed in this section also highlights that men seeking to act against men's dominations within the field of social welfare can pitch their efforts at a number of different levels. We have noted already the individual and group levels. Earlier in this study we discussed the need for men workers (and men users) to develop strategies to change practices and policies within agencies. In the material reviewed above we have begun to see that attitude and behaviour change at local, community and societal levels is also necessary. Some welfare workers may be strategically best placed to pitch their efforts at those levels: for instance, community workers, youth workers, community paediatricians, men working with men in family centres. User groups can also have critical importance here, as indeed can alliances between users and workers. None of these levels of activity is discrete: the efforts and implications of each flow into the others. We consider all these possibilities further in Chapters 7 and 8.

So far we have concentrated on sexual violence to women, partly because this is the area that has been most deeply researched in terms of the violence that is perpetrated by known assailants. However, as we have already seen, physical violence to women in the home is also a massive social problem. Although in some respects the data is less well-defined for physical assaults on female partners, it is vital that we spend some time considering this phenomenon that clearly accounts for another very large proportion of the acts of violence that occur daily in our society.

Men's physical violence to women

At the beginning of this chapter, we provided statistics about the size of the problem. Data came from both official crime figures and from community surveys. What they tell us is: even in terms of reported crime, physical violence to women in the home accounts for a very significant minority of reported assaults; secondly, the mass of physical violence to women at the hands of men they know is either not officially reported or not logged. Put at its simplest, physical violence by men to their partners is common, and largely unreported officially.

First, we need to discuss the correct language by which to describe men's physical violence to women. As we shall see, the terminology we use carries with it important implications for how we understand the formation of these violences. So, should we talk about domestic violence, partner abuse, spouse abuse or woman abuse?

The problem of language: family violence or woman abuse?

Underneath this question lies one of the most hotly debated issues in the field. That debate has direct implications in terms of how far we see this issue as one essentially about gender: which perhaps helps to explain why the argument has been so long and acrimonious.

The debate centres upon whether we should regard violence between heterosexual partners as something for which both parties are usually responsible. It originated in the 1970s with the development of the "battered husband syndrome" (Steinmetz 1977–8) which identified the fact that in arguments between partners, women struck men quite often. Since then, proponents of this approach, the so-called "family violence" school (Straus 1994), have debated at length with other social scientists drawing more heavily on feminist perspectives (Dobash & Dobash 1992, Kirkwood 1993, Kurz 1994).

The latter argue that women's physical violence to men has to take into account the following factors: the relatively greater bodily damage that men's physical violence does to women; women's violence to men has to be evaluated in the context of the overall pattern of emotional, physical, sexual and financial oppressions that men may inflict on women in relationships. To an extent, this approach is supported by the work of Anne Campbell (1993) whose social psychology research indicates that on the whole women only express their anger physically when they have reached extreme levels of frustration. This frustration may be the combined product of a wide range of oppressions including those mentioned above plus the burdens of motherhood that we discussed in Chapter 4.

Although the work of the family violence school has been useful in provoking a debate that has expanded our understanding of this issue, their approach does seem far too simplistic. It is clear that we cannot understand physical violence in the home without reference to the immense, complex webs of multiple oppression (Kirkwood 1993) that trap many women in relationships with men. Accordingly, in this study we shall use the term "woman abuse" in preference to phrases such as "partner/spouse abuse" or "domestic violence" that may mask the reality of what is going on. It is important to place the responsibility for most violence between heterosexual partners where it belongs: with men. Use of the term "woman abuse" in preference to the others, helps us to do this.

Physical abuse of women is one of many ways by which men seek to control and dominate women, and the other ways have sometimes been overlooked in the past by commentators. Kirkwood (1993) has helped us to focus with more appropriate intensity upon the critical issue of emotional abuse and emotional violence in the domination of women by men in relationships.

Why do men physically and emotionally abuse women?

As with sexual assault, there is considerable debate about this issue. All participants to the debate recognize that gender is an important variable. However, some commentators (Gelles 1994) also place considerable emphasis on the social stress that poor families are under as a factor in the genesis of physical abuse. Pahl (1985) acknowledges that more working class than middle class women use refuges in Britain but partly attributes this to the greater alternative resources that may be available to some of the latter when they are in violent relationships. The role of social stress is therefore debatable.

Various other suggestions have also been made about why men may be violent to partners. Foreman & Dallos (1993) note that theories based on a cycle-of-violence approach are problematic since many men who have experienced or witnessed abuse as children do not necessarily go on to abuse, and many physical abusers have no such history. Dobash & Dobash (1992) believe that men are more likely to be violent to partners when they think their power and authority are under threat.

Whatever their particular merits, most of these points of view share several characteristics: all acknowledge that men tend to have a need to dominate and control; they also recognize that structural factors play a part in the generation of men's physical and emotional violences.

Larry Tift (1993), reviewing the wide range of research carried out on the topic of men's physical violence towards partners, makes two important points:

That battering is a chosen behavior occurring within a larger structural context is a fact often denied by those whose research has taken an individual or interpersonal focus. A structural approach, in contrast, asserts that most often battering is behavior chosen within the context of hierarchical power arrangements that refuse women the tools for self-development. The prevalence of battering is directly related to the ideological and institutionalized strength of these arrangements.

Although some men are violent inside and outside the home, many appear to confine their violence to the private arena. Moreover, commentators such as Kirkwood (1993) have helped us to understand the way men who abuse manipulate situations, including different methods of violence, very carefully. Many men who abuse their partners choose with great care how, where and when they will be violent. This element of choice links in well with Campbell's concept of men's instrumental violence (A. Campbell 1993) that we noted above.

The issue of choice is a crucial one for our study. In Chapter 8 we shall see that choice is a similarly critical (although much neglected) factor in the process by which men sexually abuse children. To a very large extent men choose to be oppressive and they choose not to be. This seems to be true with respect to both their sexual and physical violences.

From our point of view, this is a critical insight for men engaged in the field of social welfare. It means that in terms of men's anti-oppressive activities another key task is for men to assist other men and themselves to choose not to be abusive by looking at the influences that guide their choice. This clearly links in with some of the other potential tasks that men should undertake that we have signposted earlier: the need to focus on dominant forms of heterosexual masculinity; the need to work towards changes in attitudes, behaviours and structures at a whole series of interlinked levels.

Once again, the model of power relations that seems best suited to embracing all these concerns with an appropriate degree of complexity and richness is Connell's (1987, 1995). We shall see in Chapter 8 that this model itself implies that choice and personal agency is an important element in whether a man behaves violently or not.

One of the other virtues of Connell's approach (1987, 1995) is that it fully recognizes the complexity that results from the diversity of power relations along dimensions such as sexuality, age, "race", and disability. Similarly, this is an issue that we should not overlook here in our review of men's physical violence to women. Gender is not the only power consideration that needs to be addressed by our analysis.

Difference and diversity

So far in this analysis, we have referred to the influence of social class in mediating gender relations with respect to physical violence. However, we know that difference and diversity extend far beyond this.

Kirkwood (1993) is very aware of the importance of difference. For instance, she considers the distinct political pressures that bear down on refugee women or deaf women in preventing them from speaking out.

She also refers to abusive violence that can exist between lesbian partners and the challenge that this presents to feminist analysis. Tift (1993) recognizes that the issue of lesbian battering forces us to look beyond simple gender relations in explaining personal violence. However, like Kelly (1991) he recognizes that violence between lesbian women must be seen in the context of the dominant forms of sexuality within our society: heterosexual masculinities. This need to consider the dynamics by which gender and sexuality interact in order to understand how violence in our society may be generated is now familiar to us in this study.

Similarly, the compound dynamics of "race" and gender also produce major complexities with respect to men's violences. Rice (1990) feels that white feminists have been slow to see the role of racism in precipitating attacks by white men on black women, compared with their eagerness to recognize the importance of sexism in attacks on white women. She also sees a connection between such attacks on black women and the fear originating in slavery that white men will assume they are sexually available.

Of course, as Rice (1990) adds, it is important to recognize that black women are not homogeneous and are further sub-divided by ethnicity.

Kish Bhatti-Sinclair (1994) has pointed out that amidst the mass of academic material now available on woman abuse in the home, there is so little on the experience of black women and, in particular, so little on the racism that is one of the most critical factors in their lives. She also identifies one of the main inadequacies of a white feminist approach to the issue of woman abuse: for Asian women living in a deeply racist society, the family is a major source of shelter and white feminists have generally not acknowledged this. In making this point, she is by no means denying the reality of woman abuse in black–Asian communities. On the contrary, her own study plays a major role in expanding our awareness about it.

However, we do need to recognize the power of racism in transforming situations. Rice (1990) comments that the relationship between black women and black men is not necessarily analogous to the relationship between white women and white men: ". . . black women experience sexual and patriarchal oppression by black men but at the same time struggle alongside them against racial oppression".

Moreover, she goes on to point out that one cannot assume that black men occupy the economically privileged position that feminism suggests white men do in a patriarchal hierarchy (Rice 1990). She notes that in Western industrialized countries black men have been socially and politically disadvantaged to an extent that has limited their power both in the family and in society.

Kirkwood (1993) reminds us that racism's impact upon black men may have even more direct relevance to the issue of woman abuse. Drawing upon the work of bell hooks, she describes how Afro-American men may in a sense transfer their own oppression at the hands of white society on to their partners in the form of woman abuse. In turn, some black women may then accept that violence to themselves as part of their commitment to the common struggle against racism. Of course, such a perspective might well be understandably challenged by other feminist commentators.

Last but not least, Kirkwood (1993) emphasizes that racism reduces the options available to black women in seeking assistance with woman abuse. This takes several forms. On the one hand, appeals to the police about violence in the home or racist attacks may first of all result in an investigation into the rights and status of the complainant to be in the country (Chigwada 1991). On the other hand, there is very little provision available specifically to cater for the needs of black women (Bhatti-Sinclair 1994).

Clearly, in an analysis of men's violences, dimensions of power re-garding racism, class and heterosexism interact with gender relations in complex and shifting patterns. Moreover, in Chapter 4 we saw that age, in terms of childhood, was yet another dimension to these violences. In Chapter 6 old age and disability will also enter into the equation.

Nor is diversity limited to concepts such as "race", gender, sexuality, age, disability, class. We also have to take into account the specifics (in relational and structural contexts) of men's encounters resulting in violence and the many forms that violence can take at any given moment in time:

> . . . distinct multitactical patterns or systems of battering . . . may well be associated with differing motivations (e.g. displaying power and control, countering dependency, expressing anger,

and validating self). They may also be connected with differing "causal" dimensions. Moreover, distinct battering patterns may be correlated with diverse intimate relations (e.g. noncohabiting couples, married couples, cohabiting couples, lesbian or gay couples within different living arrangement circumstances) that are differently situated in the class and ethnic structures of our society. (Tift 1993)

Any response to woman abuse by a welfare service that does not appreciate these complexities will inevitably lead to oppressive practice with service users, thereby compounding the original abuse that the service was supposed to alleviate.

In Chapter 7, we consider how oppressive power relations to be found in welfare agencies interact with those patterns of domination that we have just seen structure the issue of woman abuse.

Conclusion

We have concluded that violent adult crime is a largely, but not exclusively, gendered phenomenon. Most stranger violence occurs between men and men, and often the two parties come from similar class and cultural backgrounds. One form of man-on-man violence has been relatively hidden and yet may disclose ways of understanding a broad spectrum of men's violences: male rape. Furthermore, a large minority of the violent crimes that are recorded are perpetrated by men upon women they know. Even so, the vast majority of woman abuse is never reported.

Woman abuse can, and often does, take many forms that can occur simultaneously or sequentially: physical violence, sexual assault, emotional abuse, financial control, loss of liberty.

Men's sexual violences appear to centre strongly on those forms of oppression related to hegemonic masculinities that we have encountered so often before in the preceding chapters. To a large extent most sexual abusers of women seem to be "normal" men. A central challenge for men is to counter those attitudes permeating society from top to bottom that contextualize and create situations where many men choose that they will be sexually violent.

The factors contributing to men's physical violences to women seem more diverse (than is the case with sexual violences) and there is sharp debate as to the relative importance of different components. Various explanations for this physical violence have been put forward: intra-psychic, interpersonal, social, structural. Different combinations of these explanations may be appropriate for different cases and perhaps even for the same case over time. However, there is also evidence that many of the same processes related to the generation of men's sexual violences apply here too. Whatever other factors may also be involved in the creation of men's physical violences to women, power relations associated with hegemonic masculinities seem to play a central role once again.

Connell's analysis of power (1987, 1995) seems able to embrace the complexities of this state of affairs. Connell's model has two other advantages in relation to the material presented in this chapter. First, it acknowledges the important interrelationship between different forms of masculinity. Secondly, as we shall see in Chapter 8, Connell's model embraces the idea of individual choice and personal agency as one avenue by which positive change in oppressive practice can occur. Such a perspective underlines the vital importance of men working with men within fields of social welfare as a central strategy in the prevention of men's violences: men can help other men to choose not to oppress and they can help themselves to make the same choice as well.

At first sight, the world of Community Care seems light years away from the world of violent crime. Yet the structures of oppression that we have surveyed in this chapter also weigh heavily on the lives of adults who require care and on family members who provide that care. It is to these people that we now turn.

Chapter 6
Adult care

Introduction

Writing in 1985 and focusing on the care of older people, Janet Finch and Dulcie Groves clearly felt that the field of adult care was thoroughly permeated by gender relations: ". . . the whole process is effectively women only: low status services delivered to elderly women by low status women workers of a younger generation" (Finch & Groves 1995).

In this chapter we will try to portray the degree to which power relations associated with hegemonic masculinities do impinge on the care of adults in our society and, in particular, where men fit into that picture. We shall see that the situation is considerably more complex than Finch & Groves (1985) described, even though on the whole they were, and are, correct. That complexity arises mainly from the heterogeneity of both carers and cared for. Such heterogeneity exists partly in terms of the different labels (older people, people with learning difficulties, people with disabilities, people experiencing mental distress) that are used to describe the problems created by social responses to certain groups of people with some shared characteristics. Commentators in the field of disability studies have been especially clear about the central role of social construction in this process (Oliver 1990, Swain et al. 1993).

Perhaps more important is the heterogeneity that results from the different ways in which many forms of social disadvantage combine and impact upon peoples' lives: for instance, disadvantage deriving from "race", gender, age, sexual orientation, class, disability.

In addition, the position is further complicated by debates over finding appropriate language to encompass peoples' experiences, a process that itself reflects the complexity we have just outlined. One of those current debates centres on the utility or otherwise of the concept of "care" itself in relation to adults (Ungerson 1990, May 1992, Thomas 1993). It is neither possible nor necessary to open out that debate here. For the sake of simplicity, I shall use the term "care", but with an awareness that it can be problematic.

In the field of adult care, users of welfare services can at this point be divided into those "non-professionals" who provide "informal care" and those people who are recipients of "care" either directly from welfare agencies and/or via informal care. In this chapter we shall look at the situation of each of these in turn. Finally, we will consider the increasingly recognized problem of abuse of adults who are the recipients of care.

Informal carers

We know that the majority of people who provide formal care in various welfare agencies are women, even though the hierarchies of those agencies tend to be dominated by men and both the ethos and structures of the agencies are generally highly masculinized (Ch. 2).

However, in considering power relations within caring it is vital to look at patterns of informal care because so much adult care is provided informally. In 1985 only 8 per cent of people with disabilities over the age of 60 years in Britain were in residential or institutional care: even for the age group over 80 years the figure was only 4 per cent. It is true that a larger proportion of adults with learning difficulties was in residential care, but even then it was still a minority (35 per cent). The numbers of non-elderly people with disabilities in institutional care was lowest of all: less than 1 per cent (Parker 1990). With regard to formal services provided within the community, they too play a relatively small part in the overall pattern of care:

> Anyone who today finds themselves responsible for a handicapped child, a physically disabled or mentally ill adult or a dependent old person will have found that there is no universal minimum level of state support that can be relied upon. Rather there are unpredictable, contingent, regionally variable and rather unreliable possibilities of help. This has been called the "Lebanonization" of social care. (Baldock & Ungerson 1991)

107

Parker's comprehensive review of research on informal care concludes:

> The evidence we are able to glean from various sources suggests that available services are likely to have little overall effect for informal carers . . . few dependent people who have informal carers appear to receive services and, when they do, such services are usually crisis-oriented rather than a part of long-term support. (Parker 1990)

Women and men as carers

So how much of this massive amount of informal care is performed by women? Throughout much of the 1980s, the assumption was that informal care was virtually a female monopoly; hence the quotation from Finch & Groves (1985) that heads this chapter. However, the real picture is less simple. Hilary Graham (1993b) notes that: "In recent years, national survey data have recorded the significant involvement of men, particularly in the informal care of older and disabled spouses."

Arber & Gilbert (1989) note that 31 per cent of severely disabled older people live with only a spouse and there is an almost equal division between the genders as to which is caring for the other. In addition, there are some households (6 per cent) where a spouse and unmarried children live: in a proportion of these, men will be the main carers. Finally, 17 per cent of severely disabled people live only with members of the younger generation, generally their adult children. In just over half these households, the younger people are unmarried. Of these there are nearly as many men as women carers. Overall, Arber & Gilbert (1989) conclude that "over one third of co-resident carers are men". Similarly, in the US, Applegate & Kaye (1993) have recently placed an emphasis on the importance of male elder caregivers.

Parker (1990) endorses the view that kinship obligations and gender interact producing a reasonably clear hierarchy of obligation in relation to care of older people: spouse (to which we might add co-resident), daughter, daughter-in-law, son, other relatives, non-relatives.

We should supplement this picture with what is now known about gay and bisexual men caring for other gay and bisexual men who are dependent. In fact, very little research has been carried out in Britain on this topic. The small amount that does exist focuses on gay men caring for other gay men who have HIV-related diseases (for instance Hart et al. 1994, McCann & Wadsworth 1994). Because of the small size of the samples and other methodological problems, the authors of these studies emphasize the limits on generalizing from them and the tenuous nature of their conclusions.

Among findings that may be significant are: care may well depend on intimate relationships rather than on some nebulous concept of a "gay community" (Hart et al. 1994); location in urban areas may positively impact upon the likelihood of informal care (Hart et al. 1994); it may be that, despite the stigma of HIV and AIDS, informal care in both practical and emotional form is reasonably available to many gay and bisexual men (McCann & Wadsworth 1994); this support is from friends, partners and other relatives (McCann & Wadsworth 1994); in one study just under a half of carers lived with the person for whom care was provided (McCann & Wadsworth 1994); carers were mainly male (McCann & Wadsworth 1994); in one study carers were much more likely than carers in general to be caring for someone with the same illness as themselves (McCann & Wadsworth 1994); in the same study, most men had received some support from professional services.

It is vital not to draw any strong conclusions from this research. Some of it (particularly McCann & Wadsworth 1994) does indicate that many gay and bisexual men are receiving valuable assistance from other gay and bisexual men. This is especially important because research has demonstrated how crucial is social support to people with this form of illness, due to the stigma that often accompanies it (Green 1994). However, so localized is the material we have reviewed, that it may still be that large numbers of such men are without support. Whatever the case, we can say that this is another area of adult care where the gender stereotype of caring has to be seriously modified; and that considerable numbers of men may be primary carers in this context.

The evidence here echoes the data about men as carers in our survey of child care (Ch. 4): men can and do act as primary carers We desperately need good research about care by men, particularly regarding the quality of that care: as we have seen in relation to child care, this involves accessing the opinions of those cared for as well as those doing the caring.

Having acknowledged the considerable contribution of men as carers of adults, we do need to put that contribution in perspective. Arber & Gilbert (1989) themselves acknowledge that the majority of the carers of severely disabled people are women. Moreover, Parker (1990), surveying the range of informal care concludes that:

> Despite recent recognition of the part that men might play in providing care, particularly to their elderly spouses . . . it is still the case that, in the population at large, women provide the bulk of care. Further, on an individual level, women are more likely to be heavily involved in caring than are men. Thus, there is little evidence of any real shift in the "social division of community care". (Parker 1990)

This pattern seems to operate virtually across the board of adult care. For instance, Parker's review (1990) strongly suggests that where a spouse is not available to provide care for older people, female relatives are the main providers, including daughters-in-law for their partners' parents. Only in tasks such as visiting did adult male children make anything like a comparable contribution. Similarly, Parker reports that mothers tend to provide the main care for adults with learning difficulties, often with remarkably little support from spouses. Without wishing to draw parallels too strongly, this picture is again reminiscent of that which we saw in relation to child care in Chapter 4, whereby male parents who did share parenting tended to leave the bulk of the work, and the least pleasant parts of it, to their female partners.

As regards adult care, the impact of this state of affairs on female carers is predictable and well researched:

> Generally, female carers have been shown to be more likely to give up their jobs, lose more money and to experience more stress than are male carers. Policy makers and service providers alike have yet to acknowledge fully, let alone attempt to remedy, this very significant inequality. (Parker 1990)

We might also wonder, as did Finch & Groves (1985), whether this highly gendered picture extends to the provision of formal care to older people. In other words, do older men needing support in the community receive more than older women? Do men who are carers receive more formal support to assist them than female carers?

With respect to the first question, Parker (1990) and Arber & Gilbert (1989) demonstrate that older people living alone seem to receive the lion's share of formal support. As regards the split in services in terms of gender, once disability has been controlled for, there is little difference in level of provision as far as the public sector is concerned, although there is more in favour of men in relation to the voluntary sector (Arber & Gilbert 1989).

With respect to formal support for informal carers, it seems that it is not so much that male carers are privileged: rather, there is discrimination against female married carers (Arber & Gilbert 1989, Parker 1990).

Carers and other forms of oppression

There are other aspects of oppression and social disadvantage to be considered in relation to caring. For instance, most writing on issues of ageing ignores the question of sexual orientation (Graham 1993b). Brown (1992) highlights major issues in relation to lesbian women. Some of these may apply less to gay men. For instance, many commentators (Finch & Groves 1985, Hughes & Mtezuka 1992, Graham 1993b) have observed that in general the finances of older women depend not only on employment history but also on prior marital status: in many cases this works to the disadvantage of lesbian women as opposed to gay men.

However, in many other respects gay men and lesbian women face similar additional problems when they are older: issues of joint property; problems in relation to family support if the family are hostile to the homosexual relationship; suitability and sensitivity of formal support services such as respite care; acceptance by professional staff.

Similarly, "race" and racism have an impact on caring, although, as Graham (1993b) notes, this issue was frequently forgotten in feminist analyses of the 1980s. Both Graham (1993b) and Hughes & Mtezuka (1992) emphasize research demonstrating that the myth of the extended families of Asian people can actually mask an opposite reality: the isolation of Asian people from family and community support under the weight of a history of British racism in terms of immigration policies and employment practices.

As we noted, class has long been identified as a variable compounding the effects of ageism, disabilism and gender. Graham (1993b) identifies this issue particularly clearly, pointing out that poverty has an impact on disability in terms of its frequency and its earlier onset. Further financial deficits appear to result from the interaction of class with age as regards the common occurrence of much older people with very small incomes, especially if they are female. People in manual households are more likely than those in non-manual households to be caring informally for someone living with them, at the same time as having fewer material and financial resources to implement that care effectively (Graham 1993b). Moreover, lack of a telephone and/or transport reduces the effectiveness of kin networks where a disabled and/or older person is living outside the household.

From what has been said so far, it is clear that adult care depends massively on its informal component which is subject to numerous and heavy pressures. And those pressures are exerted differentially against women who represent the mass of informal carers.

Why are most carers women rather than men?

Some commentators have asked why it is that men take on the main caring role so much less often than women and this is clearly of relevance to our study of men as service users.

Baldwin & Twigg (1991) indicate that women's role here must be seen in the context of women's lives. Thus, caring for a dependent relative is congruent with most of the other tasks that many women undertake in both the private and the public sphere. For instance, like the professional care posts we discussed in Chapter 2, the adult care task is characterized by flexibility, low status and lack of training. Informal adult care is closely aligned to women's traditional family caring role and in particular the nurturing of children. This parallels the conjunction of the public and private domains of caring that we discussed in Chapter 2 with regard to welfare agencies.

Thus, we can see informal adult care as part of a much wider gendered division of labour that we have encountered in different guises throughout this study.

Ungerson (1987) relates these issues to cultural norms that tend to distance men from some aspects of domestic life such as dealing with excrement and nakedness. Since these kinds of activities are central to informal care, it is less likely that men might be involved. Finch (1990) to an extent echoes this idea when she says in relation to the prospect of men being more involved with adult care:

> . . . even if this were possible, it might not necessarily be a state of affairs which feminists would want to support . . . partly because one would want to defend the right of women who need care to be cared for by other women, not by men. (Finch 1990)

This latter point is surely an important consideration at the level of simply making people as comfortable about the care they receive as possible. However, there is another particular reason why one would support Finch's call for sensitivity in these matters.

We are now aware that very many adults, including older adults, will have had sexually abusive experiences in childhood and/or younger adulthood since we know sexual abuse is not a new phenomenon (Ferguson 1990, 1992); and much of this abuse will have been at the hands of men. Clearly, gender may well be an issue for older survivors, particularly in terms of intimate care. As we will see later in this chapter, some provisional British research is also demonstrating that sexual abuse in old age, both inside and outside care institutions, may be a major problem; and it seems that men may perpetrate most of this abuse too (Holt 1993, 1994). We need to bear this in mind.

Hilary Graham's work on caring (Graham 1983, 1993b, cf. Thomas 1993) offers other potential reasons why the nurturing function is so strongly embedded in social notions of being a woman. For Graham concentrates on what caring means to women themselves. As Baldwin & Twigg (1991) note, Graham regards caring as profoundly underwriting women's sense of self-identity in the same way as achieving goals for oneself underwrites the self-identity of men. Certainly in the context of Western society such a hypothesis goes some way to explaining the data that suggest many women find nurturing to be a source of satisfaction despite the hardships it entails for them. In this view the social construction of gender not only extends broadly through our society but also contributes heavily to the dominant discourses that furnish an understanding of the world for women as well as for men.

Community Care and gendered patterns of caring

If the greater part of informal adult care is indeed care by women, how then does the government policy of Community Care, embodied in the National Health Service and Community Care Act 1990, relate to that fact. It is perfectly true, as Mary Langan asserts, that the Act

> . . . virtually ignores the now widely acknowledged fact that the vast majority of carers are women, and fails to take account of demands for alternatives which do not exploit women. (Langan 1992)

However, this does not mean that those who designed the Act were unaware of who carries out informal welfare services. As Janet Finch makes clear in her analysis (1990), the presence of women as an army of carers was integral to the process by which the present policy was engendered.

113

Certainly the government realized, in John Baldock's words, that "quite small reductions in the supply of family care could have substantial costs for the public sector if it had to fill the gap" (1993). Hence, the White Paper *Caring for people* (HMSO 1989a) explicitly states that "the great bulk of care is provided by family, friends and neighbours"; and furthermore that "helping carers to maintain their valuable contribution to the spectrum of care is both right and a sound investment" (Baldock 1993).

The government has sought to encourage private and informal care. One way is via cash benefits to people who are disabled or to carers (Baldock 1993). Another strategy is the use of "paid volunteers" which takes many forms but is a development of the idea of the "good neighbour". For Baldock & Ungerson (1991) this development represents the essence of the new concept of "case management" in social welfare that focuses on the availability and cost of caring rather than its content. We discussed this trend in Chapter 2 and saw it as part of the new drive to "managerialism" (Lupton 1992) that might further alienate social welfare agencies from feminist principles and anti-sexist practice (Grimwood & Popplestone 1993). Baldock & Ungerson (1991) and Ungerson (1990) certainly emphasize that the concept of paid volunteering is in many respects explicitly based on the exploitation of women. Paradoxically, though, they also recognize that in the long run it could lead to policy changes to the advantage of women.

Relieving the burden of informal care on women

Baldock & Ungerson (1991) concede that paid volunteering could act as a bridge in the longer term to a policy change whereby all "helpers", whether formal or informal, might receive a fair wage in exchange for their labour. Ungerson (1990) believes this might well have further positive results in addition to the fact that it would offer effective support to carers. Not only might it encourage other people in the helped person's network to assist them, but it might also bring more men into caring. Furthermore, carers might well be able to pool resources to form collectives to share the stress of care. We should add, however, that Baldock & Ungerson (1991) do not envisage that this positive outcome is at all inevitable given current social policies.

Janet Finch has a much more radical long-term proposal for ending the exploitation of women within informal care (Baldwin & Twigg 1991). She questions whether the current notion of Community Care is appropriate at all given that family care for dependent adults would seem to

114

be inherently linked to sexist practices (Finch 1990). Instead, she advocates moving Community Care away from family care: care in the community rather than by it. She envisages a wide and sensitive range of residential provision allowing older and disabled people to have as independent and as normal lives as possible, well linked to their friends and families.

She emphasizes that this approach might also give autonomy to older people, people with disabilities, people with learning difficulties and persons suffering mental distress who feel trapped in family care. Some support for this argument can be drawn from Parker's data (1990) which show that some carers would clearly prefer full-time alternative provision for their relatives and some of the latter do find family care constricting.

Several commentators believe Finch's concerns are rather outdated and have been overtaken by positive developments within the field of Community Care (Baldwin & Twigg 1991, Parker 1993). It is true that there are pockets of good quality, anti-oppressive practice within Community Care but, as we saw at the beginning of this chapter, they are few and far between. In that context, it is hard to share the optimism of Finch's critics.

However, there is another important aspect to this debate: what do the people receiving care want?

> . . . disabled and older people . . . have almost without exception put their energies into achieving a better quality of life within the community (taking this to mean outside residential care) and have maintained a (critical) support of community care policies. (Morris 1991)

Morris (1991) has protested that feminist commentators have too often focused on the needs of carers rather on those cared for and her protest has recently been acknowledged by both Graham (1993b) and Parker (1993). The latter and Morris (1991) both make the point that reciprocity should be a crucial element in service provision and must be preserved if users are not to be further disempowered. This is a strong argument.

Perhaps Mary Langan offers the most sensible balance of proposals:

> Measures which make it easier for both female and male workers to carry out their caring responsibilities, and forms of community care which encourage more men to take on unpaid caring tasks should . . . be promoted. Feminists also need to challenge the assumptions about the family that underlie the community care

115

consensus, arguing that "community care need not mean family care". The provision of care in a range of residential and day care facilities, by properly qualified and well paid professionals, is essential to relieve the pressures of community care on women, both in the home and in the social services department . . . This approach must go hand in hand with a real commitment to user self-determination – we should not forget that the majority of cared-for people are also women. (Langan 1992)

This, then, seems to be an appropriate point at which to move on to consider the situation of those who receive care.

Receivers of care

Academic feminist research has attended to relationships in which care is being exchanged, describing these relationships through the perspectives of those who provide rather than those who receive care . . . It has been left to women excluded from this frame of reference to challenge the tacit alignment of feminist and carers' perspectives. (Graham 1993b)

It is true that of those adults who receive care, the majority are women and this gender imbalance seems to run virtually across the board. We have already noted that the majority of people who are disabled are female (Morris 1993) and this trend intensifies with age due to women's greater life expectancy: at 60 they can expect on average another 21 years of life – the comparable figure for men is 16 years (Hughes & Mtezuka 1992). Moreover, in terms of admissions to psychiatric units and referrals to GPs on account of mental distress, women predominate once again, though there are some interesting gender variations within these data that we will consider later (Barnes & Maple 1992, Dallos & Boswell 1993).

The various categories used to describe adults who receive care are problematic for a variety of reasons. On the one hand, such categories (for instance "people with learning difficulties") always mask extensive heterogeneity in terms of individuality and structural location (Williams 1992b). On the other hand, the overlaps between categories like "people who are older", "people with disabilities", "people with learning difficulties" also put a limit on their utility.

For the sake of conceptualization, I shall discuss receivers of care within those categories but it is important that readers do not assume that this conceptual map corresponds directly to the diversity of lived experience. In particular we shall see that once again the interplay of different forms of oppression is complex.

People who are older

We have already noted several of the relevant issues here, many of which impact upon one another (Hughes & Mtezuka 1992, Baldock 1993, Graham 1993b): women's greater longevity than men's; their financial vulnerability depending upon marital status and employment history; the greater likelihood of women living alone; women's vulnerability to disability and illness partly as a function of their longevity; the potential differential impact upon some or all of these factors for both women and men of being working class or black or homosexual. However, the health of older men and women requires further comment.

As Hughes & Mtezuka (1992) note, although men in each social class up to the age of 65 years are twice as likely to die, older women in the community (especially those who are single) seem to experience more chronic conditions than men with consequent loss of mobility and other physical limitations. Despite this, some studies suggest that men are twice as likely to report their inability to wash clothes, prepare meals or to sew. Moreover, it seems that men are less likely to report general satisfaction with their health. It has therefore been suggested that men might go into institutional care on account of disabilities that women cope with in the community. After considering the possibility that agencies have lower expectations of men's ability to cope, Hughes & Mtezuka (1992) comment:

> However, it is also likely that, after a lifetime of socially-constructed dependency of all forms, older women themselves have low expectations and more easily accept the consequences of disability. Conversely, they may have also learned that they have to simply get on and make the best of things, which they do but often at no small cost to themselves.

The different experiences of old age between men and women are clearly difficult to classify without stereotyping, given the complex interaction of "race", class, sexual identity, gender, age and disability in each person's life. Moreover, the credits and debits of growing older tend to be complicated in themselves.

For instance, some men who are used to placing employment outside the home at the centre of their existence might find retirement and growing older to be very stressful; others might see it as an opportunity. By contrast, old age for many women does not represent any diminution in the previous domestic tasks demanded of them. For some women this may represent a terrible burden in the context of what we have said about old age, women and health. On the other hand, for some women (and in certain cases perhaps the same women), such domestic routine may represent not only a continuing link with a time when they were younger but also a framework for maintaining kin and friendship contacts now (Baldock 1993).

People with disabilities

Again, we have looked at some of the relevant issues already in terms of the interactions of class, poverty and disability (Graham 1993b). However, there is more to be said about disability in relation to being a woman and/or being black (Begum 1992, Morris 1993).

The compound impact of these oppressions takes numerous forms. For instance, in the case of being black and being disabled (and to some extent in being a woman too), discourses around genetics and social Darwinism can merge together. Of course, the reinforcement of adverse belief systems as a result of the conjunction of different forms of oppression poses a major problem for men too who are, for instance, black and disabled.

Moreover, gender and disability can combine in ways that are especially problematic for men:

. . . although gender and disability operate as structures of oppression for both disabled men and disabled women, this happens in different ways, primarily because of the way in which dependence/independence are key parts of the social meanings of what it is to be a woman or a man. The fact that dependence is a key part of the social construction of gender for women and of the social construction of disability means that women's powerlessness is confirmed by disability. In contrast, a man who is disabled will experience a conflict between the two roles and may attempt to use masculinity as a way of resisting the disabled role. (Morris 1993)

Morris (1993) and Taylor (1993) provide many examples of the way welfare services' responses to these compound sources of oppression are inadequate. Of course, we cannot divorce this inadequacy of response from the power relations that structure welfare agencies. For, as we saw in Chapter 2, they too reflect forms of domination associated with hegemonic masculinities: not black, not disabled, not old, not homosexual or bisexual, not poor, not women. At a concrete level, many welfare agencies demonstrate this complex pattern of domination in the identities of the people who exercise power to a greater or lesser extent within them. Given these patterns of oppression that we have seen structure welfare agencies, it is hardly surprising that their responses to the needs of people who are older or disabled are often inadequate.

These points have been made especially clear in the case of disability by the emphasis that commentators who are disabled have placed on the social construction of disability. Commentators such as Oliver (1990), Oliver & Barnes (1993) and Morris (1993) are seeking a different framework in which the provision of services can occur, one that centres on the needs of the person who is disabled as defined by themselves; and in which the service meeting those needs is also shaped by what we have called the "user" in this study.

This approach, like the importance of reciprocity that we saw Morris (1993) emphasizing above, should be a central element in all anti-oppressive practice. As such, the anti-oppressive activity of men that is the subject of this study must embrace both reciprocity and the principle of user-centred services. In previous chapters we have started to indicate issues of oppression where users can work together to create change. This is already happening (Beresford & Croft 1993), and many of these efforts are focused on areas of adult care. We will consider these important themes in later chapters where we will also find that there are limits on how far they can be pursued in some work with men.

People with learning difficulties

In a summary of the stigmatizing experiences that people with learning difficulties may well encounter, Williams (1992b) tells us that:

> [They] have often been denied the right to integrate with others, the right to marry, the right to parenthood, the right to vote, the right to freedom from harassment, violence and abuse . . . Many people with learning difficulties are denied paid work, or else

119

are highly exploited in the paid work they do . . . and they often experience substantial poverty . . . Their behaviour is often stereotyped in devaluing, negative and often contradictory ways – as child-like, dangerous, promiscuous, volatile or insensible . . . Furthermore, many state policies and institutional practices continue to intensify some of these aspects of oppression.

Clearly, all these factors may bear down on both women and men. However, some of them feed more directly into male stereotypes (for example dangerousness) and others into female ones (for example promiscuity) and we can expect to see an accentuation of negative attitudes around these gender assumptions.

As regards mediation of negative attributes assigned to people with learning difficulties by other sources of stigma, many of the examples given in the section on people with disabilities apply here as well. For instance, the mutual reinforcement of negative images about infantilization applies to learning difficulties, women and black people (Williams 1992b). So too have myths around genetic inferiority and the need for eugenic intervention. Williams (1992b) points out that at different times in British history these stereotypes have contributed to disproportionate numbers of all these groups being classified as having a low IQ: for instance, working class women in the early twentieth century; black girls and boys in the 1960s.

Given what we have heard in this study about the way welfare agencies often replicate and reinforce dominant images of masculinity and femininity, it is no surprise to find it happening in this sphere as well. For instance, Williams (1992b) reports an Irish study that demonstrated how rehabilitative services taught social skills for independence along strictly traditional gendered lines thereby restricting the life opportunities of both men and women – and limiting how far any of them could cope alone on a daily basis.

As regards racism and learning difficulties, close parallels can be drawn between the experiences of black people (women and men) in this field and the experiences of black people with physical disabilities: lack of resources; difficulties in access; myths around black people "keeping themselves to themselves" (Williams 1992b).

People who are experiencing mental distress

There is no doubt that there is overall a clear gender imbalance in terms of who is treated for psychiatric problems both within psychiatric units and at the general practitioner level: women preponderate (Barnes & Maple 1992, Dallos & Boswell 1993).

Why are men less likely to be defined as experiencing mental distress?
Various reasons have been suggested as to why men are less likely than women to require social welfare services in this area. Barnes & Maple (1992) acknowledge that the process by which problems are defined as being "mental" in origin is part (but only a part) of the answer:

> . . . women are in general more likely to go to their GP when they have worries about their health than are men. Also they are more likely to identify their own problems as those of their emotional state than are men.

This is in itself an interesting phenomenon and it connects with discussions in earlier chapters about men's general unwillingness to engage with welfare services (O'Brien 1990). In the light of the consideration we have given to men and masculinities (particularly heterosexual masculinities) in previous chapters, we can suggest some hypotheses about this lack of engagement on the part of men:
(a) a tendency to emphasize control over one's own life and over those who share it;
(b) a consequent avoidance of powerful professional figures who might threaten that sense of power and control;
(c) a tendency to seek emotional invulnerability mainly by withdrawal from emotions other than anger;
(d) a tendency to regard emotions, relationships and care of family as women's domain.

If women do present themselves more than men in ways that allow psychiatric diagnoses to be made about them, they are still not responsible for those diagnoses. The way medical (and other welfare) professions view women and mental health is a major factor in the engendering of "mental illness".

As we have seen on numerous occasions in this study, social welfare agencies cannot be understood without reference to the gender relations that permeate both them and the society in which they are situated. Moreover, as we explored in Chapter 2, the caring function that osten-

121

sibly underpins the activity of those agencies tends to replicate domestic gender oppressions, thereby reinforcing their patriarchal nature.

In Chapter 2 we saw that this was just as true of the medical and nursing professions as of other welfare systems. Although numbers and status of personnel are only one part of the process by which patriarchal relations are reflected and reproduced, they are an important part. We saw that men massively preponderate at middle and senior levels of the health service. In the particular context of the mental health services where the majority of users are female, the fact that, as Jeanette Henderson (1993) notes, over 80 per cent of psychiatric consultancies are held by men mirrors familiar power relations. This is the structural background to what follows.

For instance, Barnes & Maple (1992), reviewing available research, demonstrate that the social construction of "mental health" adopted by medical personnel is deeply rooted in prevalent gender stereotypes. Consequently, within that social construction there is a clear differentiation between concepts describing a "mentally ill" man and a "normal" man; there is much less difference in descriptions of a "mentally ill" woman and one who is "normal". The implications of such stereotyping are clear:

> The irrational, subjective woman by her very nature is closer to madness than the scientific, rational male who not only controls most of the external world, but also has greater control over his own physical and mental well-being. (Barnes & Maple 1992)

They conclude that it is therefore hardly surprising that psychiatric and medical diagnoses label more women than men as having mental health problems.

However, this is only half of the labelling process. In Chapter 5 we saw how women could be drawn into the mental health services when they failed to conform to stereotypes of passivity and femininity: in particular, how men's crime was more likely to be processed via the criminal justice system whereas women's was more often dealt with as a psychiatric aberration.

We also saw that this gendered process was heavily mediated by other dimensions of oppression: to some extent by class, but most strikingly by "race", given that "the psychiatry practised is western, white, and ethnocentric" (Henderson 1993). For instance, we saw that the processing of black men (particularly Afro-Caribbean men) by the mental health system in the context of crime differed substantially from that of white men.

These sexist and racist processes extend well beyond criminality as several commentators have demonstrated (Barnes & Maple 1992, Dallos & Boswell 1993). Thus, Henderson (1993) concludes that:

> Women and Black people are pathologised and disempowered by psychiatric discourse and practice. They are more likely to be "misdiagnosed" and have longer hospital admissions (often compulsory) and to receive physical treatments such as ECT and major tranquilisers . . . Any challenge to the hegemony of organisations such as the Royal College of Psychiatrists (RCP) is fraught with difficulties.

Davis et al. (1985) add:

> . . . there is little dispute about the general response of the medical profession to problems that are defined as psychiatric. The use of the prescription pad results in millions of women becoming dependent upon the products of a highly profitable drugs industry. This industry has never been backward in its advertising. It demonstrates that what they offer can keep women coping with: child care; high-rise living; or the pressures of squeezing paid employment, unpaid domestic labour, and sleep into a twenty-four-hour day.

So a double jeopardy of labelling catapults more white women than white men into the psychiatric system.

The impact of men confronting their mental distress

It might be argued that men's emotional pain (originating, say, in past or current life experiences) brings them into contact with the public authorities in different ways: via violence to the criminal justice and child protection systems. Moreover, men's violence has associations with other behaviours that also appear to be particularly characteristic of them: alcoholism, drug abuse, suicide (Barnes & Maple 1992). This scenario has led some commentators to regret that men cannot, in a sense, follow a similar path to women in using the mental health services to alleviate their emotional pain (Barnes et al. 1990).

It may well be true that some men would benefit if more of them could approach mental health services for help. However, evidence from this study suggests that the view expressed above is questionable on a number of counts.

123

First, although men's inner emotional pain may sometimes be part of the complex processes by which men's violences are generated, this study has already demonstrated that numerous other factors are involved in those processes. Many of men's violences are often carried out with great coldness and calculation, with instrumentality: child sexual abuse (Ch. 8); abuse of women (Ch. 5); sexual abuse of adults with learning difficulties and older people (see below in this chapter). Stress is not generally associated with most of these violences. Moreover, the perpetrators of these violences usually do not possess different psychological profiles from other men.

Secondly, in previous chapters we have seen that societal beliefs among men about the acceptance of violence as a legitimate way of relating to women and to other men can be linked to the way dominant heterosexual masculinities are created. One element in that process of creation may be a reaction by some men to their insecurities, including sexual insecurities, which results in an emphasis on: strength, violence, objectification, control. It may be true that with such a personality profile a man might express emotional pain in violence. However, there is nothing to suggest that men need to be in emotional pain to be violent, controlling or emotionally cold.

Thirdly, given what we have seen, we must be sceptical about the positive benefits of treatment within the mental health system, even though no doubt some people benefit from some therapies with some therapists. After all, we have seen in this chapter and the previous one that the mental health services frequently appear more concerned with social control than personal care. There is no guarantee that the mental health services would always assist a man with his emotional pain.

If men want to do something about their violences at the personal level, our evidence suggests they have several avenues, including: work with other men about how to choose not to be violent; work with other men in exploring other ways to relate to human beings. However, this is work for all men, not merely for those in emotional torment.

Sources of women's mental distress

We have already noted that women preponderate in terms of admissions to hospital on psychiatric grounds. However, we now need to be more precise about the pattern of admissions (Dallos & Boswell 1993). Barnes & Maple (1992) provide a succinct summary:

> Amongst single, widowed and divorced people, the rate of admission to psychiatric hospital is higher for men than for

women. But amongst married people the rate of admission is much higher for women than men and the predominance of married people in the adult population means that the overall rate of admission is higher amongst women than men . . . The number of men and women admitted to hospital with a diagnosis of schizophrenia is similar, but women are twice as likely to be admitted to hospital with a diagnosis of depressive psychosis or psychoneuroses.

This information is important on several counts. First, it strongly suggests that environmental factors are vital to the differential diagnoses of men and women, particularly as regards depression. Secondly, the fact that marital status seems correlated with very contrasting outcomes in the cases of women and men may give us pause for thought about who might benefit most and least from the institution of marriage, especially in view of what we learnt in Chapters 4 and 5.

We can be specific about the kind of stresses that create more depression in women than in men. The team led by George Brown and Tirril Harris have studied women's depression for almost 20 years. Some of the main stress factors that they have identified include: being at home full time with several small children without paid employment; and social disadvantage (Davis et al. 1985, Harris 1993).

Hilary Graham (1993a) places all this in a wider context when she discusses the strains on women in fulfilling their dual role as family "health-keeper and housekeeper".

Graham's work (1993a) has emphasized that the financial pressures on families is increasing generally, and alarmingly so for families in poverty. The reasons are familiar to us from Chapter 4: greater unemployment; more reliance on low-paid, part-time work; the way employment, benefit and child care policies impact upon the growing number of one-parent families (Millar 1994). For a variety of structural reasons these pressures are intensified for many black families (Graham 1993a, Millar 1994).

These very practical stresses on women have to be seen in the context of a myriad of other attitudinal social pressures with negative effects upon women's self-esteem, a factor that Brown & Harris identified as crucial in their model of depression (Harris 1993). Not surprisingly many of these attitudinal pressures are deeply sexist. For instance, the emphasis that society places on childrearing as a benchmark for women's success as human beings sets many women up to fail given the environment within which they are expected to fulfil that task. Second, the great importance attached to an unrealistic perfection in the female body has a similar impact (Davis et al. 1985).

In Chapter 3 we saw that the welfare services often put extra pressure on women in families when they become involved on grounds of child protection. This may well exacerbate problems by reducing a woman's self-esteem further (Barnes & Maple 1992), which not only damages the woman but might also limit her power to protect her children from an abusive father (Hooper 1992, Smith 1994, Ch. 8 below).

Henderson (1993), reviewing the literature, catalogues other potentially destructive and insensitive professional psychiatric responses in the particular context of women service users who have a history of having been sexually abused as children. In fact many of her comments apply to mental health issues in general: the use of mixed wards that may cause women to feel even more insecure (and with good reason); male health and social work staff dealing with women where this may be threatening to some women; professionals' disregard of service users' views and feelings; the denial of reality as perceived by the service user.

Nor should this be a minor consideration in terms of the number of women service users who have a history of sexual abuse: as Henderson (1993) notes, some studies suggest that at least 50 per cent of women who receive psychiatric treatment have been sexually abused at some time in their lives. We should not be surprised by this figure given the general prevalence statistics we reviewed in Chapters 3 and 5.

To summarize: in addition to the labelling processes that draw more women than men within the ambit of the mental health services, there are also reasons for believing that many women may also actually endure more mental distress because of the nature of the social pressures bearing down on them. Both the labelling processes and the social pressures are heavily structured by power relations associated with hegemonic masculinities. Welfare agencies such as health and social services that have a similarly oppressive profile therefore frequently replicate and reinforce the same patterns of domination. This is a picture that we have seen in many of the previous chapters in this study, relating to other areas of welfare.

Before we end this survey of adult care, we have one more, very relevant but largely unexplored, topic to address: the emotional, physical and sexual abuse of adults who are receiving care.

Abuse of adults receiving care

The statistical evidence from Britain is deficient in relation to all aspects of this issue and more deficient in some than others. The evidence that does exist clearly indicates that there may well be cause for concern. The evidence also leaves no doubt that further research is absolutely essential.

People with learning difficulties

In Britain there is probably more awareness of the issue in relation to learning difficulties than in other adult sectors of social welfare. It is reasonably well established that all forms of abuse of people with learning difficulties occur both in home and out of home environments and examples are coming to the attention of the British media quite regularly (Williams 1994).

What is particularly striking about the research in this area is the degree to which it has considered the extent of sexual abuse of adults with learning difficulties and this work has been proceeding for some time (Brown & Craft 1989). In other areas of adult care, sexual abuse seems to be the last possibility to be considered in research.

In North America, a large amount of effort has gone into studying sexual abuse in the area of learning difficulties and disability in general, with disturbing results (Sobsey 1994).

In Britain, Brown & Turk (1992, 1994) are halfway through their major study but have provided preliminary results. They note that due to methodological problems, their data probably underestimate levels of sexual abuse to a great extent.

Most abusers in their study were known to the persons abused, 32 per cent being other service users. However, Brown & Turk (1994) point out that this finding may be skewed as such abuse is probably less well hidden than abuse perpetrated by more skilled abusers. About 18 per cent of abusers were family members and about 14 per cent were staff members or volunteers.

About 60 per cent of those abused had moderate, severe or profound learning difficulties: i.e. the most vulnerable people seemed to be particularly targeted. In over 97 per cent of cases reported, the abuser was male. Brown & Turk (1994) have some interesting comments about this finding that parallel our own discussions in Chapters 2, 3 and 5 and so I will quote them at length:

127

Services for people with learning disabilities, with their predominantly female workforce and male managers, replicate dynamics of power in the home. Raising the abuse of power in staff
teams is inevitable if the reality of sexual abuse is to be made
clear to staff, but against this backdrop of inequality it is risky
and complicated. Discussion can get diverted by questions about
the minority of "women perpetrators", or dissolve into badinage
of the "you just hate men" variety . . . People with learning disabilities cannot afford for men in management positions to back
away from the issue, since allegations will often be passed up the
line to them and they will need to take formal action on behalf of
both women and men who have been the victims of such assaults
. . . Meanwhile, there are important practice issues to be considered about the circumstances under which male staff are encouraged to offer personal care to women and men service users and
about what is to be done to safeguard both parties in such interactions. Male workers express concern that they will be wrongly
seen as abusers and are often left to work in the absence of good
practice guidelines.

As we will see, these are vital issues across all fields of social welfare.
We will address them directly in Chapter 8. For the time being, we
should note that in this study those abused included both women (73
per cent) and men (27 per cent).

One final thought about the particular vulnerability of some adults to
sexual assault is also raised by Brown & Turk (1994). In their sample,
very few cases went to court and, in fact, no action at all was taken
against alleged perpetrators in almost half the cases. This parallels the
situation in child sexual abuse cases with reference to both children generally and those with disabilities specifically.

People who experience mental distress

By contrast, this is the most under-researched area in terms of abuse.
Very little indeed has been written about abuse within institutions. We do
have more idea about the alarming frequency with which users of
therapy in the community are abused, particularly sexually, by welfare
professionals (Frenken & Van Stolk 1990, Rutter 1990, Russell 1993).
For instance, in 1992 the BBC programme *Public eye* (Public eye 1992)
included details of a survey commissioned by the University of Warwick

of 300 clinical psychologists practising as therapists in Britain: 4 per cent said they themselves had been sexually involved with a patient; 22 per cent said that some of their patients had been sexually involved with other therapists; and 40 per cent said they knew of other patients who had been sexually involved with therapists.

Earlier studies have also suggested an alarming situation (Ussher 1991), with up to 15 per cent of therapists admitting to sexual relations with patients and 50 per cent engaging patients in physical contact that the therapists defined as "non-erotic", such as kissing, hugging and touching. When one considers the evidence mentioned above suggesting the very high numbers of women in the mental health system who already come to it with a history of sexual assault, then this behaviour seems especially heinous. Moreover, one is left with exactly the same thought as Ussher: "What is astounding is the high percentage of thera-pists who actually own up to sex with their patients. Is this merely the honest few?" (Usher 1991).

Although not all abusing therapists are men (Russell 1993), there are indications that gender is a very important factor in this form of abuse (Rutter 1990). One commentator who has focused on that gender dimension is Jane Ussher (1991):

> There are no connections made between abuse inside and abuse outside the consulting room. It is presented as an aberra-tion rather than an experience of many women's lives in many contexts. What is ignored is the gender issue, the misogyny, the misuse of power.

And of abusing therapists she says:

> These men are not aberrations. They do not behave in a way that deviates greatly from men in other positions in society. Path-ologizing or ridiculing them conveniently ignores the fact that sexual contact between powerful men and powerless women is part of the fabric of our society. Erotic stimulation is provided by the imbalance of power. Women are blamed for the resulting sex. Why should therapy be any different?

If this level of abuse by therapists may be occurring out in the commu-nity, then it is inconceivable that there is not also a large problem within residential and day care settings, given the relatively "total" quality of the environment there, and the issues of power alluded to earlier in this chapter. In 1992 the mental health charity MIND launched their very successful campaign entitled "Stress on women", one of the results of which has been the campaign report *Eve fights back* (Darton et al. 1994). That report does focus on this issue in institutional settings:

> MIND is receiving mounting evidence that women often do not feel safe in psychiatric hospitals and other mental health settings. Staff, visitors or other patients can be guilty of harassment and abuse. It may take the form of outright abuse through violence, or some more subtle form of coercion; for instance, use of threats or bribes to obtain sex, abuse of a position of trust by a professional or constant unwanted sexual remarks or looks . . . Women are most at risk – although men can also be abused. For black women and lesbians, sexual harassment or abuse can go along with unacceptable remarks about race or sexuality.

Yet the amount of systematic research carried out in this country is minimal: the MIND report mentions one small study, a survey of 100 psychiatric patients of whom 60 had been sexually harassed, 10 sexually assaulted and 2 raped (Darton et al. 1994). Sometimes lack of information can tell you a considerable amount and this seems to be one example: why is this matter not being researched as a matter of urgency?

People who are older

In this area, some research has been carried out in relation to specific forms of abuse while other forms remain largely unexplored.

It is now acknowledged in Britain that physical abuse, emotional abuse and "financial abuse" are considerable problems, although only quite a small amount of focused research has been carried out: Ogg & Munn-Giddings (1993) and Penhale (1993) provide summaries. Further data are desperately needed. More research into these aspects of abuse has been carried out in the United States (Steinmetz 1994, Pillemer 1994), although many issues remain unresolved there too.

Some of the data from the United States and the United Kingdom are relevant to this study. It may be that acts of neglect are perpetrated by both genders or perhaps more often by women since it may involve acts by spouses. Acts of physical abuse may most frequently be carried out by men on women, often adult children abusing a parent (Ogg & Munn-Giddings 1993, Penhale 1993). There is considerable debate as to how far this represents the result of perceived stress on carers (Steinmetz 1994) and how far it is a product of the "deviance and dependence of care-givers" (Pillemer 1994). However, Ogg & Munn-Giddings (1993) comment:

> The emphasis on characteristics of individuals and families has been at the expense of wider sociological perspectives where structural factors such as race, class, gender, poverty, and ageism have more often than not been ignored. No explanation of the causes of elder abuse can be complete unless due attention is given to the structural inequalities that pervade all aspects of old age.

Where there has been almost no research in Britain and very little in the US is the area of sexual abuse of elders. That absence in itself is an interesting phenomenon: why has it been neglected?

In Britain, one practitioner/researcher has begun to build up a database on this issue and provide a sophisticated analysis (Holt 1993, 1994). Malcolm Holt's research is ongoing and is not yet at a fully quantifiable stage. Nevertheless, he has gathered data on, and analyzed, about six hundred cases and some interesting potential patterns are beginning to emerge, three of which I shall mention.

First, the vast majority of perpetrators in his sample are men, though those abused are men and women in a ratio of 1 : 6 (Holt 1994). The perpetrators are heterogeneous in terms of their roles: sons, brothers, formal care staff, partners, friends, neighbours. There are a few cases of sexual abuse in gay relationships. A small minority of abusers are female, including two cases of sisters.

Secondly, very old and very frail people appear to be the usual targets of perpetrators. Older people exhibiting dementia seem particularly to be abused. Holt (1994) hypothesizes that in some cases, it may be that the sexual abuse is producing the behaviours that are being diagnosed as dementia.

Thirdly, this abuse occurs both in people's own homes and in residential/day care settings: i.e. both professionals and non-professionals are abusers (Holt 1994). Both in-home and out-of-home abuse is mainly perpetrated by men.

If these patterns are supported by Holt's future research and other studies, then they would fit quite well with what we know about sexual abuse in other areas of social welfare.

As regards abuse of elders in general, we have to acknowledge that so far the prevalence levels discovered are "relatively low", as Ogg & Munn-Giddings (1993) state. However, they qualify this by adding that:

> . . . one cannot rule out the possibility that the low figures reflect in part an underestimation of the extent of the problem due to the socially desirable response-rate effect from the sensitive nature of the topic.

To summarize: much more research about abuse is needed in all these fields and we cannot make over-firm statements on the information we have. Some provisional conclusions, however, are possible. It seems there may well be a major problem of sexual and physical abuse in the areas of learning difficulties, mental distress and old age.

Judgements about gender of perpetrators have also to be provisional. Once again, it is hard to ignore the issue of gender in the case of sexual abuse in all the areas surveyed here. The picture is more confused in relation to physical abuse and neglect.

We surely have enough evidence in this chapter, and in this study as a whole, for us to be able to say that people can be subjected to men's sexual violences from the cradle to the grave (Turnbull 1994), both inside and outside the welfare services. We can also discern a pattern whereby those people who are oldest or most frail or whose learning difficulties are most profound seem particularly to be targeted by abusers. Once again, this reveals the calculation that characterizes many perpetrators: and this in turn implies some element of choice on their part.

Holt (1994) suggests that welfare agencies should develop protective services for adults requiring care. This is an important suggestion. Men who are workers or users seeking to challenge those oppressions associated with forms of hegemonic masculinity should assist in implementing such services. Hopefully those services would be able to avoid the negative, oppressive features of current child protective services in England and Wales.

Conclusion

Relations of domination associated with hegemonic masculinities are clearly of primary importance in the field of adult care just as they have been in the fields of violent adult crime, child care and child protection. We have seen those patterns, with variations, repeated over and over. What has also been common is the tendency for welfare services to compound those relations of domination, which is not surprising because the agencies are structured by them too.

Of course, there are not only variations but also some disjunctures in these patterns and the disjunctures are crucial to the argument of this study. In this chapter we saw that informal primary caring by men, although still a minority activity, was a significant contributor to the overall resources available. In carrying out this function, the men involved were deviating in important respects from dominant formations of masculinity, particularly dominant models of heterosexual masculinity. We have already concluded in previous chapters that one task for men who are workers and/or users in welfare systems is to re-examine and reform the characteristics by which they define their masculinities. In this chapter we again have examples of how masculinities can be adapted to emotionally productive and creative ends. (See also Applegate & Kaye 1993.)

Of course, if men are to develop their capacities for caring and nurturance as informal carers, it has to be done in ways that will not result in additional abuse of people who require care. For this chapter has again thrown up strong indications that more men than women exploit such caring roles to be violent. Men must be involved to a greater extent in caring in their families for the sake of women, and also for their own sakes. However, this increase in men's caring has itself to be done in ways that ensure the safety of recipients of care. Precisely the same issues apply to child care in the family (Ch. 4).

Consequently, men involved with all aspects of social welfare must work with the widest possible range of men and boys to help them look at their own masculinities and at how these relate to oppression: with a view to assisting them to think about other, more benign, forms of masculinity that they can create for themselves. In Chapters 7 and 8 we develop further the themes that men can pursue in individual work and groupwork for preventative purposes. There is no shortage of opportunities to carry out this work but what is sometimes lacking are the resources (people and time) to do it. So men must also strive to have an impact upon welfare agencies' policies and practices, and an impact on government agencies, so that resources are made available for this work. In turn, this requires men to try to change attitudes at local, community and societal levels. Society needs to understand that men's violences are an immense social problem that requires an equally large injection of resources to reduce or eradicate it. Once again we come to the conclusion that work by men involved with welfare services is required at all levels and these levels are interlinked.

The scope for a worker to commit abuse in the welfare services is immense: the needs of those people using the welfare services and the way such services often do not meet their needs, results in a tendency for many users to be especially vulnerable to abuse. Consequently some men who want to be violent, particularly sexually violent, are likely to be attracted to welfare services. The majority of men working in welfare services will not abuse other people but in Chapter 8 we will see that we have immense, possibly insuperable, problems distinguishing those welfare workers who will abuse from those who will not. Throughout this study, evidence has come to light demonstrating that sexual violence to people inside the welfare services by people working there, mainly men, is considerable. This is not acceptable, especially in services designed to be safe. So in Chapter 8 we will consider what stringent measures can be taken in the welfare services to protect users from the violence of men.

In this chapter we have alluded to pockets of anti-oppressive practice where user-centred services are being developed, fully incorporating principles of reciprocity between welfare workers and users so important to the self-esteem of the latter. We have said that user-centred approaches and principles of reciprocity are central to anti-oppressive practices and therefore have to be incorporated into the activity of men, which is the object of this study. Men who are users can incorporate these features either in their own work for change or in alliance with women who are users. A number of practice models are also now available that are designed to facilitate the collaboration of welfare workers with users in anti-oppressive frameworks. In Chapters 7 and 8 one of our tasks is to define the possibilities and limitations for collaboration of men with men within such frameworks.

Chapter 7
Men against oppressions: woman abuse

Introduction

In previous chapters we have observed that power relations of domination associated with hegemonic masculinities deeply structure the lives of
people who use welfare services and similarly structure the operations of
those services themselves. Consequently, we have seen that the interaction of service provision with the lives of service users often, though
not always, results in an intensification of the oppressions to which users
are subject. It is the contention of this study that men who work in the
welfare services and men who use those services have a responsibility to
challenge those power relations both inside and outside the welfare
services.

Of course, not all men benefit equally from the operation of the structures of domination: hence the concepts of "subordinate masculinities"
and "marginalized masculinities" developed by Connell (1987, 1995).
Moreover, there are no powerful men whom we can turn to and simply
say that they and they alone represent hegemonic masculinity. As
Connell makes clear, the situation is far more complex than this and
most, perhaps all, men are implicated in the operation of hegemonic
masculinities:

> The public face of hegemonic masculinity is not necessarily what
> powerful men are, but what sustains their power and what large
> numbers of men are motivated to support . . . There are various
> reasons for complicity . . . it seems likely that the major reason is
> that most men benefit from the subordination of women, and
> hegemonic masculinity is the cultural expression of this ascend-
> ancy. (Connell 1987)

In putting forward that view, Connell (1987) was echoing what Carrigan, Lee and himself had also suggested earlier:

> the culturally exalted form of masculinity, the hegemonic model, so to speak, may only correspond to the actual characters of a small number of men. Yet very large numbers of men are complicit in sustaining the hegemonic model (Carrigan et al. 1985).

It is important that men seeking to challenge the complicity of themselves and of other men should regard this task in terms of responsibility rather than guilt. The latter often tends to be destructive, negative and immobilizing: and doing nothing to change the situation is yet another form of complicity.

Throughout this study we have also seen that the generation of oppressive power relations is closely connected with what happens between men. We can develop that observation in several different, but linked, ways. First, we can recall Hearn's observations (Hearn & Parkin 1987, Hearn 1992) about the centrality of dominant forms of heterosexual masculinity not only to hegemonic masculinity (Connell 1987) but also to the generation of men's violences; and the way those dominant forms might express a reaction to homosexual desire and sexual uncertainties that exist between men.

Secondly, we remember the research of social psychologists in Chapter 5 that emphasized the importance, at peer group and societal levels, of shared attitudes and beliefs in the generation of men's violences: attitudes and beliefs closely associated with dominant forms of heterosexual masculinity. Even earlier in the study we examined the structures of domination in agencies, including the networks of advantage between men, which worked to the detriment of many women and some other men in those organizations.

All these factors indicate that what happens between men is crucial to the generation and maintenance of men's dominations, including their violences. It is not surprising, then, that an anti-oppressive approach for men should identify men working together for positive change as a central strategy. In social welfare, this can take a number of forms: men workers together; men users together; men workers as therapists to men users; men workers as facilitators to men users; men workers and men users as collaborators. All these permutations are valid in different settings and for different purposes. In this study we have already mentioned situations where some of those options are possible.

The study has also demonstrated that meaningful change in the field of social welfare requires action by men at different levels both inside and outside agencies: individually; at a group level; at different agency levels; at locality/community level; at governmental level; at societal level. These levels are not in practice discrete: changes at one level impact to a lesser or greater extent on all other levels. So in reality, for instance, men working together in a group to help each other develop forms of masculinity that challenge those that are hegemonic are not unconnected with men working to change agency structures. Different men will be active in whatever areas they feel are appropriate for them at any given moment in time. What is perfectly clear from this study is that there is no shortage of opportunities for men involved with social welfare agencies as workers and/or users to take part in this anti-oppressive project.

All the above can be drawn from what we have seen in this study so far. We already have here the basis of a framework for men's anti-oppressive activity in the field of social welfare. In this chapter and the next we develop this framework further by seeing how it can work in practice. Two particular issues will come into focus during this discussion. First, what tools are available to men engaged in this activity? Secondly, what are the dilemmas and limitations on this activity? For there are major problems in men challenging hegemonic forms of masculinity (Connell 1995).

We start this process, then, by considering the ways in which social welfare (and related) agencies respond to the intensely gendered subject of men's violences to women.

Agency responses to woman abuse

The courts and the police

Studies of these agencies (Foreman & Dallos 1993, Gillespie 1994, Gregory & Lees 1994) have confirmed that widespread sexist assumptions have operated here: the alleged tendency of women to withdraw complaints against violent partners, the alleged propensity of women to fabricate allegations against men, and the alleged degree to which women "provoke" violent assaults. In the past neither the courts nor the police were proactive in instituting the Domestic Violence Act (Gregory & Lees 1994).

However, Gregory & Lees (1994) demonstrate that in the 1990s the police have tended to change their dominant discourse, which was to disbelieve women. Gillespie (1994) notes that this positive change of emphasis is largely the result of successful public campaigns by feminist action groups and grassroots organizations: and that for many feminist commentators the changes do not go far enough.

Nevertheless, these moves on the part of the police are significant in the context of our study not only for what they represent in themselves but also for what they say about the processes of change. Gregory & Lees (1994) after noting the problems that feminist activists have in facing the apparently monolithic power of state institutions comment as follows:

> Yet in view of the complex and contradictory ways in which the legal system operates, there is room for a variety of approaches to reform, which are not necessarily mutually exclusive, nor in conflict.

This highlights the possibility that apparently monolithic power blocs within institutions may often afford much room for manoeuvre to those seeking change by virtue of the complexity of institutional structures and the contradictory flows of power within them. In such situations people both within and outside organizations can usually develop alliances and networks inside them by which to create positive change.

We are talking here about the nature of power and in particular poststructuralist conceptions regarding it. Such conceptions can be problematic for those engaged in anti-oppressive projects. This has become most apparent in relation to feminism where the fragmentation of interests implied by postmodern approaches can threaten the idea of a collective project against oppression (Nicholson 1990, Ramazanoglu 1993).

However, some commentators who are influenced by feminist perspectives have emphasized the opportunities that poststructuralist perspectives can offer in terms of possibilities for change. These opportunities may include tools for deconstructing dominant discourses (Tong 1989) and using networks of power relations to counter oppressive practices:

> The gaps, silences and ambiguities of discourses provide the possibility for resistance, for a questioning of the dominant discourse, its revisions and mutations. Within these silences and gaps new discourses can be formulated that challenge the dominant discourse. This theory of discourses and their mutability

provides an accurate understanding of the task of feminism. Feminists have attempted to fashion new discourses about the feminine, discourses that resist the hegemony of male domination, that utilize the contradictions in these hegemonic discourses in order to effect their transformation. In this task the perspective of postmodernism is a help rather than a hindrance. (Hekman 1990)

Or, again, here is Sawicki (1991) writing specifically about the use of Foucault's politics of difference: ". . . one can make generalizations, identify patterns in relations of power and thereby identify the relative effectiveness or ineffectiveness, safety or danger of particular practices".

In referring to such feminist postmodernist approaches, it is important not to over-mystify what are in fact common strategies used by people seeking to create change in agencies where there are complex systems of power: identifying contradictions in the way power is held in organizations and exploiting those contradictions; seeking out potential allies, including apparently unlikely ones who may nevertheless share common objectives. Above all, one should never assume that powerful organizations are monolithic in their structures or patterns of power distribution. On the contrary, one can usually assume they are not. These approaches can be adopted in men's anti-oppressive activity along with other strategies that we discuss later in this chapter.

Returning to the practice example above relating to the police, Gregory & Lees (1994) indicate that similar changes have not been effected in the court systems. On the contrary, between 1985 and 1991 the conviction rate for crimes of rape and sexual assault fell from 24 per cent to 14 per cent. They note that public opinion is now being educated and canvassed in an attempt to extend the change in attitudes and practices to the courts.

Social care agencies:
social work, probation, health and community work

In this survey, we shall see that services for those abused and those abusing are both fragmentary, spread across all these fields, and informed by different, often conflicting, ideologies about the origins of woman abuse. These characteristics in themselves probably say quite a lot about the resistances that can be met when the operation of power relations associated with hegemonic masculinities is challenged.

Many of these considerations apply for instance in relation to social work agencies. As Foreman & Dallos (1993) note, social services have no statutory mandate to intervene in situations of woman abuse except insofar as statutory duties around mental distress or child protection become relevant. In a survey of welfare agencies carried out by the author and colleagues (Gray et al. 1995), social work agencies were quite explicit in stating that it was difficult for them to provide services for women sexually abused in adulthood unless there were child protection considerations. Studies indicate that this is a function of lack of resources and sexist attitudes on the part of agencies (Foreman & Dallos 1993).

Furthermore, O'Hara (1993) suggests that even in the context of child care cases, social workers may be insufficiently responsive to the plight of mothers. She regards this failure as partly arising from the fact that welfare agencies focus on issues of individual/family pathology or on stress due to social disadvantage when assessing situations of risk. In terms of both child protection and woman abuse they place too little emphasis on structural gender oppression and its linkage with men's individual violence to women and children. This was also a conclusion that we ourselves reached in Chapters 3 and 5. (See also Mullender & Morley 1994.)

Black women may well find social care services more unsatisfactory than other women even when there are clear child care issues involved (Dominelli 1988, Ahmad 1990, Ahmed 1994, Bhatti-Sinclair 1994).

Groupwork and individual work with abusive men

Services from social welfare agencies, either statutory or voluntary, may also take the form of individual and/or groupwork with abusive men and this work is often carried out by male workers or a combination of male and female workers. In looking at these services, we need to make some distinction between those directed at sex offenders and those for men who physically abuse their partners, while recognizing that such a division in terms of the men themselves may be partly artificial.

Work with sex offenders There is an overlap here between services for adults who assault adults, adults who assault children, and adolescents/children who are themselves sex abusers. Although the latter two groups belong properly to the subject of the next chapter, for our purposes many of the issues are the same across the three groups and so we will deal with them together here to prevent repetition.

There are rapidly developing services for sex offenders, largely under the auspices of the prison and probation services. Malcolm Cowburn (1993) reports that most probation services in England and Wales are now providing some form of groupwork programme for sex offenders. There is considerable literature on this topic and some feminist and pro-feminist analyses of them (Dominelli 1991, Cowburn 1993, Perrott 1994).

There are several critical questions that we need to ask about these services. First, why is this a growth area in terms of service provision? Why is the government in the form of the Home Office providing funding and what are the implications of this? Some commentators fear that resources devoted to this work by central and local government may be depriving services for abused women of resources at a time when public spending is under severe pressure, and some of these commentators are from within the probation service (Perrott 1994). Of course one can correctly argue that it is vital to prevent offenders re-offending. On the other hand, there are methodological problems in assessing how far such offender programmes do enable men to control their criminal behaviour (Fisher 1994).

Secondly, we might, with Cowburn (1993), query how far these treatment programmes have explicit value bases. He questions the extent to which treatment programmes address gender as a critical issue in offending behaviour. Cowburn also points out that few programmes acknowledge the racism and homophobia that need to be explicitly addressed in both the programmes and the criminal justice system. As regards homophobia, Cowburn notes that some gay "offenders" may in fact be so labelled on account of convictions for their part in sexual acts with consenting peers. He also notes that in primarily white, heterosexual groups black and gay men will have great difficulty in being able to participate usefully.

Dominelli (1991) endorses these comments in terms of racism, adding that there are few black probation officers and the white officers in her study had little awareness in their work of issues of either gender or "race". Cowburn (1993) states explicitly: "If we accept that sexual offending has its roots in the use and abuse of power, then all methods of work must address gender, race and sexual orientation." And he includes in this issues of leadership. Cowburn's work is an example of good quality anti-oppressive practice by men for men that this study is seeking to encourage.

The content of programmes differs widely. Most seem to acknowledge the importance of patriarchal relations, although the extent of this acknowledgement is extremely variable. Cowburn's programme (1993) places more emphasis and time on looking at patriarchal relations than most others. Given the evidence that we reviewed in Chapter 5 regarding the processes that contribute to sex offending by men, Cowburn's approach seems fully vindicated. Using that evidence we can identify themes that programmes with sex offenders should pursue, though not necessarily at the same time:

(a) Offenders must be assisted to take full responsibility for their offences. After all, they chose to sexually assault.

(b) Offenders must be assisted to place their offending in the wider context of oppression that operates not only at structural levels but also in their general behaviour.

(c) The myths and attitudes shared by men, and often by women too, which reinforce men's violences must be challenged by information, argument and example.

(d) If choice is an important factor in whether men abuse or not, then work must also focus on assisting offenders to choose not to abuse. There are many potential avenues to pursue here. Two of them might be: assisting men to understand what the consequences of their violence are for other people; assisting offenders to construct strategies for avoiding situations where re-offending is more likely. This usually entails helping them to understand the precise processes by which they come to choose to offend.

(e) If men's oppressions are bound up closely with the performance of behaviours associated with some dominant forms of masculinity, including dominant forms of heterosexual masculinity, then work must be done to assist men to develop the performance of masculinities less related to violence, control and objectification. This is a major task that may well extend beyond the timescales of the other themes listed here. Indeed, it may not be possible to pursue it thoroughly until after some of the more confrontative themes above have been well completed. For this task often entails closer, more intimate work between therapist and offender than is appropriate when tackling the other themes that should take precedence over this one in terms of timescales. Even so, completion of the other tasks above should have some impact on the offender's perspective regarding his masculinity. This can then be built upon.

Changing the performance of different masculinities is not essentially about men bolting new forms of masculinity on to themselves. It is about assisting men to locate those different forms of masculinity in themselves and then extending their performance of them. For I am suggesting that we men all perform numerous masculinities at different times in our lives, indeed at different times in each day. Our range of options is enormous if we are freed from the belief that we have to conform to particular ones by, for instance, societal values, our friends, our insecurities. In work with offenders the process of exploring these issues will be ongoing, although, as noted above, it may not take centre stage until later in the programme, whether on a one-to-one basis or in groupwork.

A final question we might want to ask about treatment programmes for sex offenders is how the leadership/therapist role is to be decided. Both Perrott (1994) and Dominelli (1991) refer to female probation officers having to work with offenders when they are deeply uncomfortable about doing so for personal and/or political reasons. As Perrott (1994) comments: "Undertaking the work is in itself a compromise for many feminists who believe it is a male problem that should be resolved by men."

One can understand that point of view very readily and it is abusive to a woman for her to have to work with sex offenders if she is uncomfortable. On the other hand, there is no doubt that a woman therapist can have a particular impact on sex offenders if she presents a model of a female who is in control of her own life. However, it also has to be acknowledged that when confronted by such a powerful model, some abusers may react by seeking to inflict emotional, and sometimes physical or sexual, violence on a woman therapist. Certainly women engaged in this form of work should be offered excellent support in terms of supervision and consultancy: it may well be many of them will prefer that support from other women.

Men therapists do have a clear responsibility to be engaged in this work either by themselves or co-working with a female colleague, which is the preferred option of many programmes (Morrison et al. 1994). Men's responsibility, as we have said before, is to challenge those power relations associated with hegemonic masculinities in which most (all?) men are implicated. Furthermore, some men may bring particular assets with them into this work with sex offenders. We know that relationships between men usually have a central role in generating and reinforcing those attitudes that promote violence to other human beings (Ch. 5). Men working with sex offenders can therefore harness these powerful processes for the purposes of halting that violence. We also saw in Chapter 3 that there is evidence men therapists may sometimes be more able to engage men in therapy. Finally, of course, a man therapist may be able to model other versions of masculinity for the offender: if such a therapist is co-working with a woman then they can place that modelling in the context of female/male relationships.

On the other hand, the common elements that exist between a man therapist and a male sex offender pose a great difficulty. Dominelli (1991) stresses that a major problem of men working with men abusers is their propensity for collusion with the latter. Dominelli emphasizes that it is so easy for male workers to collude because, as we saw in Chapter 5, many offenders are "ordinary guys". Welfare workers often share a common sexism, racism, heterosexism with sex offenders, even if in the case of workers those prejudices are muted.

Moreover, it is important to place the collusion of male therapists/workers in a structural context: we are after all not simply talking about the foibles of individual men. This phenomenon is another manifestation of "organization sexuality" and those oppressive structures which, as we saw in Chapter 2, permeate both society and welfare agencies.

In the case of working with sex offenders, the answer to the issue of collusion is perfectly clear: there should be no collusion on any count. Offenders must be confronted with their responsibility for their offending and offered no escapes from that responsibility by therapists, unwittingly or otherwise (Morrison et al. 1994).

Some precautionary strategies are available that can limit the risk of men therapists colluding with sex offenders' attitudes when working with them. First and most basic, men workers engaged in these activities need to have done a great deal of work on themselves initially. That "work" on oneself should have followed similar contours to the themes identified above for dealing with offenders: acknowledging one's own tendencies to oppress; linking that with oppressive systems more widely; challenging the oppressive attitudes and beliefs that we men tend to share; working out in practice how we will not be oppressive; seeking to transform the oppressive masculinities that we may be performing in much of our lives.

In addition, there should always be a supervisory/consultancy team observing and videotaping work with offenders, whether that work is with an individual or a group. If it can be arranged, that supervisory team should either be all female or predominantly female. Moreover, those women supervisors should not only understand the principles behind work with sex offenders but, preferably, should also be actively working with survivors of sexual assault: either in what we label "professional" agencies or in rape crisis/women's aid settings. For those women who work with survivors may well be most highly motivated and able to detect collusion by men therapists. This is a model similar to one in the United States described by Dobash & Dobash (1992).

However, as we noted above, collusion is not a purely individual characteristic: it partly reflects the oppressive assumptions and structures of the agencies in which men work. Thus, we need to recognize that consultancy/supervision of men therapists is only one response to the problem. The oppressive structures of agencies must also be a target of change for men engaged in anti-sexist and anti-oppressive work; and not least in work with sex offenders. One strategy that has been employed in some agencies is for local women's organizations to have a major role in the management of projects engaged in work with sex offenders. As we will see below, this strategy can be problematic if the women's organizations are not given real power. Men working to challenge oppression have a role in trying to move agencies to the adoption of policies such as these.

Work with men who physically abuse their partners   Most of the issues discussed in the last section are relevant here too. For instance, many commentators have expressed concern that resources diverted to working with men in this field may also be at the expense of services for women (Lees & Lloyd 1994, Pringle 1994a). Similarly, there is doubt about how far treatment programmes incorporate a clear value-base, including a definite commitment to anti-oppressive and anti-sexist practice. Lupton (1994) writes about:

> . . . the growth of work with male abusers which tends, with some notable exceptions . . . to focus on the personal inadequacies of the men and their need to achieve greater control over their feelings and behaviour. The problem is the extent to which such behaviourist approaches, in conjunction with an emphasis on social factors such as poverty, stress and unemployment, make the violent response of the individual male at the least "understandable" and, at the worst, to some extent, "excusable". The fact that many women experience these pressures and do not resort to violence, and that many men who batter their wives and partners do not experience them, may be ignored . . . it does nothing to confront the larger problem of men's abusive power over women.

In the light of the evidence surveyed by this study we would totally endorse Lupton's view (1994). Moreover, projects that work with men who batter partners vary considerably in their outlook, their objectives and their funding. Some projects focus on more preventative work (for instance, The Everyman Centre); some on community-oriented approaches (for instance, Domestic Violence Intervention Project (DVIP)); while, increasingly, others are developing a more "professional" orientation by forming multi-agency partnerships with a strong probation and statutory ethos (Lees & Lloyd 1994).

Not surprisingly in view of these disparities, there is variation in the degree to which projects focus on countering men's violence as a primary aim. For example, Lees & Lloyd (1994) suggest that DVIP places more emphasis than Everyman in putting women and children's safety first: Everyman is committed to stopping men's violence but also has the aim of helping men re-evaluate their attitudes to masculinity, sexuality, relationships and violent behaviour. The evidence of our study demonstrates that these two objectives are not separate, although the safety of women and children must be the paramount consideration.

Lees & Lloyd (1994) suggest that there seems to be a trend towards the growth of multi-agency semi-statutory projects with relatively secure, part-public funding. This may be at the expense of the other forms of provision whose funding tends to be less secure. This development could be problematic given that the former projects usually focus on men at the point of prosecution and conviction rather than earlier when perhaps their violence is less entrenched.

Another parallel with sex offenders is that it is difficult methodologically to measure how far work with men who batter is effective. In particular, we noted in Chapter 5 that it is becoming increasingly apparent that men may often stop battering but instead terrorize their partners through emotional abuse, financial control and restriction of liberty (Kirkwood 1993). In other words, they may merely substitute one form of abusive behaviour for another.

Issues over the gender of workers dealing with physically abusive men are virtually the same as those relating to sex offenders and so we will not add to our comments above.

Likewise, the themes that we have suggested above should be central to work with sex offenders are also applicable to a large extent in work with physical abusers. This reflects our conclusion in Chapter 5 that the very complex processes generating both forms of violence are similar even if they are not always identical. Obviously in adapting those themes for work with men who batter their partners, workers may want to incorporate other issues.

I have suggested elsewhere (Pringle 1994a) that projects working with physical abusers, like those addressing sexual assault, need to have very close links with women's groups: that preferably women's groups should have some management oversight of the work that men therapists are doing with men abusers. Some projects do incorporate such management links but there is concern that these may be loosening over time (Pringle 1994a). The movement towards multi-agency semi-statutory projects at the expense of community-oriented projects working with batterers could accelerate such de-linking. To an extent we may see this process as a trend towards professionalization of services: as we will see shortly, the same trend is discernible in other areas of work associated with violence to women. Given what we have concluded about the importance of user-led services and what we revealed about professionalization in Chapter 2, this trend may well be a cause for concern. In practice what it may partly represent is retrenchment against feminist and pro-feminist approaches to welfare provision.

Services for women abused by men

Certainly, what is generally lacking in statutory therapeutic provision for survivors of men's violence are women-centred services. The survey by Gray et al. (1995) established that there was little statutory provision for adult survivors of child and adult sexual assault. Moreover, where survivors could obtain professional services (either from the health or social work agencies) they tended to prefer voluntary, survivor-focused or survivor-led provision.

In terms of sexual assault in adulthood, the major woman-centred providers are Rape Crisis Centres. These are now under considerable stress for a number of reasons. The sheer mass of women coming forward for help is one obvious source of stress. Another is the "new managerialism" (Lupton 1992) in the public sector of welfare which produces a consequent desire on the part of the latter to use funding pressure to make Rape Crisis more bureaucratic, more accountable and more "professional" (Gillespie 1994).

At the same time alternative services are beginning to develop that are directly linked to the public sector: Victim Support Schemes (VSS) (Gillespie 1994) and Sexual Assault Referral Centres (SARCS) (Foley 1994). Both these alternative services conform to the needs of "new managerialism" more neatly than Rape Crisis Centres and both, as it happens, tend not to approach sexual assault from such a clear feminist perspective. Both VSS and SARCS tend to focus on assaults primarily in terms of rape trauma syndrome (RTS). The latter is a controversial approach that has been criticized by a number of commentators on several counts (Foley 1994, Gillespie 1994), not least that it may deflect attention from the structural, patriarchal context of sexual assault to more individual, pathologizing frames of reference.

Rape Crisis has also come under pressure for, on the whole, not providing services to men who are survivors (Gillespie 1994)). As our survey showed (Gray et al. 1995), there is a desperate need for services for men survivors of both adult and child sexual assault. However, the fact that services for men are lacking does not imply that Rape Crisis has to be the agency that meets this need. It is surely valid for Rape Crisis to maintain their service to women and for other existing or new agencies to develop services for men. If these services do become available from other agencies, there is a justifiable fear that they may be at the expense of services for women. It is vital that both kinds of service are available but not to the detriment of one another. We consider this issue further in Chapter 8.

Finally it is important to emphasize that the survey by Gray et al. (1995) found a profound lack of statutory or voluntary provision in the North East of England for black people who have been subject to men's violence, though some developments are now occurring. We cannot be sure whether this is representative of the country as a whole.

Housing services

We saw in Chapters 4 and 5 that difficulties in meeting housing needs were crucial in keeping women with men when they wanted to leave them. These difficulties are partly a function of the way employment, benefit and child care policies conspire to limit the potential income of would-be lone mothers. They are also a function of central and local government housing policies, as Foreman & Dallos (1993) note: a combination of enforced sales of housing stock and local housing policies can imprison women in violent relationships. In this situation, the Women's Aid Federation and the Women's Refuge movement have played a critical role in assisting women and in countering those oppressive relations in many official agencies that replicate the patterns of oppression many women endure in the home.

One problem about refuge provision is that there are relatively few refuges that cater specifically for the needs of black women. However, Shama Ahmed (1994) emphasizes how much black women's groups have achieved in setting up autonomous refuges and safe places. We might also consider what is available for women seeking refuge from violence within a lesbian relationship. Moreover, men may endure violence in some gay relationships and clearly, escape may be blocked by lack of alternative accommodation. On the other hand, as men, many of them will have access to greater income than women in a similar position.

Movements towards professionalization are threatening Women's Aid and refuges in the same way as we saw above that they threaten both Rape Crisis Centres and community or volunteer-oriented men's projects. Lupton (1994) describes how a shortage of resources enables statutory agencies to put pressure on refuges to bureaucratize and to restrict themselves to targeted services, similar to the process that has already occurred in the statutory agencies themselves (Ch. 2 above). Such changes are inimical to feminist approaches that have underpinned the work of most refuges.

Lupton (1994) places this trend in the context of a renewed resistance by the social welfare establishment (funding bodies, the Central Council for the Education and Training of Social Workers, some prominent academics, Department of Health, Home Office) against feminist approaches in welfare. Clearly, what is happening to Rape Crisis and voluntary men's groups committed to pro-feminist practice could be seen as part of the same process. She regards the movement towards purchaser/provider models of service provision as being likely to accelerate the general assault on the integrity of feminist practice in favour of more hierarchical, masculinist managerial practices.

If Lupton is correct, as I believe she is, then this has major implications for our study that is after all seeking to find ways in which men as service users and workers can align with one another in anti-sexist and anti-oppressive practice. In essence, what Lupton is describing is the dismantling of such an alignment as existed (uneasy though it was) between feminist and pro-feminist survivor-focused agencies and the state sector. On the other hand, we have seen in previous chapters that a more general movement towards user-led services is beginning to develop, largely although not exclusively in the field of adult care. This movement can be a source for the development of men's anti-oppressive action against patriarchal relations. However, the trends that Lupton describes are a warning that these activities need to be progressed with considerable skill and strategic acumen: for resistances to them are massive. Nor should this be a surprise to us given the depth and breadth of oppressive power relations associated with hegemonic masculinities that we have reviewed throughout this study.

General implications for men's anti-oppressive practice

So far in this chapter we have seen that familiar, oppressive power relations structure not only the form of services available in the field of woman abuse but also patterns of non-availability of services, especially for survivors of such abuse. On both these counts, there are clearly issues that men involved with welfare agencies could, in their practice, address in challenging those relations of power.

I want now to use our foregoing review to draw out some more general issues that are relevant to the whole subject of men as workers in, and men as users of, social welfare services.

The need for an anti-oppressive approach

In this chapter, as in all those preceding it, we have observed the way oppressive gender relationships are part of complex dynamics of domination that involve other forms of oppression: issues of "race", sexual orientation, class, disability, age. If we privilege one form over the others when we seek to counter oppression, we will simply mirror the operation of those hierarchical power structures that are meant to be the object of change. Moreover, such privileging is a nonsense in practice as compound systems of oppression do not allow one dimension to be simply isolated from the others for attention. So, for instance, if men seek to develop services for men who have been sexually assaulted in childhood or adulthood, they must consider how issues of "race", culture or sexual identity impact on that provision. Or, again, we may recall Cowburn's excellent programme for sex offenders (Cowburn 1993) that fully addressed issues of "race" and sexual identity. It has to be said that the evidence of this study suggests that men's work with men frequently does not demonstrate the breadth of vision we are advocating. For instance, we may recall what various commentators above said about the nature of much provision in the probation service. The conclusion to be drawn from this discussion is that when men involved in social welfare as workers and/or users seek to challenge relations of domination associated with hegemonic masculinities, their efforts must take cognizance of all dimensions of oppression. Such an approach is also the logical conclusion to be drawn from Connell's analysis of power relations (1987, 1995) that underpins the framework we are developing here.

Countering men's oppressions generally

This study has catalogued an overwhelming level of oppression perpetrated within structures of domination associated with hegemonic masculinities. These oppressive practices take numerous forms, extending from the cradle to the grave, and are located in diverse sites, not the

least of which are social welfare agencies themselves. It is so overwhelming that changing the situation may seem hopeless. A different and more
constructive view is to say that opportunities for men to do something
about this state of affairs are almost endless. This latter view is the one
we adopt in this study.

In this chapter we have seen that men are joining in the struggle
against woman abuse: some by working on themselves and with men
who abuse; some (who abuse) by seeking help to change themselves;
some by seeking to develop in a progressive fashion the structural
frameworks of the agencies and localities within which they operate.
While none of these efforts are without their problems, nevertheless they
clearly represent positive steps forward that need to be multiplied.

Because the forms of oppression that are the subject of this study are so
widespread and entrenched, there are many other avenues by which men
can more broadly engage in changing this state of affairs. In previous
chapters we noted numerous issues that men in social welfare could
tackle. There will be many more that we have not mentioned. I now want
to address some of those broader avenues that some men in social welfare are beginning to develop and that require far greater expansion.

Working with men and boys: preventing oppression

As we will see, there is evidence that there is an increasing amount of
work being done by men with men and boys outside the specific field of
abuse, much of it with the prevention of oppressive behaviour as one
objective. However, far more could be done in a range of settings.

One-to-one work with men is an obvious method of engagement.
Groupwork is another important approach and is suggested by several
factors that we touched on in our earlier discussion about working with
sex offenders. We know that peer pressure is crucial to the development
of oppressive behaviours in men and boys (Ch. 5 above, Pollard 1994,
Campbell & Muncer 1994). We also know that feelings and relations between men may be crucial to understanding the way many men behave
towards women and children (Chs 1 and 2 above, Carrigan et al. 1985,
Hearn 1992, Kimmel 1994). Finally, we know that group activity is a common way of men and boys relating to one another, although not normally
as a method of countering oppression (i.e. in pubs, sports teams, gangs).

O'Neill (1990) has usefully surveyed general, anti-sexist social work
and community work with men and boys in 1989/90. Although literature available to him seems to have been limited, he found groupwork
going on in a variety of settings, largely in community and youth work.
Groupwork with men by men is also now developing in family centres.

This has been surveyed by Colin Holt (1992) and to an extent by Sandy Ruxton (1991). At the same time Holt (1992) also reviewed individual work with men in family centres.

In recent years the journal *Working with Men* (WwM) has not only provided a wide range of very useful resources in this field but also chronicled the broad extent of groupwork and individual work being developed throughout the country in a wide variety of settings. For instance, current practice includes family centre work (Chandler 1993); groupwork on men and offending (Murphy 1993); peer education of young men in terms of health promotion (WwM 1993); social and sex education for men with learning difficulties (Hazlehurst 1993); support groups for men with testicular cancer (Williams 1993); counselling for men who are infertile (Entwistle 1993); using football matches as a focus for a safer sex campaign (Brown 1994). This suggests that the range and creativity of work with men and boys has increased considerably since O'Neill's survey six years ago.

One observation about much, although by no means all, of this creative material is that it describes projects that are outside the day-to-day routine practice of certain welfare sectors. For instance, there is relatively little reported about men's anti-oppressive work being done with men by field social workers in statutory services. We know that some individual field workers do practise from this perspective in their day-to-day activity (Bowl 1985). However, the lack of material about this practice may well reflect an overall lack of activity in this sector of welfare work.

Certainly, throughout this study we have commented on the increasing limits being placed on the work of staff in statutory social work agencies. Men's anti-oppressive activities in statutory social services seem to need particular expansion. There may be many reasons for this suggested lack of activity (Hazlehurst 1994). One of the most important is surely the chronic shortage of resources in statutory social work and the targeting of services that flows both from this and from ideological factors: themes that have emerged and re-emerged in this study.

Men working in statutory social services need to place special emphasis on the necessity for working together concertedly to adapt structures in their agencies so as to release time and space for them to develop their anti-oppressive practice. That practice can exist without more resources but it will be heavily limited. Change is also required in the structures within which the statutory agencies operate more generally. This can be achieved via the agencies themselves and also through public campaigns on particular issues. Such work is vital with respect to all sectors of welfare: it is even more vital for statutory social services. All this work at different levels may look like a huge task. However, not everyone has to do everything and we will see that some valuable work is already beginning to be done at each level. Later in this chapter we focus on strategies that may assist men to create structural change within their agencies. We also start to consider how changes at different levels can be linked.

Let us now return to the material above that reports the anti-sexist and anti-oppressive work that is being performed across a considerable number of other welfare sectors. In reading these diverse accounts several points made by both O'Neill (1990) and Holt (1992) are borne out. First, to engage men initially it is sometimes necessary to use venues, settings and techniques (problem-solving, action-oriented tasks) that are regarded as being more typically masculine. Secondly, once men are at ease in groups or individual sessions, they are often keen to look at issues that are emotionally difficult and sensitive for men, including issues of sexuality and gender.

In the light of the material that has been surveyed in this study, it is clear that certain themes are particularly relevant to the content of work with men or boys that is aimed at general prevention of oppressive behaviour: and these are applicable to both individual work and groupwork. They are similar to those that we defined as necessary in work with men who sexually or physically abuse. Clearly, the manner in which the themes are dealt with in general work with men and boys will be different in terms of pace and style from work with actual abusers: discussion and challenge rather than confrontation is more appropriate in this work, and we discuss below precisely what we mean by challenging.

Because we have mentioned these kinds of themes earlier, we will only summarize them here in the form applicable to more general preventative work with men and boys:

(a) They should be helped to acknowledge their own tendencies to act oppressively.

(b) They should be assisted to link that oppression to the more general oppressive structures and behaviours in society.

(c) The societal and peer group attitudes that endorse men's and boys' oppressive behaviour should be challenged by information-giving, debate and by example.

(d) They should be assisted to think in very practical terms of situations where they tend to act oppressively and devise strategies for avoiding those situations and changing their behaviour.

(e) They should be assisted to consider what being a man or a boy means to them. By looking more closely at themselves and at the situations of other men/boys they should be encouraged to develop wider repertoires of behaviour and models of masculinity not associated with violence, control and objectification.

(f) These themes above should be dealt with in a way that allows all forms of oppression, not only sexism, to be addressed continuously.

A precondition of engaging men workers in this kind of activity with men and boys is that one should have already pursued these themes with oneself. Workers can do their own work in one-to-one settings (for example co-counselling or simply via friendship) and/or in group settings (for example men's support groups) within agencies and outside.

It is not being suggested that each of these themes should be addressed in all anti-oppressive individual or groupwork with men or boys, nor to the same depth. Much depends on the characteristics of the people being worked with, the setting, the precise focus of the work, the length of time available and probably many more variables specific to each situation. Nevertheless, these are the components of anti-oppressive men's work or boy's work that the evidence of our study has thrown up.

Developing commonalities between men workers and users

Holt (1992) and Ruxton (1991) make a further important point about work with men: it can be enhanced by men facilitators and members of groups sharing their commonalities as men. However, one should be realistic about the difficulties of this breaking down of barriers: power differences acting in both directions between group members and facilitators (such as culture, age, disability, sexual identity, income, class, the status of "professional" knowledge, control over access to welfare resources) are not managed simply by good intentions. They have to be tackled by openness about these power disparities, by adopting clear strategies for minimizing their impact, and by a hard-won trust. Even then a perfect power balance is unlikely to occur.

Yet work between men who are workers and users, where barriers can be reduced in the way we have just described, is an important strategy for anti-oppressive practice. Such a reduction in hierarchical barriers between professionals and non-professionals is by its very process potentially anti-oppressive. Moreover, if one reason why men may avoid contact with welfare services is their fear of professional power (as we suggested might be the case in an earlier chapter), then this strategy may facilitate men's engagement with such services.

In addition, as we saw in Chapter 6, commentators in the field of adult care (Morris 1991, Walmsley 1993) have been particularly sensitive to the value that reciprocity can have in social welfare exchanges between welfare workers and users: and conversely how a lack of reciprocity can have an adverse impact on a user's self-image, no matter how benign the service provision. This observation applies equally to work with men.

There are a number of models of practice that claim to enhance partnership between welfare workers and users and that men working collaboratively can draw upon for ideas. Most are useful and I will mention them in a moment. However, one relatively new approach, social constructionist therapy (Steier 1991, McNamee & Gergen 1992, Shotter 1993), which claims to promote partnership with users, has to be treated with considerable caution on three grounds. First, it seems to replace one form of hierarchical expertise with another (Lax 1992). Secondly, it has little to say about the very real forms of social oppression that bear down on the users of welfare services (Bhaskar in Shotter 1993). Thirdly, it seems to eschew any concept of a value-base (Gergen & Kaye 1992) and this is inimical to anti-oppressive practice. So, at this stage, the social constructionist therapy model seems to have only limited relevance to our project of forging collaboration between men as workers and as service users.

However, men workers seeking to engage more collaboratively with men or boys can now access a range of other models that are genuinely based on principles of mutuality. These models are proven, easily available and well documented, so I will not expand on them at length here. They have been developed by radical and/or feminist social welfare commentators and include: feminist and user-led groupwork (Butler & Wintram 1991, Mullender & Ward 1991); Rogerian counselling techniques (Mearns & Thorne 1988); radical networking/community-oriented social work (Barber 1991); radical casework (Fook 1993); and models of citizen involvement (Beresford & Croft 1993).

There are, of course, particular conditions relating to work with men that make the wholesale transfer of feminist and radical strategies problematic. For instance, feminist and radical strategies presume that users are disempowered in some form or other. We have agreed that masculinity is a heterogeneous phenomenon and at any given moment in time some masculinities will be less charged with power than others. Feminist strategies may often be transferred relatively unproblematically to work with subordinated or marginalized masculinities.

However, we have to recognize that anti-oppressive work with men often entails considering what to do about the oppressors and potential oppressors in society rather than the oppressed.

Connell (1995) makes a similar point: men's counter-sexist practice runs directly against the interests they share in society. This is different from the anti-oppressive practice of, say, women or black people. Despite this, he suggests that men's anti-sexist project can progress if it exploits two "strategic possibilities" within present gender relations. Both of these are being capitalized upon in this study. The first consists of those tensions within the multiple and contradictory masculinities that characterize current social relations – "crisis tendencies" that open spaces whereby masculinities may be transformed. This is reflected in our study by our attempts to enable men, collectively and individually, to develop more positive forms of masculinity in their public and personal lives.

Connell's second "strategic possibility" focuses on "alliance politics" between the anti-sexist project of men and other social movements or interest groups, including those of women (Connell 1995). Thus in our study we emphasize the crucial importance of men networking both inside and outside welfare agencies to promote their anti-oppressive purposes. We will develop further both these themes later in this chapter and in the next. However, at this point we need to consider the immediate implications of the fact that the object of men's anti-oppressive practice is men themselves.

Two implications of this discussion are particularly important. First, some of men's anti-oppressive practice is concerned with how to use power more positively. However, we need to acknowledge that some of it also has to be about men relinquishing power individually and structurally. By contrast, much work by women with women is about how to take power and that is often a critical difference between anti-oppressive work with the two genders. Secondly, men must be continually on guard in case the strategies they devise to achieve positive anti-oppressive change simply replicate oppression in other forms: as men we should never underestimate the intransigence of the dynamics of hegemonic masculinities in our own practice or in the structures that provide the context for that practice.

Although I do acknowledge the real value of the diverse and creative efforts carried out by men with men which is recorded in WWM and the studies mentioned above (e.g. O'Neill 1990, Holt 1992), I have several qualms about elements within that work in the light of the comments I have just made.

Problems in developing men's work and boy's work

First, in the literature noted above, the advantages of men acting as facilitators/therapists for other men are sometimes overstressed while the problems of this role are underemphasized. For instance, it is true, as some of the literature suggests, that men may sometimes have a more constructive impact on other men than women could achieve when giving men an anti-sexist message; and it may well be appropriate to take advantage of this phenomenon (Pringle 1990). However, in choosing this strategy we have to be careful not to reinforce men's devaluation of women's authority and the full range of roles that should be open to women. If we are not very sensitive to this danger, then the process we adopt to communicate our message may be at odds with the anti-oppressive content of that message.

One of the greatest problems in men's work and boy's work generally is the ease with which men facilitators/therapists may collude with men's or boy's oppressive attitudes. It is a problem we have already mentioned in relation to work with abusers but it is by no means confined to that specialist area and I now want to think about it in terms of more general work with men and boys. Each act of collusion is an active reinforcement of oppression, not just a momentary lapse to be dismissed as unimportant. This is particularly the case in a group setting where men or boys may well test the facilitator's attitudes, and any endorsement of oppression by the latter, no matter how unintentioned or minor, could have an exceptionally negative impact.

Similar, though perhaps less elaborate, precautions to those recommended in working with abusers are needed in this more general area to keep a check on what men workers are saying and doing. These precautionary strategies might include some combination of, for example, co-working with a woman facilitator, having women as consultants, videotaping work done.

This point clearly applies to work with men and boys where the explicit objective is to prevent oppressive attitudes and behaviour. However, we are suggesting that it should also apply to work by men with men and boys that is not explicitly about such prevention. We would argue that the issue of men's oppression is such a massive problem that all welfare work with men and boys on whatever topic should still have prevention of oppression on its agenda as a secondary aim.

In Chapter 8 we shall see that there are additional reasons for monitoring men's individual work and groupwork with men and boys in the ways described here. Moreover, it needs to be stressed that these sorts of precautionary strategies have considerable value in their own right. If adopted, they are general aids to good quality therapeutic work, whether done by men or women. Consequently, I believe men working with men or boys should welcome them as procedures of general good practice.

O'Neill (1990) highlights another dilemma in men's work and boy's work for facilitators: if one confronts oppressive attitudes or behaviour too strongly one may lose the engagement of the person being confronted. On the other hand, if one does not confront sufficiently, then one may well be colluding.

This is a dilemma that applies to all anti-oppressive work. Collusion on the part of facilitators is never justified to any extent. However, that does not immediately catapult facilitators to the other extreme of having to confront in ways that have destructive results. Challenging is perhaps a better term to use rather than confronting and there are numerous strategies that facilitators can devise for challenging oppressive behaviour, none of which need include aggression nor alienation of the person being challenged. The aim of challenging is to produce a positive change in the behaviour of the person being challenged. Different strategies will be appropriate for different situations and part of the skill of facilitation is knowing how to match the two in order to produce a positive result.

Extending anti-oppressive work with men and boys

My second criticism of some anti-sexist men's work and boy's work described in the literature noted above is that the actual challenging of men's oppressions may not always be as firmly placed on the agenda as it should be. After all, this study has demonstrated that oppression exercised by men is one of the most widespread and pernicious problems that our society faces and has to be challenged.

We have clearly shown that this oppression is not the responsibility of a few "deviant" individuals but is intimately connected to the way masculinities develop and to the way the contours of hegemonic masculinities structure our society at all levels. Work that contributes to challenging this oppression must be actively carried out wherever men engage with men or boys in the field of social welfare. Sometimes anti-oppression will be the explicit central reason for work with men or boys and there is a need to expand this massively. At other times men's work with men will focus on more discrete topics such as, for instance, health issues.

As we said above, actively challenging men's oppression of other people should clearly be on the agenda even when the central focus of the work is a topic not overtly concerned with such oppression. Too often it is relegated to being a minor issue on the agenda or even avoided altogether because it is felt by facilitators to be too painful and uncomfortable and might disturb the safety of the group. As we have seen, there are many strategies for challenging oppression in individual work and groupwork that can avoid alienation of participants.

The breadth of the problems arising from power relations associated with hegemonic masculinity is so considerable that anti-oppressive work with men and boys on an individual or group level should be systematically expanded and not allowed to be piecemeal as at present. It warrants concerted and well-funded government campaigns in schools, the full range of health and social work settings, community and youth centres, and numerous other welfare locations. After all, we are talking about one of the most pervasive social problems in our society.

Support for men working with men and boys

Those men engaged in this work also require good support for it can be painful and stressful. Some material has been written about providing support for men or women working with abusers (Erooga 1994). However, these considerations need to be extended to the broader forms of work undertaken by men with men and boys.

All the comments in this section are applicable to welfare workers committed to combating sexism and oppression in their day-to-day practice with men service users (Bowl 1985). Yet, how much support do social welfare agencies provide to men using the perspective advocated in this study for their practice? In social work qualifying courses teaching of anti-oppressive practice has been as advanced as in any other social welfare profession, and more advanced than in most. Yet the reality is that once social workers have qualified and entered practice it is largely down to them as individuals to continue working anti-oppressively. Generally speaking, support for men engaged in this form of practice is often poor across social welfare services.

For instance, how many social welfare agencies actively encourage men's support groups for those wanting to work anti-oppressively? How many of these agencies proactively provide training for staff in anti-oppressive practice?

All these comments draw our attention to the fact that men who are welfare workers engaged in active anti-oppressive practice cannot survive alone in agencies (or in society) where relations of domination structure hierarchies (Ch. 2). Part of men's anti-oppressive practice must be to develop supportive networks for themselves as bases for challenging those structures; and to persuade agencies to provide resources for some of those supportive networks.

Countering structural oppression in welfare agencies

I will briefly outline some knowledge bases that workers, or users, can draw upon in devising strategies to adapt procedures, policies and structures within agencies.

The unfinished

Janis Fook (1993) has taken the relatively conservative concept of "casework" and developed it into a sophisticated tool for radical practice. She explicitly recognizes how this skill also needs to be deployed in relation to agencies:

> It is preferable . . . if working from a radical perspective in a non-radical setting, to attempt to radicalise that setting in some way. The politics of "the unfinished" . . . is a useful stance to take . . . small-scale changes are viewed as a vital part of the large-scale, still as yet "unfinished" social change which is aimed for. Small-scale changes are, therefore, important and should not be devalued simply because they are not large-scale changes. All change in this sense is valuable, as long as small-scale change does not become a substitution for large-scale change and thereby function to deflect structural changes which still need to be made. (Fook 1993)

Systems theory

This can be useful for helping to understand how power is distributed and alliances are formed in agencies. For instance, Marie McNay (1992) discusses how it can be used to analyze systems beyond the family.

Poststructuralist perspectives on power

Systems theory can be used in conjunction with Foucauldian perspectives to map out the most effective forms of intervention and alliances. We reviewed this approach at length earlier in the chapter when we discussed the response of the police to woman abuse, so I will not repeat it again here. The central point is that no organization is monolithic in its structures of power and there are always opportunities for exploiting contradictions in complex systems.

160

Social constructionist therapy

We have seen above that at present this approach is limited in terms of anti-oppressive practice with users. Nevertheless, it does offer some valuable insights about how to build alliances with individuals in agencies and to work positively with agency structures. For instance, the idea of framing one's objectives within the appropriate "grammar" so that they are more compatible with the objectives of potential allies within agencies is useful: to create common "narratives" with potential allies about objectives for change.

Networking

This skill is central when workers and/or users seek to effect change in agencies. Clearly, it can be combined with the other strategies suggested here. Commentators such as Barber (1991) and Beresford & Croft (1993) have documented usage of these and other associated approaches in the context of user empowerment. Those texts (which do not focus specifically on men) detail strategies whereby men can mobilize energy and support with other welfare workers in their own agencies.

Networking with other workers at various levels within different agencies can provide a range of advantages to men seeking anti-oppressive change. It can provide emotional/practical support in the form of work-based or non-work-based support groups that is essential. As we have seen, such groups can assist individuals to challenge their own tendencies to oppress. Allies and members of support groups can bolster each other's resolve when resistance to change seems insurmountable and can assist in preventing collusion with oppressive agency practices. Furthermore, networking clearly offers greater leverage in seeking procedural and other structural change in an agency. It also facilitates information exchange and building up of data to support a case for specific change which is an important strategy to utilize. Finally, and not least, networking can reduce the risk of individuals being "picked off" by managements as "cranks" or "trouble-makers".

Networking with the public media can be a powerful tool in making a case for change on a specific issue but needs to be handled with care. Sometimes it can be disastrous to do this without the sanction of the agency and contact with the media may need to be framed to management in such a way that it is regarded as of benefit to the agency. Different approaches to the media will be appropriate in different situations. For user groups in particular, surprising an agency by involving the media may sometimes be a valuable tactic. On other occasions, letting an agency know that an approach to the media is imminent can produce change.

Men seeking alliances with women and women's groups in agencies may be an extremely positive action in terms of promoting networks for structural change, if such alliance-making is felt appropriate by the women. Many women may be suspicious of men who are working on a pro-feminist agenda and of men who are eager to network with them. These suspicions are thoroughly justified on two counts. First, men's anti-sexist projects often tend in practice to have had sexist outcomes for women. Secondly, as we said earlier, men historically seem to be good at forming their own "clubs" and these traditionally have had the purpose of reinforcing the oppression and exploitation of women. A men's anti-sexist and anti-oppressive network may be seen as just another men's club by some women who could be potential allies. And unfortunately in some cases the women may be right. For men need to ensure that their networks or support groups do not become venues for mutual self-congratulation and the advancement of men's power games, or a mechanism whereby men colonize and annex anti-oppressive work that women have already developed. This does happen. Networks can provide support and safety for men working anti-oppressively but that must not be at the expense of honest challenge and criticism by men of men in those networks.

So women's suspicions of men networking are well grounded. Therefore, it is important that men working together for change in an agency should liaise with women doing likewise and not work against their efforts nor annex what they have achieved.

As noted above, it is useful for men to develop networks outside and inside their agency as these may fulfil different functions that are difficult to combine in one venue: for instance, personal support and strategic planning.

Using men's gender and institutional power constructively

Men as men may have considerable influence within their organizations individually and collectively: not simply by virtue of their gender but also because of the complex way that gender relations interact with status and hierarchy in most agencies (Ch. 2). This is not desirable in itself and indeed should be an objective of change. However, insofar as this situation exists, it should be used constructively by those men to whom it applies in strategies for improving agency structures.

Some of the references to men working anti-oppressively with men in welfare agencies cited earlier also contain examples of men seeking to make an impact on agencies (Bowl 1985, Ruxton 1991). However, few of them provide evidence of a systematic attempt to influence agency procedures, policies and structures in the way that is being advocated here. In most cases influencing agency structures has been an *ad hoc* activity, growing rather haphazardly out of the attempt to work with service users anti-oppressively and encountering structural barriers thereby. Instead, the analysis of our study has indicated that change in agencies is not an optional extra in men's anti-oppressive practice: it is an essential component and efforts for change must be systematic and concerted.

This has particular salience for men working in some agencies where the scope for putting into practice the goals advocated here will be especially limited. We are thinking, for instance, of men working within social services departments. We have seen evidence throughout this study of the increasing constraints being placed on the parameters of social work, particularly statutory social work, including even the dismantling of that concept (Clarke 1993).

In all agencies men need to work at structural change both to counter oppressive practices and to free up resources to enable themselves and others to implement services that are needed. In the context of social services departments this is absolutely crucial, since what we are advocating here will, to a considerable extent, be unattainable unless that structural work is initiated. The strategies detailed above may assist in this process.

As we have seen before and as we will see again, anti-oppressive change has to be sought at numerous different levels, right from our own individual actions up to the level of societal attitudes and legislative reform. Each level impacts on the others. Men can be involved in change at all these levels but obviously no one has the time to be active in each of them. Different men networking with other men will be doing what they can, where they can, in line with Fook's concept of the unfinished (1993).

However, it is vital that as far as possible men's networking is aware of, and links in with, what other men and women are doing elsewhere, perhaps at different levels. If this does not occur, there are two dangers. First, "the wheel will go on being reinvented": the overall task we are setting ourselves is massive in relation to the resources available to us and we must learn from each other; we cannot afford not to. Secondly and even worse, we may block each other's efforts.

Working with users for change: empowerment or exploitation?
We have reviewed some of the strategies by which men workers engaged on an anti-oppressive project may seek to change and challenge

the structures that function within their agencies. A final strategy for effecting such change is particularly powerful and especially problematic. It therefore requires some particular comment. Consulting service users and researching their views can provide valuable material for workers by which they can try to persuade management to adapt structures. There are many instances of this practice (for example Jones et al. 1988). It is an especially effective strategy now when legislation and governmental guidance (allegedly) encourages user partnership and empowerment in the context of "Community Care" (Ch. 6). It may well be that information gathering and consultation are appropriate and useful strategies in some situations, as Beresford & Croft (1993) indicate. However, it is not unproblematic.

Beresford & Croft (1993) remind us that there are two different approaches to user involvement: consumerist, which is service-led, and democratic, which is citizen-led. They regard information gathering as closer to the former than the latter. Beresford & Croft do not necessarily reject consumerist approaches that can embrace elements of empowerment. However, they do point out that consumerism's relationship with user empowerment is ambiguous and it is often aligned with the managerialism that is now developing apace in health and welfare agencies under the influence of "Community Care". In Chapter 2 we saw how feminist commentators linked this managerialism to the further masculinization of social care systems (Grimwood & Popplestone 1993).

Consequently, while consulting users to bolster workers' attempts at adapting agency structures can be a valid and valuable tactic, we have to be careful that the process is not disempowering for, or exploitative of, service users.

Changing societal and community attitudes

We saw in Chapter 5 that the problem of woman abuse could only be successfully countered by a multidimensional approach. The same is true for dealing with men's oppression across the spectrum of social welfare. So far we have considered how men can engage with this issue at individual, group and agency levels. In Chapter 5 we presented evidence that suggested attitudes about gender, masculinities, power and violence at community and societal levels falsely minimized the actual seriousness of men's violences and actively encouraged them. How then can men working in the field of welfare or men who have been users of welfare services also be active anti-oppressively at these community and societal levels?

This issue is linked with what has been said above since work at each level feeds into the others. For instance, men working with men individually and in groups on anti-oppressive practice will necessarily be engaged in attitude change that feeds into community and societal beliefs about oppressions perpetrated by men. However, there are at least three more direct means of influencing attitudes at community and societal levels and we will consider them here.

First, community awareness and attitudes can be influenced by community groups. In the area of woman abuse we have seen that community-oriented projects may work with abusive men, have links with women's groups and have an impact upon awareness of the issues around men's violences in their locality. In Chapter 8 we look in more detail at how a group of service users with the collaboration of a few welfare workers went about raising awareness regarding child sexual abuse in their city with remarkable success.

Secondly, men who are practitioners, academics and service users can influence community and societal attitudes by means of teaching, training, public presentations and use of the media. This can be small-scale or larger scale. There are numerous opportunities for the former and sometimes occasions when the latter is also possible. For instance, a public meeting on the subject of "Is there a future for men in families?" was held in Edinburgh by the Zero Tolerance Campaign and Edinburgh City Council in March 1994. Papers were given by Liz Kelly, Bea Campbell, Dave Morran (of the Change Project, Stirling, who works with men who abuse women) and myself. The papers were followed by a discussion with the audience. This event was well reported in the Edinburgh and Scottish press and opened up many issues for wider community debate.

Thirdly, in the light of the evidence in Chapter 5, large concerted public campaigns about men's violences are vital. What form might these take and what role is there for men in them? In Britain we have an existing model of such a campaign to help us answer those questions.

The Zero Tolerance Campaign was initiated by the Women's Unit and the Women's Committee of Edinburgh City District Council in November 1992. It followed a study of a similar project in Canada and some research carried out in Edinburgh's secondary schools that revealed both a wide acceptance of violence against women by boys and much ignorance on their part about the reality of violence in the home (Foley 1993, Salond 1994). The focus of the campaign is violent crime against women and children and its approach to this issue has been three-pronged:

active prevention of those crimes; adequate provision of support services; appropriate legal protection for women and children suffering from violence.

It has developed a range of creative, striking and compelling campaign materials. These were deployed in a very high profile manner in Edinburgh using full-size posters on street hoardings and posters on the public transport system. The campaign also used the press and broadcast media as well as extensive networking nationally and internationally to promote their work.

The results have been spectacular in terms of responses from frontline women's services, the media, other local authorities in Britain, and from overseas.

All this is impressive. But what is equally important is that in research evaluations of public responses to the campaign in Edinburgh (by the Glasgow University Media Studies Unit), all indications are that it has had a considerable impact in making people, of both genders, more aware of the size and nature of the problem. The vast majority of the public were supportive of the campaign, with only a small minority feeling alienated from it. This is particularly relevant to us because the campaign has, in well thought out "messages", been very clear indeed about placing responsibility for this kind of crime on men.

How far can men be involved in such initiatives as Zero Tolerance? In view of what we said earlier about the dangers of men colonizing and annexing women's anti-oppressive practice, it would not seem appropriate for men to copy what Zero Tolerance is already doing so well. On the other hand, the campaign is challenging men to change what they are doing and to help other men to change. Men clearly have a central role in responding to that challenge and can meet it in all the ways we have already discussed and that we will be considering further in the next two chapters.

As we have already noted, the different sites and levels where abuse of women, children and men can be challenged impact upon one another: society, communities, welfare agencies, groups, individuals. The output of one feeds into all the others. The Zero Tolerance Campaign asks questions that men working with men should be asking each other (and themselves) in whatever they do. Earlier in this chapter we mentioned that men working anti-oppressively at different levels of activity must be aware of, and link up with, each other and with women engaged in similar projects.

Zero Tolerance offers a good example of this. It is important that men working to end men's violences from within voluntary agencies, community work, social services, education services, should find out what Zero Tolerance initiatives there are in their localities and how they can link in with them. Perhaps the material on display in the community can be used as the basis of group discussions with men in a variety of settings. Perhaps men workers in a particular setting could arrange for a public meeting of men based on Zero Tolerance material if it is on display in their community. These are only a couple of examples; many more are possible. Of course, in line with what we have also said above, such work should always be co-ordinated with local women's groups and other men's groups. From this work more services might eventually result.

Once again though, resources should be available to fund work with both women and men. Services for men should not be provided at the expense of those for women: otherwise we simply replicate the prioritization of men's needs over other people's that already characterizes so much of our society. We will say more about this in the next section.

Respecting and preserving resources for women and other oppressed sections of society

In the course of this chapter we have seen several examples of situations where services that are desperately needed for men might be developed, in a difficult financial climate for public spending, at the expense of services to women or, indeed, to others such as people who are black, lesbian, gay, disabled or older.

We also saw that many feminist-oriented services for women are already under threat due to financial pressures and due to the development of alternatives that focus more on women's pathology than on their structural oppression by men. There does indeed seem to be an anti-feminist backlash.

Men who are workers or users must carefully scrutinize where the financial support and personnel are coming from when men's services are being established and not rob potential or existing provision from other service users.

This issue is of course linked to all the others we have addressed. For instance, diversion of resources to men's services is more unlikely if management of agencies is less masculinized; likewise if women and women's groups are given some consultancy or management control over men's services.

Conclusion

These then are general issues about men as service users and workers in social welfare agencies drawn out of our earlier discussion about work with woman abusers. Those issues will be amplified and added to by our discussion of child sexual abuse in the next chapter. Our conclusion in this chapter is that men workers and users do have a large role to play in the field of social welfare working at a variety of levels against all the oppressions associated with the exercise of hegemonic masculinities.

However, there are many difficulties about this role and most of them can be reduced to one central problem: how can we prevent men's anti-oppressive practice replicating in unintended forms the power dynamics that it ostensibly seeks to challenge?

As regards men and boys as service users, the size of the problem of men's violences in our society suggests that social welfare agencies should move in two directions. First, they should work alongside as many men and boys in as many settings as possible to challenge relations of domination exercised in our society by hegemonic forms of masculinity; and develop the positive contribution that men and boys can make to relationships and to society. Men can fulfil this role both in specially dedicated services and in routine practice. But they need space to do this and acquiring that space from agencies is another task for men.

Secondly, they should work to increase services for those people most oppressed by that hegemony, including: women, the poor, black people, people with disabilities, gay men and lesbian women, children and people who are older. These services must be defined and implemented in democratic collaboration with service users. As we have seen, men have a major role to play in both these movements even if that role is not always without its problems.

Chapter 8
Men against oppressions:
child sexual abuse

In the last chapter we identified crucial areas of welfare activity where men workers and users might have particular roles to play and that require urgent expansion: working at individual and group levels with men and boys, changing agency structures, having an impact on community and societal attitudes to combat the huge social problem of oppression by men. In that chapter we recognized that there are some significant dilemmas about carrying out such work. In this chapter we shall see that there are others.

Explaining men's sexual violences

First, we need to consider a vital question that this study has not yet answered. Throughout the study we have seen that one particularly pernicious form of men's oppression occurs repeatedly both within welfare agencies and outside: men's sexual violences. We need to ask what is the process by which these violences are generated. In the previous chapter we suggested some themes that both work with abusers and preventative work with men and boys needed to address. Those suggestions were based on evidence that we had found in the course of our study: evidence drawn from practice; and evidence drawn from social psychology research studies into men's violences. If in this chapter we can develop a theoretical model that explains the processes by which men commit sexual violence, then this may offer a means of confirming whether our empirical suggestions about treatment and preventative work are valid.

169

The explanation of men's sexual violences is a field of controversy and complexity. We will focus on data relating to child sexual abuse which are substantial. However, we will continually relate this to what we know about other sexual violences. For our objective is to develop a model that is relevant to all forms of men's sexual violences, not only to child sexual abuse.

The facts about child sexual abuse (CSA)

First, the vast majority of CSA perpetrators are heterosexual men or boys, and this holds true whether we are talking about abuse of girls or boys (Ch. 3). This imbalance in the proportion of male perpetrators mirrors what we also know from the limited research about abuse of adults, male and female, including adults who are older, who have learning difficulties or who are experiencing mental distress (Ch. 6). Sexual violence is preponderantly (but not exclusively) perpetrated by males.

Secondly, the psychological profiles of most child sex abusers are not significantly abnormal: certainly it is not possible to separate them out of the population as a whole by using such profiles. This issue was explored in the Warner Report (HMSO 1992) which sought to find ways of screening out abusers from welfare work. That report concluded that no profiles existed by which potential abusers could in fact be screened out of the general population. We have seen that similar findings also relate to men who sexually assault adult women (Ch. 5).

Thirdly, our society contains an extremely large number of men or boys who have sexually maltreated children in one form or another. This judgement is based partly on the prevalence figures that we discussed in Chapters 3 and 4. It is supported by two other pieces of data. First, Dawn Fisher (1994) cites research which, using a telephone sample of men, estimated that 10 per cent of them actually admitted sexually abusing a child: and we have to remember that many abusers would probably not disclose this. Secondly, Fisher has reviewed research studies relating to men's willingness to commit sexual assault against adults and children and concluded as follows:

> These studies clearly demonstrate that a significant percentage of the "normal" male population believe it acceptable to carry out a sexual assault, and report the likelihood of doing so if they could be assured of not being detected or punished. A percentage also report having actually carried out forced sexual assaults

against both women and children. Given that the samples used tended to be male college students, and the likelihood that subjects would be prone to under-report, the base rate in the general population is likely to be significantly higher. (Fisher 1994)

Taken overall, the picture of men's sexual violence that emerges is that a very significant minority of the male population sexually assaults girls and boys as well as women and, as we saw in Chapter 5, also some men. Moreover, although further research is desperately needed, there are also clear indications, for instance in Chapters 3 and 6, that many perpetrators are quite prepared to abuse children and adults whom they regard as the most vulnerable in the population. It is very possible that some perpetrators target them precisely because of their perceived vulnerability. Sexual violence by men is perpetrated upon people quite literally from the cradle to the grave (Turnbull 1994).

Having said all this, we need to emphasize at this point that the majority of men and boys in our society do not become engaged in sexual abuse. Such a statement naturally leads us back to our original question: how, then, are men's sexual violences generated? We will now review answers that have been given to this question in the past and consider why they have been inadequate. This will take us on to develop a more comprehensive and sophisticated model of explanation.

A critique of previous explanations for child sexual abuse

As we have said, various explanations have been put forward but most are problematic (Pringle 1990). Briefly, we can say that there is no significant research link between class, personal stress or geographical location and child sexual abuse (Finkelhor 1984, Finkelhor et al. 1986, Glaser & Frosh 1993). Explanations based on particular family configurations were the dominant model in Britain of the 1980s (Furniss 1991) but have now been widely critiqued mainly because they failed to take into account power dynamics within the family and because we now know that much abuse does not take place in the "nuclear family" anyway (McLeod & Saraga 1988, Kidd & Pringle 1988, Will 1989, La Fontaine 1990, Pringle 1990, Kelly et al. 1991, Glaser & Frosh 1993). That family model is now given much less credence in Britain: in most of western Europe it remains dominant (Pringle 1993b).

Individual-oriented explanations of the crude variety, to the effect that abusers are ill or grossly abnormal, have been exploded by the evidence that we have seen regarding abusers' apparent "normality". More sophisticated individualistic explanations still have much currency, in particular the idea that having been sexually abused as a child increases the risk of a person becoming an abuser later in life.

Although we cannot discount this hypothesis completely it has been effectively critiqued (see Finkelhor et al. 1986, Pringle 1990) on a number of grounds: how is it so few women are abusers? How representative are the prison populations on which it is based? Are prisoners capable of inventing abuse histories for themselves to justify/mitigate their crimes (Cashman 1993)? Are the percentages of abusers who allegedly have histories of abuse in their lives very significant when we now know that perhaps 20 to 25 per cent of all men in Britain have such histories anyway? We might add that one British study (Waterhouse et al. 1993) found that only 10 per cent of their sample of perpetrators had such a history of abuse. Although having a history of abuse may be a factor in why some men or boys go on to abuse, it seems there are so many serious methodological problems with this hypothesis that it would be unwise to place much weight upon it at present.

Explanations focusing on the lack of rights of children and the power of adults over them (Ennew 1986, La Fontaine 1990) do have their place. They are particularly important in pointing out that the structural processes of oppression responsible for the abuse of women may not be precisely the same as the processes responsible for the abuse of children, especially as we now know that so many boys are also assaulted. These explanations that focus on the powerlessness of children indicate quite correctly that we perhaps need to think about ageism as well as sexism in the generation of child sexual abuse. Given the evidence that we reviewed in Chapter 5 about the sexual abuse (largely perpetrated by men) of older people, people with learning difficulties and people who have experienced mental distress, we should perhaps think about the conjunction of not only ageism but also disabilism with sexism in the generation of men's sexual violences.

However, explanations that focus largely on the powerlessness of children have two major flaws. First they do not attach sufficient importance to the issue of gender given the remarkable imbalance in the number of men and boys who abuse. Secondly, as we saw in Chapters 3 and 4, it is now apparent that a large amount of child sexual abuse is committed by people who themselves are not adult, predominantly boys.

On the whole most current commentators have now turned from monocausal explanations of child sexual abuse to multifactorial ones.

For instance, many commentators would now probably identify Finkel-hor's influential "four factors/four preconditions" framework of sexual abuse as a useful way of explaining the phenomenon (Finkelhor 1984, Fisher 1994). However, this framework is so broad and all-encompassing that it surely offers a way of describing what is happening in the process of sexual abuse rather than providing the tools for analyzing why it happens.

It has to be agreed that sexual abuse is probably too complex to be wholly monocausal in origin. Nevertheless, it has been argued that one causal model of sexual abuse can be regarded as the most important in the majority of cases. That model is based on feminist perspectives of men's violence, perspectives particularly associated with radical feminism (MacLeod & Saraga 1988, Kelly 1988, Driver & Droisen 1989, Saraga 1993). It regards the same patriarchal processes as being responsible for child sexual assault and woman abuse. The model also links these with overarching structural gender oppressions within society and connects with a range of other oppressive behaviours such as sexual harassment and emotional abuse (Kelly 1987, 1988).

Such a model, unlike the others we have reviewed, is consonant with the central fact that in our society there are very large numbers of perpetrators, the vast majority of whom are heterosexual men or boys, functioning as "normal" psychologically and socially. They are our friends, our colleagues, our families, our partners: they might be you or me, particularly if we are men.

In the past, I myself have supported the importance of this model (Pringle 1990, 1993c). Although I still regard it as the most vital compo-nent of an explanation of men's sexual violences, I have come to see that it has limitations and needs to be supplemented in various ways. Cer-tainly it has been criticized from a number of perspectives. Some of these criticisms are more valid than others. Let us first examine a critique of the feminist model that is, I think, misleading. For the feminist model has been attacked for not having anything to say about women who abuse, nor about the sexual violence of lesbian women and gay men. To a con-siderable extent this charge is not justified. As we have seen earlier in this study some commentators have usefully addressed women's sexual violence (including lesbian violence) from feminist perspectives (Kelly 1991, Matthews et al. 1991, Matthews 1993).

As regards gay men and sexual violence, some gay commentators have also considered this in the context of patriarchal relations and of feminist analyses.

Gay men and sexual violence

We saw in Chapters 3 and 5 that sexual violence towards women, men and children of both genders is primarily a problem of male heterosexuality rather than homosexuality.

However, sexual violence is still an issue for gay communities in terms of pederasty, sadomasochism and gay pornography (Edwards 1994). Gay commentators have considered how gay men may construct their identities and cultures in complex ways that both replicate and resist dominant patriarchal conceptions of masculinity (Blachford 1981).

Moreover, some commentators have looked at gay sexism and sexual violence in the context of what Gough (1989) and Edwards (1990) call the "masculinization" of gay men in the 1970s and early 1980s (Gough & Macnair 1985, Shepherd & Wallis 1989).

Edwards's more recent study (1994) illustrates the complexity of the issues around pederasty, sadomasochism and pornography in relation to gay men. In particular he demonstrates the myriad ways in which patriarchal discourse is reshaped, transformed and sometimes thereby resisted by some gay men. This is a process, by the way, which in itself may have much to say to all men regarding the need (which we have emphasized in this study) to redefine dominant heterosexual masculinities into more positive and creative forms (Carrigan et al. 1985, Hearn & Parkin 1987, Connell 1995).

In terms of the specific relationship between gay men and patriarchal relations, it is clear from this brief discussion that the picture is far more complicated than patriarchal relations simply dictating aspects of gay masculinities: up to a point, the latter have the power to transform patriarchal discourse. Even so, there is no doubt that feminist analyses of men's violences have had considerable relevance for gay commentators seeking to understand gay violences (Edwards 1994).

So the criticism that the feminist model is irrelevant to lesbian and gay violence and the abuse of children by women is not really valid. There are, however, more substantial drawbacks to the feminist model and it is to these that we now turn.

Criticisms of a feminist model

I will consider these criticisms in terms of child sexual abuse and of adult sexual assault since the model claims to be relevant to both. This model goes a long way in explaining on a macro scale why men and boys commit sexual abuse against women and girls: as such it is extremely valuable and must remain as the foundation stone of an analysis of why men and boys sexually abuse. However, it needs to be adapted and supplemented for a variety of reasons. First of all, it fails to tell us why the majority of men and boys do not abuse.

Moreover, additional analysis is also required if we are to explain why a large number of boys and a considerable number of adult men are sexually assaulted by heterosexual males: we need to consider the nature of dominant forms of heterosexuality as well as masculinity to understand why both adult and child sexual abuse happens.

Nor does the feminist model fully explain why abusers seem to target the most vulnerable members of society: for instance children of both genders and people who are older, have learning difficulties, or have experienced mental distress. As noted earlier, we need to address how issues of ageism and disabilism fit in to the processes of men's sexual violences.

Finally, I do not think the feminist model in itself provides a convincing linking mechanism between macro-level structural gender oppression on the one hand and the micro-level oppressive actions of individual abusing men on the other. As this study has amply demonstrated, there seems no doubt that such a linkage does exist: the problem is that the feminist model has not satisfactorily explained it. The social psychology perspectives, upon which we drew in Chapter 5, went some way towards mapping out that middle ground between the macro and the micro. However, in Chapter 5 we concluded that they too did not fully bridge the gap.

My own efforts in the past to fill this gap between the macro and the micro have been inadequate (Pringle 1992) and have been critiqued (Carter 1993). For I relied on a rather crude socialization explanation of how men learn to be violent and oppressive. We need to develop a more sophisticated explanation than this of the processes by which men's sexual violences are generated and it is to this that I now turn.

Men's sexual violences: the importance of "choice"

The socialization model that I adopted (Pringle 1990, Pringle 1992) was vague. It did not address the shifting, dynamic variations in men's sexual behaviours that exist both at any given moment in time and also across time and space. My attention was focused on sexism while other elements of oppression in this process were ignored: racism, disabilism and ageism. Most of all, I made very little reference to dominant forms of heterosexuality which, as we have seen, along with sexism seem to be central to the generation of men's sexual violences.

Finally, my socialization approach was far too deterministic. I assumed that the great weight of patriarchal oppression over millennia implied that there was little scope for men to change their behaviour in any major way in the short-term. The hope I offered was that men should start to work on changing both themselves and patriarchal structures now, so that men's propensity for sexual violence might over generations be challenged. In retrospect, I now acknowledge that such a view represented a determinism about men that bordered on essentialism.

In the present study we have reviewed evidence that suggests that my approach was both too simple and too bleak. We have seen that the room for manoeuvre in terms of men adapting themselves in a positive fashion and of seeking change in oppressive structures is more considerable than I conceded in the past. As regards change at the more personal level, we have seen that individual choice is a factor that both myself and other commentators have perhaps understated in the past.

In Chapter 5 we saw that men who abuse adult women are often extremely careful to choose where, who, and when they do it. In Chapter 6 we saw that men who abuse often carefully choose to abuse adults whom they regard as the most vulnerable. We also saw in Chapter 5 what Anne Campbell (1993) had to say about the instrumentality of men's violences.

The picture in the field of child sexual abuse is precisely the same. We have learnt much from perpetrators about the way they go about committing child sexual abuse. Generally, men do not offend on the spur of the moment: they target the child carefully and "groom" her or him with patience and attention to detail. Abuse is carried out very skilfully and often judiciously (Salter 1988, Ryan & Lane 1991), even if it occurs in a relatively public place. We need to remember that the statistics available to us indicate that the vast majority of sexual abuse is never detected (Fisher 1994). There are many possible reasons for this. An important one seems to be the calculation that abusers demonstrate in the way they abuse. Perpetrators are choosing with great care whether they abuse at any given moment in time.

None of this evidence suggests that we are dealing here with either uncontrollable biological urges or an irresistible need to conform to powerful socialized patterns of behaviour. Nor is this evidence totally consonant with the theory that sexual abusers are prey to an addiction once they begin to offend (Furniss 1991).

It is not being suggested that we can expect all men who sexually abuse to choose not to do so in future. Choice is partly a function of perceived potential gains and losses. Each person's estimate of these can vary depending upon several factors: the environment around them; the relative values they attach to the different forms of gain and loss that apply to them; the past and present life experiences of each individual. These factors are linked in complex ways. Unfortunately, as we noted above, we cannot explain the nature of those links: we still have a gap between structural and personal oppression; between the macro and the micro.

What we can say is that all men (and boys) make a choice at some level about whether to commit sexual abuse; and that choice is always potentially open to change. This is important because it allows us to escape from the pessimistic determinism of the blanket socialization model that some commentators, including myself, previously adopted. The implication of our current analysis is that by working with men and boys, we may have an impact on the choices they make. This does not imply that we should be too optimistic about the ease with which men and boys will choose against abuse. The determination with which some abusers go on abusing with or without treatment is enough to puncture any naïvety about this. In some cases it will not be possible to have sufficient impact on the factors impinging on a person's choice to produce a positive outcome. Nevertheless, as we have said, the fact of choice always exists and is always open to potential change.

Having said all this, we still need a convincing model of the processes that link structural systems of oppression to expressions of sexual violence by individual men. If we possessed such a theoretical model, we could use it to identify the themes that we would have to address to try to influence a person's choice about whether to abuse. Of course, in the last chapter we already identified such themes using the practice material and social psychology research results we reviewed in Chapter 5. If we had an adequate theoretical model we could see whether the themes it suggested matched the ones we have developed based on practice and empirical research. In the next section we begin to build this theoretical model that can explain the way men's sexual violences are generated.

Men's sexual violences: linking the macro to the micro

This model will be convincing if it fulfils three criteria: it must incorporate the concept of choice as an important factor in the generation of men's sexual violences; it must be able to include multiple forms of oppression (heterosexism, ageism, disabilism) as well as patriarchal relations in that process of generation; finally, it must be able to explain why there is such variation in the degrees of abusive behaviour manifested by different men as well as across time and space.

In the course of this study we have uncovered much evidence in general about oppressions at structural and personal levels. The analysis we adopted to make sense of this picture was that of Connell (1987, 1995). If we now apply Connell's analysis to the specific topic of men's sexual violences, then we find that it also fulfils the criteria that we have just set.

The concept of hegemonic masculinities incorporates not only the domination of men over women as a major force in the structuring of power relations but all the other dimensions of oppression (Connell 1987), not least heterosexism:

> The most important feature of contemporary hegemonic masculinity is that it is heterosexual, being closely connected to the institution of marriage; and a key form of subordinated masculinity is homosexual. (Connell 1987)

Connell's approach, moreover, posits a much more fluid, dynamic process of shifting power relations impinging on the individual than is implied in either socialization or sex role models:

> . . . a personal life is a path through a field of practices which are following a range of structural conditions which routinely intersect and often contradict each other . . . The structure of personality is not the structure of an object. It is a particular unification of diverse and often contradictory practices. (Connell 1987)

Liddle (1993) has applied Connell's work (1987) to the specific issue of child sexual abuse. For Liddle the value of Connell in this context is not only the detailed link he makes between the structural and the individual, but also the connections he forges with "the emotional and other complexities which seem to occasion matters of sexual desire and attachment". He attributes this range of linkages to the fact that Connell analyzes gender relations by focusing on three sets of structures together: the division of labour; the structure of power; and, most important of all from Liddle's point of view, the structure of cathexis that relates to the social construction of sexuality.

Liddle (1993) convincingly demonstrates how in Connell's model

(1987) the differences between men and women in terms of structures of desire are compatible with a greater propensity in men to engage in abusive sexual relations. These differences correspond quite closely to characteristics that I identified in my earlier work (Pringle 1993a) as being more typical of men: ". . . the need for control, the inability to express emotions other than anger, and a tendency to objectify the world". In the context of Connell's model (1987) I would identify these as characteristics of hegemonic masculinities. Liddle (1993) notes that in the creation of such masculinities several themes are writ large: imperious sexual desire plays an important role and is strongly linked to a sense of personal adequacy and success; numerous conflicts and uncertainties over dependency and personal adequacy remain that may be resolved by satisfaction of sexual desire.

We should note that this corresponds closely to the importance that Hearn (Hearn & Parkin 1987, Hearn 1992) places on men's uncertainties about their sexual desires and the reaction to this that may occur in the formation of dominant heterosexualities. Earlier in this chapter we saw the way some gay men have responded to the influence of these dominant forms. That response was complex and included some quite subtle transformations and thereby resistances to dominant masculinities (Edwards 1994). The creativity that some gay men have used to subvert dominant forms of masculinity, while still incorporating them, demonstrates that the options open to all men in transforming hegemonic forms of masculinity may be far wider than is often assumed. Those working with men and boys should remember this. We will take this point further later in the chapter.

Returning to the application of Connell's analysis (1987) to men's sexual violences, we can see that it offers a far more sophisticated method than socialization or sex role theories for understanding how structural relations of domination are translated into individual behaviour. The complexity and richness of this analysis allows us to understand why it is that some men may commit sexual abuse and other men do not. On the other hand, even with this model we still cannot predict which men will sexually abuse and which men will not. In fact this analysis makes it clear that prediction may always be impossible because of the complex interaction of variables involved in the generation of men's sexual violences. It is certainly not a model that could be accused of being monocausal.

So far we have seen that Connell's model (1987) satisfies two of the three criteria set out earlier: it explains the diversity of men's abusive behaviour and it embraces all forms of oppression in explaining the generation of men's violences. What of our third criteria? Where does choice fit into Connell's model in terms of men's sexual violences?

Liddle (1993) suggests that Connell's analysis (1987) intrinsically "promises to locate individual bodies and subjects within the real constraints that surround them, but also to leave room for the operation of creativity and resistance". He goes on to conclude that within Connell's model the room for manoeuvre may not be identical for everyone "but the element of choice is of considerable importance nonetheless"; and "the role of individual choice and decision also needs to be given centre stage, and it is here that the feminist claim 'the personal is the political' seems most compelling" (Liddell 1993). This importance attached by Liddle to the concept of choice in the generation of men's sexual violences seems to match precisely our view on the issue of choice that we defined earlier and that we constructed on the basis of evidence drawn from practice.

Our model explaining the way men's sexual violences are generated seems to be complete. It has been based on material drawn from what we know about men's sexual violences across the board, not simply on data about child sexual abuse. Therefore, it is applicable to the wide spectrum of those violences and is not confined to violence perpetrated against children.

The model centres on the complex operation of power relations associated with hegemonic masculinities throughout Western societies. Patriarchal structures of domination represent part of this but all other forms of domination are also implicated. In particular, dominant forms of heterosexual masculinity are closely associated with hegemonic forms of masculinity.

Within the operation of these structures, individual choice still has an important role to play in determining whether a man is sexually violent or not. However, the room for manoeuvre in that choice will vary according to the way numerous other variables impinge on his decision, variables that necessarily include previous and current life experiences. One clear implication from all this is that no simple prediction of which men will and which men will not abuse is possible.

Having developed this theoretical model, we can now compare it with the themes for work with men and boys that we suggested in the last chapter based on practice and research material.

Preventing men's sexual violences

In the last chapter the themes that we suggested for treatment and preventative work with men and boys included: assisting men and boys to acknowledge their own capacity for acting oppressively; demonstrating the links between oppressive behaviour and structural oppression; developing strategies to avoid oppressive behaviour in specific sorts of situation; challenging societal attitudes about women, violence, sexuality, masculinity that reinforce oppressive behaviour; understanding how traditional peer groups for men (in pubs, sports teams, gangs) are important in generating and reinforcing men's oppressive belief systems; helping men think about what masculinity means to them and to reshape it in more positive and creative ways. We emphasized that such work should embrace all forms of oppression including racism and heterosexism.

It seems clear that in many respects these themes are consistent with our theoretical model explaining the processes by which men's sexual violences are generated. We will give one example of this compatability.

One theme we identified in the last chapter based on empirical and research material was to help men redefine what masculinity means to them. This is closely connected with Connell's concept of multiple masculinities (Connell 1987, 1995). There are characteristics of dominant forms of heterosexuality that may incline men to: objectify others; strive to control; express anger in preference to other forms of emotion; resolve their insecurities by imposing their sexual desire. If alternative options by which men might define their own masculinities are explored with them, more positive approaches to various aspects of life are possible for men: sexual relationships, friendships, parenthood, work, leisure. We have noted that the way some gay men creatively subvert dominant heterosexualities while still incorporating them may suggest possibilities by which men identifying themselves as heterosexual can subvert those dominant forms too. Moreover, as we saw in Chapter 7, Connell (1995) has specifically identified transformations of masculinity through exploiting the "crisis tendencies" in gender relations as a way forward in men's anti-sexist practice.

So, the themes on which treatment and preventative work with men and boys should focus have now been confirmed by both empirical evidence and use of a theoretical model.

However, this model is not only useful in helping us to define work with men and boys. It also assists us to make sense of another major issue. For throughout this study we have had cause to make reference on a number

181

of occasions to sexual violences perpetrated by men working within the social welfare system (Chs 2, 3, 6).

Sometimes that violence is inflicted by men upon colleagues in agencies (Ch. 2). We have seen that structural action is required to stop this violence (for instance effective harassment policies). The model we have just developed also indicates that another way of countering this violence is for all men workers to address their own tendencies to be oppressive, using the themes we suggested in the last chapter and confirmed here. This may assist them to choose not to be sexually oppressive to colleagues.

In this chapter, though, I want to shift the focus on to the sexual violences that men workers may perpetrate against service users. In Chapters 3 and 6, we emphasized that this was a major problem in relation to children and adults. The attention that men workers should pay to their own attitudes and behaviours, recommended in previous paragraphs, is also important in preventing this form of abuse.

We also need to ask what other action can be taken to halt or at least effectively minimize abuse of those who use welfare services? Over the years, many answers to this question have been suggested and put into operation. It is our contention that the actual impact of these measures has been very limited and there is a particular reason for that ineffectiveness. We will also argue that more effective measures are possible but have largely been ignored.

Scandals in caring?

As we have seen earlier in this study (Chs 3 and 4) there is evidence, largely from the United States, that sexual abuse of children by welfare professionals may be at worrying levels (McFadden 1984, Finkelhor et al. 1988, Fanshel 1990, McFadden & Ryan 1991, Margolin 1991, 1993, Benedict et al. 1994). Foster care, nursery care, day care and residential care have been the areas subjected to most statistical scrutiny.

In Britain, the plethora of major sexual abuse scandals making the headlines in the media have related to residential care and to some extent nursery care. However, there is no reason to believe that the other areas mentioned above will be any safer than residential or nursery care. On the contrary, some of them, especially foster care, offer an even greater degree of intimacy and isolation for potential abusers to exploit (Pringle 1993a). That may also explain why there has been no comparable scandal about foster care in Britain, even though there are frequent individual reports in the press about foster carers who abuse or who are alleged to abuse.

Of course, it is unfortunate that virtually no systematic research into abuse in welfare settings comparable to the American research has been carried out in Britain. One might ask oneself why that should be? Why are British agencies not eagerly funding research into this issue, given continual press reports about abuse across the welfare spectrum and given the data that are being collated in the United States? The answer probably lies in the material we reviewed in Chapter 2, which discussed the resistance of agency responses and related this to issues of organization sexuality and the masculinism of agency hierarchies.

There are three reasons why we should expect particularly high standards of safety in social welfare settings. First, when adults entrust their children (and children entrust themselves) to public care, or to care purchased by the state for them, they have a right to know the children are as safe as is humanly possible. The same applies to adults who for one reason or another require care. Secondly, a considerable proportion, though not all, of these children and adults will probably have had some form of adversity already in their lives: that indeed may be why some of them are seeking welfare services. Those services should exist to alleviate adversity not massively compound it, which is what occurs when abuse happens. Thirdly, if an abuser operates within the welfare services then it is extremely likely that he will gain access to very large numbers of children or adults whom he can abuse. One abuser can wreak multiple havoc in a welfare setting. We should emphasize that for this very reason it is highly likely abusers will deliberately gravitate to welfare work.

Reducing sexual abuse: the official line

So how effective at stopping this sexual abuse are the strategies that have been suggested repeatedly by official reports investigating these numerous scandals? As we said in Chapters 2 and 3, the fact that these scandals have continued and the reports have gone on replicating themselves, indicates that the strategies may well be ineffective. However, let us consider them in a little more detail.

Elsewhere I have examined these issues in depth (Pringle 1992, 1993a, 1994c). Here I will mention only two of the existing strategies to illustrate their limitations. First, police checks and social services checks on job applicants (HMSO 1992). Of course, these should always be carried out because they may pick out a few abusers who have a record of some sort. However, we know from the massive prevalence survey results which we have reviewed earlier that the vast mass of sexual abusers never come to the attention of any authorities whatsoever, let alone have a record. So checks on job applicants will only deal with a tiny fraction of abusers.

My second example is greater supervision of staff. This is advocated by both the Hunt Report (Hunt 1994) and other commentators (Ruxton 1994). Once again, this may have value but it is only limited. We know that a skilled perpetrator seems capable of abusing, for instance, very young children even when there are staff in the same room. The Hunt Report (Hunt 1994) itself acknowledges this.

We have already seen earlier in this chapter that the Warner Report (HMSO 1992) acknowledges it is impossible to use psychological profiles to effectively screen out abusers at job interviews. The model we have developed to explain the process by which men's sexual violences are generated indicates that this process of generation is so complex and involves so many interacting variables that predicting abusers at some point in the future is also highly unlikely.

Other strategies have been put forward by inquiry reports and they are all similarly limited (Pringle 1993a, 1994c). One of the latest reports is the Hunt Report (Hunt 1994). Its prescriptions are virtually the same as those of all its predecessors. The only major difference about this report is that it is striking in its honesty about the limitations of its recommendations. The Report says that staff who are in charge of groups of children anywhere:

> daily live with the knowledge that their schools or associations can have no perfect defence against the determined, covert measures that a paedophile may take to infiltrate into their small society, often under a cloak of friendliness, innocent charm or altruism . . . All that one can realistically hope to achieve, by collecting the evidence that emerges after events such as happened in this case, is to point to factors that may in future give rise to the slightest possibility of prevention, or at least, early detection.

The Report has to be admired for its honesty ,and in terms of its own rec-ommendations it is telling the truth. But is this the best we can really do? If it is, then that is a message with appalling consequences for our chil-dren. In fact, I have argued elsewhere (Pringle 1992, 1993a, 1994c) that other measures are available that none of the British official reports have ever recommended and that do offer the possibility of reducing considerably (though not absolutely) the levels of sexual abuse in welfare settings.

If one reads the Warner Report (HMSO 1992), which specifically addressed this whole issue, one will find that it never even mentions the issue of the gender of perpetrators. It is not unusual in this. The Hunt Report (1994) does mention gender but only briefly as an aside. This neglect of one of the most distinctive features of sexual abuse is remarkable. Once again, for an explanation of this one probably has to return to the material on organization sexuality that we surveyed in Chapter 2. If we make allowance for the small numbers of men working in some areas of welfare, then there is very clear evidence (again almost all from the United States) that men account for a very large proportion of sexual abusers in fields as diverse as foster care, residential care, nursery care and day care (Finkelhor et al. 1988, Ryan et al. 1988, Fanshel 1990, Margolin 1991, 1993, Nunno & Reindfleisch 1991, Rosenthal et al. 1991).

We must finally bear in mind that given what we have seen about sexual violence throughout this study, it is almost inevitable that the sexual abuse in the welfare system that is now starting to come to the surface with great regularity, represents only a fraction of that which is actually occurring. This is a sobering thought. What other strategies for preventing abuse in welfare settings, then, does a perspective focusing on the gender of perpetrators indicate?

Reducing sexual abuse: a gender-centred perspective

We have already said that men working in welfare settings should carry out as much preventative work on themselves as possible using the themes mentioned earlier as a framework. Agencies should facilitate this by providing time and space for men's support groups, employment of consultants, and relevant training. Of course none of this provision should be at the expense of other services to users or to staff. Moreover, men workers must also network together and liaise with women colleagues (as far as the latter feel is appropriate) to change those oppressive structures detailed in Chapter 2 that reinforce and condone the abuse of service users that is our present focus.

Having said all this, what other gender-centred strategies for staff can we suggest? Once again, I have dealt with this issue elsewhere (Pringle 1992, 1993a, 1994c), and so will only summarize the arguments here.

Training

All staff (and parents) should be taught that sexual abuse can occur in any welfare setting and that, as the Hunt Report (1994) says, the abuser can be a popular, likeable member of staff. This message would have to be given in a careful balanced way. It is important to emphasize that in the field of welfare, as outside, the majority of men will not be sexual abusers but that a significant minority may be; and that unfortunately we have no way of telling which is which.

In line with what we have said earlier about the importance of choice as a factor in whether a man abuses, we suggest training for staff, particularly men staff, designed to help them to choose not to abuse. This could be done using a variety of training methods: practical suggestions; discussing the issues about men's masculinities; raising their awareness about the damage that abuse inflicts on those who are abused. Of course, many men undergoing such training would probably choose not to abuse anyway, regardless of the training. A few men may well still choose to abuse even after the training. But for some men it might make a difference at a future date, in which case it is worth doing with all men staff. In fact, my ex-colleagues at Barnardos and myself designed a training programme similar to this in 1987 (Davis et al. 1987, Pringle 1990).

However, training men not to abuse can play only a part, and probably a relatively small part, in devising strategies to reduce the amount of sexual abuse committed by men in welfare situations. We know that many existing abusers who are caught choose to go on abusing after they have received far more intensive therapy/training than is being suggested here for welfare staff. Moreover, it may well be that those men who enter the welfare professions with the intention of abusing vulnerable people will continue to choose to abuse no matter what training they receive. Even so, the form of training I am advocating might assist some men not to abuse who otherwise would go on to do so.

Adapting the behaviour of men workers

This is a strategy designed to help protect children from being sexually abused by men workers and to protect men workers from having their actions misinterpreted as being abusive. We need to say a little about this latter point.

There is much evidence that children make deliberately false allegations about sexual abuse only very rarely indeed (Salter 1988). What is probably more common is for children who have a history of sexual abuse in their pasts to see abusive patterns of behaviour in the actions of staff when that is not the case. They honestly misinterpret the staff's actions perhaps because those actions remind them of the circumstances leading up to their previous abuse (the "grooming" we have mentioned earlier) and this makes them think it is going to happen again. We need to remember that when this occurs, the children do believe they are about to be abused: the effect on them is the same as if it were about to happen. So it is important to avoid this situation for the child's sake and for the sake of the staff member who may be accused of abuse.

What makes the position more difficult is that staff may well not know when a child has a history of abuse in the past. For instance, there is evidence in the United States that about 75 per cent of children entering the care system have such a history (McFadden & Ryan 1991). Any child might have such a history, so men workers must exercise care in working with all children. What is clear is that men workers are more likely to encounter misinterpretation because it is also more likely that any child with a history of abuse will have been abused by a man. This is not to deny that a few children may have a history of having been sexually abused by a woman, or by a woman and man together. Providing an environment in which these children may feel safe can be particularly difficult to achieve.

So, men workers should adapt their behaviour to protect children from actually being abused, to prevent children feeling they are being abused, and to protect men workers from misinterpretation of their actions by children. Adaptation can take many forms, ranging from quite minor changes to major ones in specific situations. The precise level of adaptation depends on the particular situation.

In order to begin thinking about how to gauge the correct amount of adaptation to particular situations, I have suggested some guiding principles (Pringle 1994c) in the form of questions. The more a particular setting requires that the issues raised in this list be taken into account, the more extensive may be the need for men staff in that setting to adapt their way of acting.

Staff (in particular men) and agencies should consider these questions when they are trying to assess a situation:
(a) What is the age of the children here and how will that impact on their ability to say or show if they feel discomfort or abuse?
(b) What is the children's developmental level and what effect does that have in those respects?
(c) Are there other issues that might make it harder for children to express discomfort or abuse, such as some physical disabilities?
(d) Are there reasons for thinking more children in this setting might have a history of sexual abuse?

(e) What level of physical and/or emotional intimacy with children by staff is required in this setting?
(f) What level of staffing is available here to make children feel more secure?
(g) Above all, what are the children in this setting telling us (in words and actions) about what would make them feel safe?

It needs to be borne in mind by readers that these are only preliminary suggestions: it may well be that a debate about them would be a useful development in helping us move forward.

In using these questions, we need to be very clear about one issue. For these questions might be interpreted as suggesting that "problems" in the children create a greater risk of them being sexually abused and that therefore in some way the "problems" are responsible for the abuse. This is not what we are saying on two counts. First, when abuse occurs the only person responsible is the person who abuses. Secondly, insofar as characteristics of the child are relevant to the situation, it is those characteristics in the context of the child's environment that are important.

For instance, where a child is deaf, it is the environment that the agency provides for the child that may cause that child to be unsafe. How far does the agency provide resources for the child to assist her or his communication? How far does the agency train staff to be alert to the child's needs and to facilitate the child's communication, including if the child feels discomfort about touch or has been abused? (Kennedy & Kelly 1992). Insofar as there are "problems" that make sexual abuse more likely for some children, those problems lie in the response of the child's environment to the needs of the child and not in the child herself or himself. That is a general principle which applies to all children.

We need to remember that children may not feel able to tell a staff member if they do feel uncomfortable about the latter's actions, or to tell another staff member if they have been abused, even when there are no other barriers to communication. Consequently, agencies and staff should think in terms of making more changes to staff behaviour rather than less, particularly as far as staff who are men are concerned.

Moreover, there are some adaptations to staff behaviour that are probably wise in virtually all settings. For instance, in professions working regularly with children serious consideration should be given to the issue of how far men staff should use touch as a means of communication with children. A degree of wariness should also be considered regarding touch used by female staff, particularly where cues of possible discomfort are picked up from the child.

Regardless of the issues around misinterpretation, we have to remember that children who have suffered any form of violence at the hands of adults in the past, may find touch uncomfortable. Because of the potential impact of these past experiences on their self-esteem, such children are often the least able to express their unease about touch to adults. Most of the past experiences, but not all of them, will have been at the hands of men.

It may be objected that these possibilities restrict men's avenues for communicating at a deeply emotional level with children. While touch is such an avenue, it is not clear that strong relationships with children can only be developed using touch. I would suggest that one's overall demeanour and respect for children is what really counts with them. Touch can certainly play an important part in this but it is not my experience that it is essential.

Another potential adaptation to behaviour, depending on the particular situation as assessed using the principles listed above, might be for men in some settings always to work alongside women colleagues. In settings where considerable intimate physical/emotional care of children is necessary, then consideration should be given to women staff playing the major role in this activity, perhaps with men staff in a supportive capacity.

In some very specific welfare settings, many of the issues addressed in the guiding principles will come together at the same time (i.e age, developmental level, degree of intimacy, other disabilities, level of staffing, likelihood of children having a history of sexual abuse). In such situations, the risks to the child's safety may be so great that we need to consider the possibility of restricting the access of men to work in those settings. As I said above, it is not possible to be prescriptive here: every setting should be assessed on its particular characteristics. However, I would suggest that the types of settings where restricting men's access would be most appropriate for further debate include: work with very young children in nursery care and day care; working with children with severe disabilities or with severe learning difficulties; work that focuses specifically on children and young people who have been sexually abused.

It may be objected that such restrictions will deprive children of valuable contact with men. The response to this is twofold. First, absolute restrictions on men's access would occur in relatively few settings and only where the environmental risk to the child is very high. Moreover, in practice, there will be very few children, if any, who would be deprived of all contact with men in their lives by these suggestions.

The specific debates about this issue will always be extremely difficult partly because they necessarily involve subjective and/or controversial judgements on which there is no universal agreement, such as: what is an acceptable level of risk? How is it to be assessed? How far does the agency accept that gender is an important risk consideration? To what extent does the agency accept that sexual abuse is one of our society's greatest social problems by virtue of its size and potential for emotional damage? Those debates in relation to this topic will also be particularly fraught because they strike at the heart of power relations associated with hegemonic forms of masculinity and hence of "organization sexuality".

The question of limiting the role of men in some areas of social welfare is not new. For instance, Frosh (1988) has argued that men welfare professionals should not be involved in either disclosure work or medical examinations where children have been sexually abused by men. Ruxton (1994) also seems to agree that men should be absent from the early stages of "treatment" of such children and young people. On the other hand, Frosh never envisaged a situation where a professional might abuse a child: he was only concerned with the child's discomfort about being with a man. Moreover, we are considering this issue in terms of a wider spectrum of social welfare than did either Frosh or Ruxton.

All this does, however, need to be put in perspective. First, it is not being suggested that restrictions on men's access to welfare positions should be widespread. As I have said, this possibility should only be considered where the environmental risks of sexual abuse are particularly high according to the criteria indicated. Secondly, this rather limited restriction and the broader suggestion about adaptation of men's behaviour for the safety of children and staff in some settings are put forward for debate. The worrying aspect of all this is that until recently the topic of sexual abuse by welfare personnel and the issue of men was not even on any agenda.

The corollary of what is being suggested is that women in some cases will need to fill the gaps where men's involvement is restricted to various degrees, and this may be seen as sexist. It is not my brief in this study to talk about what women should be doing in social welfare. It would also be presumptuous of me. My focus here, as a man, is on men. However, I will make three short comments about the implications of these proposals for women. First, as we have just seen, it is envisaged that men will still play a major role in welfare work albeit with some limitations. Secondly, insofar as women would complete tasks not done by men, this is being discussed in the context of a work setting not a family one: these are tasks that women would tackle by choice and for payment. Thirdly and perhaps most importantly, this change for women would occur as only a small part of larger developments. As we saw in Chapter 2 some feminist commentators (for example Grimwood & Popplestone 1993) believe it is imperative that women should hold far more positions at all levels of management in social welfare agencies and that the management ethos should become less "macho". Women and men, separately and together, can work towards this goal as part of the transformation of oppressive structures. The role of women doing some tasks that men have done before has to be seen in the context of this overall picture.

There is a separate implication of this approach to making children safer that connects with material we looked at in Chapter 7. In that chapter we recommended use of strategies such as videotaping of sessions, use of consultancy teams (largely composed of women), co-working with women, management involvement of women's groups in situations where men are working with men or boys for treatment or broad preventative purposes on an individual or group basis. These strategies have two purposes. First, many of those strategies represent simply good practice that will produce better quality results for service users and workers. Secondly, they were put forward as ways of reducing the risk of men therapists/facilitators colluding with oppressive attitudes or behaviour. In the light of the material discussed in this section, it becomes apparent that these strategies serve two further purposes: helping to reduce the risk of men therapists/facilitators committing sexual abuse against service users; reducing the risk of men workers behaving in ways that may be misinterpreted by men or boys as abusive.

It should be stressed that the strategies advocated in this chapter do not claim to offer the prospect of eradicating child sexual abuse in welfare systems totally, only of reducing it significantly. Some perpetrators will be so determined to abuse that no efforts will be able to stop them completely. Moreover, we are very aware that, as we have fully acknowledged elsewhere in this study, some women do commit sexual abuse. Even although their relative numbers are small, their absolute numbers are not (Finkelhor et al. 1988, Pringle 1994c). So there will be some women in welfare systems who will also abuse. Agencies need to be alert to their presence. However, statistically, men workers pose a considerably greater threat than women workers, even although it is still true that the majority of men will not be abusers. It is because they represent a greater statistical threat that particular measures, such as those advocated here, need to be taken with men. A substantial reduction in sexual abuse within welfare settings, which is what we are seeking, is far better than the pessimistic outlook predicted by the Hunt Report (Hunt 1994) above.

Before moving on, we should make one final point. We have focused here on services to children because we have considerable data in that field, albeit largely from the United States. The data regarding sexual assaults on adults that we drew together in Chapter 6 were less firm. However, they gave us cause for concern and in certain respects, although not all (Penhale 1993), reflected the data on children. In particular, there seemed to be considerable evidence that men again preponderated as perpetrators within the welfare services. Clearly, it is impossible to make definite recommendations until we have more research to draw upon. However, given that there seems to be a similar gender pattern, perhaps a debate along these lines could begin to open up in the field of adult care too. We saw in Chapter 6 that Brown & Turk (1992) are already asking questions about gender in the area of adults with learning difficulties.

We now turn to a series of other issues in the area of child sexual abuse that have wider applicability to the subject of this study.

Services for children and young people who have been sexually abused

Organization of services

As Esther Saraga has noted (Saraga 1993), in Britain the bulk of welfare resources are channelled into investigation and assessment of "cases" and there is little in the way of "treatment", "therapy" or help for the person who has been sexually abused. Such provision as exists is very patchy. This is amply confirmed by recent research carried out in the North East of England (Gray et al. 1995).

Saraga (1993) and other commentators (McLeod & Saraga 1988, 1991, Frost & Stein 1989, Armstrong 1991, Parton 1991, Hudson 1992, Langan 1992, 1993a, 1993b) portray investigations and assessments as being highly bureaucratic and managerial with a heavy emphasis on processing cases as rapidly as possible. In previous chapters we referred to difficulties with the official guidance documents *Protecting children* (HMSO 1988b) and the *Memorandum of good practice* (Home Office 1992): both documents reflect these trends and contribute to them.

Saraga (1993) tries to make sense of all this in several ways. For instance, she interprets these bureaucratic responses as agencies having a need for clarity of purpose and direction; which in child protection cases is often spurious due to their complexity. We can also view this through the lens of gender and the oppressive relations of power we surveyed in Chapter 2.

Who should provide services?

It may be useful to summarize a few findings from a survey of adult survivors of child sexual abuse (Gray et al. 1995) regarding which services they would prefer to turn to for assistance. There is no intention of claiming that these answers are "definitive": the sample was limited (36 respondents) and certainly not random; it may well be that the concept of obtaining a "definitive" answer regarding such questions would anyway be misplaced.

Almost all respondents felt it was important that the person offering them assistance was also a survivor. That applied whether the source of help was a voluntary or statutory agency. The vast majority of respondents, though, preferred to seek help from voluntary agencies. Many of them had already experienced oppression at the hands of statutory services (for instance, insensitivity, not being listened to). There are issues here of commonality and reciprocity between workers and users.

There were few men respondents, an issue to which we return shortly. Of the men in the survey, none expressed a preference for assistance from a man and this included one respondent who had been abused by a lone female. Consequently, this response on the part of men may reflect both their abuse histories and gendered assumptions about women as carers. None of the women respondents had been abused by lone women, though a few had been abused by heterosexual couples. No woman preferred help from a man; some expressed no preference; most preferred assistance from a woman. Finally, very few of the respondents were black. This seems to reflect a lack of resources for black people, a lack of awareness about their abuse, and a considerable lack of research relating to it (Bogle 1988, Rouf 1990, Wilson 1993, see also Ahmed et al. 1986, Dominelli 1988, Ahmad 1990, Barn 1993, Saraga 1993).

Clearly, there are many issues raised by these data that require further research. However, one other piece of data is available here. We carried out a parallel survey of social work and health agencies to ascertain what services were available to survivors (Gray et al. 1995). Few agencies reflected any of the gender concerns of survivors and even fewer offered anything for black people.

Services for men and boys

The lack of men in our sample (Gray et al. 1995) partly reflects the reluctance of abused men and boys to come forward for assistance, which has been attributed to several factors: shame at having been a sexual object; anxieties about whether they are gay or will be thought to be gay by others (La Fontaine 1990, Glaser & Frosh 1993).

These negative feelings about self may well reflect the way being an abused man or boy is socially perceived as contravening some dominant forms of heterosexual masculinity: within the latter, after all, issues such as controlling rather than being controlled, activity rather than passivity, sexual penetration rather than being penetrated tend to be emphasized.

However, the relative absence of males in our sample also seems to reflect a lack of services for men and boys (Gray et al. 1995). This is even more true of men who have been sexually assaulted in adulthood. For men with a history of sexual abuse either in childhood and/or in adulthood there are some survivor-created helplines and groups around Britain. However, these largely rely on individual initiative, have poor support systems, and their funding is normally tenuous. Some public agencies (for example the police) are exploring ways of being more responsive as increased numbers of survivors come forward and as male rape has been recognized legally (Price 1994).

It is clearly important for men working in welfare agencies not only to continually put this whole topic on the agenda in terms of priorities but also to be alert to it in all work with boys and men. This applies across the welfare spectrum. Moreover, initial disclosures of abuse of men and boys are often made to welfare agencies that are not "front-line" in dealing with sexual violence: for instance, housing projects, drug and alcohol projects, youth projects (Price 1994). Further research on the size and nature of the problem of males who are abused will be important, partly as a tool for pushing for a more concerted response to the issue.

It may well also be possible for alliances of men users and welfare workers to push for services together. We should bear in mind that many men workers themselves might be survivors. However, the prospect of alliances between men workers and users who are each survivors may be limited by the inhibitions on both sides. These inhibitions have their roots, as we saw above, in the social perceptions of an abused man that contravene the dictates of dominant forms of heterosexual masculinity.

Once again, if the issue of males who have been abused does rise up agendas and services are made more available, it is important that the resources for these services are not simply diverted from women's services. The efforts of men to have this need met by agencies must be directed at obtaining additional resources.

In seeking to develop services for men and boys sexually assaulted in either childhood and/or in adulthood, we must bear in mind that such services also need to be geared to men and boys who are black or who are gay.

Services for children and non-abusing parents

Practice experience demonstrates that where sexual abuse has occurred in the "nuclear family", support for the child from the non-abusing parent (almost always the mother) is critical to the future wellbeing of the child (Hooper 1992, Helm et al. 1993, Smith 1994, Bernard 1994). Non-abusing mothers are often the best "therapists" for their children, provided they have advice when they need it and adequate social and structural support. Gaining the latter is often a major stumbling block due to the hostile benefits, employment and child care policies that disadvantage lone mothers (Chs 5 and 7). There is good practice guidance about how to help these parents to assist their children (Smith 1994) and there are firm recommendations about how to support them as lone mothers (Hooper 1992, Chs 5 and 7 above).

Non-abusing parents remain a low priority for welfare services (Hooper 1992, Pringle 1993b). When we compare this situation with the position regarding work with sex offenders where central and local government funding is targeted relatively heavily, the contrast is striking – particularly as there is still uncertainty about the effectiveness of offender treatment programmes (Ch. 7). This contrast in resourcing between offenders and non-abusing parents may partly reflect, once again, prioritization of control over care issues in the welfare bureaucracies and also gendered assumptions about caring by those agencies. In both cases we are referred back to issues discussed in Chapter 2. Our view here is that there should be financial support for offender programmes and support to non-abusing parents.

As with informal carers of adults (Ch. 6), we need to remember that not all non-abusing parents are female. This is particularly the case in situations where sexual abuse occurs outside the immediate household, which as we have seen is quite common. In the next section we look at some practice material relating to such parents that raises many valuable issues.

People Against Child Sexual Abuse (PACSA)

I have discussed and agreed the material in this section with PACSA. This organization is a group of people who began to gather together in Newcastle upon Tyne in the second half of 1993. Many of them were parents of children who had been involved in investigations into sexual abuse perpetrated by a trainee nursery nurse, Jason Dabbs. It was this case that led to the Hunt Inquiry and the subsequent Hunt Report (Hunt 1994, Campbell 1994) mentioned earlier. During those investigations and the inquiry, a number of parents had formed their own support and pressure group that was extremely successful in: influencing the course of official events; having the needs of their children met; raising awareness about sexual abuse in their community. This had been a highly empowering experience for many of those parents, most (but not all) of whom were mothers.

Some of those parents (all mothers) wanted to build on what they had achieved in terms of developing community awareness and seeking to change the structures within which child protection practice functioned both locally and nationally. They were also interested in supporting others who had undergone similar experiences. Hence, their meetings in the second half of 1993. They were joined by a few welfare workers (social workers, community workers, paediatrician), an academic, and a writer/broadcaster, some of whom had also been involved with the previous support/pressure group. Soon the new group attracted other parents and survivors of sexual abuse from around Tyneside. Some of these people had experience of abuse by welfare professionals, some of abuse within the family, some of abuse by other adults known to the family. The majority of those meeting together were, and are, women. Having said that, a small number of men are also involved either as parents, partners of survivors, or professionals.

The group decided to call itself by what it is: People Against Child Sexual Abuse (PACSA). The group has been highly successful. It has provided support to parents and survivors in individual cases and to parents who were involved in another very large local multiple abuse investigation. The group organized a major conference (which was free) in Newcastle in May 1994 to raise awareness about the issue of sexual abuse and the importance of welfare agencies listening to what survivors and non-abusing parents are telling them they need. Three hundred people from Tyneside and Britain attended that conference (including social agency managements). This in turn has created a much wider network, leading to PACSA people speaking around the country about the same issues and helping similar groups that want to develop elsewhere. They have also taught on a social work training programme at a local university. A new conference is planned for 1995. The group has acquired considerable funding from statutory and charitable sources. PACSA has had a major input to the work of a regional inter-agency network on abuse. A PACSA helpline has been set up and is running in new premises. Also, PACSA members are receiving training in counselling.

The group has always been, and is, explicitly directed by the parents and survivors. Virtually all the major initiatives noted above have been generated and achieved by them. The parents and survivors form the majority of both the core group and the wider network. They also hold all the official positions. Having said this, we need to remember that the categories of "parent", "survivor", "professional" are not discrete. It is possible to belong to two or all three of those categories, which bears out the tenuous nature of boundaries that are drawn between "workers" and "service users", as we said at the beginning of Chapter 2.

Everyone brings to the group what they have to offer in terms of its different purposes. The professionals and non-professionals are aware that in this mix of group members there may always be a tendency for the former to try to dominate. Because of this awareness, it rarely happens and when it does the parents and survivors have learnt how to deal with it quickly and sensitively. On the whole, professionals act as resources to be used as the other members of the group think fit and on the basis of mutual agreement.

The official positions are held by women. The group meetings have a general structure but are always very fluid. The overall ethos of the group is highly democratic, warm, energizing and supportive. A group meeting may cover a wide range of functions: planning future action, dealing with immediate crises, designing funding applications, discussing current issues around the topic, and last but not at all least offering personal support to different group members.

Not all the people involved with PACSA always attend the meetings: many people can be called in to fulfil different functions. This applies to men and women. The men do not seek to dominate: they would not get very far if they did, anyway. Like everyone else they provide different things at different times. It is probably fair to say that they generally offer practical assistance more than active emotional support. However, they are engaged at an emotional level and this is recognized by both the women and the men. Expression of feelings does not seem to be inhibited by their presence and they too express them at times, and by no means necessarily only anger.

It is probably fair to say that the issue of gender and sexual abuse has not been a central focus of PACSA's work. However, it is inevitably raised and there is no problem about this as far as either the women or men are concerned: everyone more or less simply accepts the fact that most perpetrators (although not all) are men or boys.

Partly because of the experiences that the various parents and survivors have had over the years, they are very confident in dealing with large welfare hierarchies and are expert in using all the strategies we discussed in Chapter 7 to effect structural change: exploiting contradictions in the structure of those organizations; networking; the media; data collection; use of political contacts. Perhaps at an earlier stage, they might have used professional resources to facilitate some of this. Now it is not necessary. As we noted above, they are starting to stimulate similar initiatives elsewhere in Britain.

I shall pick out some major themes relating to this study that the experience of this group illustrates.

Gender issues

First, the gender dynamics of the group are significant. We know from plentiful research (Spender 1985) that in mixed groups familiar patterns of male domination can easily reassert themselves. This has not occurred here. Partly that is a function of the small number of men. However, it may also be a function of the fact that all of the men in this venue adopt models of masculinity that are in some ways quite far removed from dominant forms: quietly caring and emotionally in tune; offering practical assistance, never forcing it but placing it at the disposal of the women.

It is probably impossible to find clear reasons for this. It may just be luck. However, we can put forward two hypotheses. First, all the men one way or another have been extremely close to the distress and pain of sexual abuse. All of them have been deeply affected by this. In the group or in activities organized by the group where the focus is abuse, their sensitivity is ready-formed.

Secondly, all of the men are aware that the vast majority of the distress with which the group is dealing is created by other men. As we said above, gender of perpetrators is not a major issue for the group. However, it may still be that the men's background awareness of men's preponderant responsibility for sexual abuse makes them particularly aware (not necessarily consciously) of the importance of being sensitive in their behaviour to others of either gender. It is hard to know how far these effects feed into other aspects of the men's lives. For many people working with sexual violence, it is never far from their minds whatever they are doing.

What this situation seems to indicate is, once again, that the potential options for re-forming and reshaping masculinities are virtually endless (Hearn & Collinson 1994). Each man can draw upon numerous potential masculinities within himself in creative ways if he is freed of his inhibitions to do so. That freeing up can occur in various ways: being exposed to something deeply emotional is one way. On the other hand, there are also many examples where being exposed to deep emotion has simply frozen men. It may be, as Barker (1994 and Ch. 4 above) seems to suggest, that men's approach to masculinities can sometimes be unfrozen if they are already fulfilling certain roles not wholly consonant with dominant heterosexualities such as being a lone parent or caring for a sick or disabled partner (Applegate & Kaye 1993). This analysis obviously mirrors Connell's observation (1995) that we have already mentioned on several occasions: tensions between contradictory masculinities can create space for transformations in masculinity. However, it is also important that our analysis does not oversimplify the processes that are occurring in these transformations. Connell (1995) goes to great lengths to express the complexity and richness of men's experiences in his research on the life-histories of various categories of men. We need to acknowledge that a similar complexity and richness of experience will characterize the lives of the men we are discussing here.

Probably careful, slow groupwork between men is one of the best avenues for freeing up men's approach to their own masculinities, particularly where the factor of reciprocity can come into operation: where a degree of trust can build up and any boundaries are appropriately relaxed to allow men to play with different masculinities, to practise them.

It may also be that groupwork with men who have had, or are having, specific kinds of experiences would potentially make particular progress in reshaping men's repertoire of masculinities: for instance, men who are non-abusing parents or who are the partners of women sexually abused in childhood. This work can be part of the support that such men could give each other if they felt it was appropriate.

Another promising situation might be working with men who are new parents in family centres. In earlier chapters we discussed how important it is for men to work with men to help them become more involved in child and adult care, but in ways that are safe for dependants. Part of this work could be to use the men's experiences of parenthood to help them explore aspects of their masculinities that had not been opened to

199

them before, and thereby give them a wider repertoire of options upon which to draw in different aspects of their lives.

Perhaps if more men had been in the PACSA group, the nature of the dynamics might have changed. It is hard not to feel that the fluid, democratic quality of the group owes something to the preponderance of women. Its spirit is certainly very reminiscent of what is expressed by Butler & Wintram in *Feminist groupwork* (1991) and to some extent Mullender & Ward (1991) even though it is a "natural" development not reliant on any academic knowledge. Given what we have just said above, though, it is quite possible that a men's group could develop (albeit with more difficulty) a similar way of working: indeed, some of us may have experienced this in men's groups.

Users and workers

The dynamics of this group similarly show how the very real problems of user/worker collaboration can be overcome (Beresford & Croft 1993). In many ways this group conforms to what Beresford & Croft refer to as the democratic model. It demonstrates many of the issues that they raise in their framework that is a useful resource for workers seeking to advance this form of empowering collaboration. What is clear from the PACSA experience is that the process can be accelerated where both workers and users are aware of the possible pitfalls of collaboration and the prerequisites for it. That is why a firm statement of these pitfalls and prerequisites such as is provided by Beresford & Croft (1993) or Barber (1991) can be so useful.

It may be that in the field of child protection resistance to user empowerment and involvement is sometimes greater than in other areas of welfare work. As Beresford & Croft (1993) note, "Child protection is the most contentious area of social work practice and raises wider issues of participation with particular intensity." We can partly attribute this to the special closeness of child protection issues to power relations associated with hegemonic forms of masculinity. We have discussed that point earlier and in this context it becomes easier to see why child protection bureaucracies might resist those service users who seek to introduce issues such as working with emotional pain, caring, loosening control, and gender oppression on to public agendas.

Several commentators have already demonstrated that it is possible to achieve positive movement on some of these issues with respect both to child protection generally (Mullender & Ward 1991, Beresford & Croft 1993) and to sexual abuse in particular (Mullender & Ward 1991, Helm et al. 1993). It may well be, however, that the PACSA group (and the parents' support and pressure group that preceded it) represents one of the most successful examples of a participatory approach in Britain.

Obviously men users as part of mixed gender groups can learn from this example and others provided in the literature mentioned above. Men as workers collaborating with men as users can also develop campaigns to create services to fill the many gaps in provision for men that we have noted in the course of this study.

Use of strategies to effect structural change and responsiveness in large bureaucracies

We have already mentioned the details of these in Chapter 7, so will not specify them again. It is important to remember that although the people of PACSA learnt some of these strategies from allied professionals, most of them they developed very quickly from their own experience of dealing with powerful organizations. Clearly, such strategies are useful to workers, users and combinations of the two.

In Chapters 5 and 7, we discussed the need for men to be engaged in efforts to change community attitudes that encourage men's sexual violences. In Chapter 7 we noted some ways in which men might pursue that objective. In this section, we have seen another example of how men working with, and in support of, women can become involved in making such an impact. In principle, it would be quite possible for men involved in a project such as PACSA to carry out similar community liaison and promotion work about gender and sexual abuse, as long as they liaised with their women colleagues and did not try to annex or block their work.

Conclusion

In this chapter, focusing on the issue of child sexual abuse has allowed us to extend and deepen our analysis in a number of ways.

First, we have developed a theoretical process by which to understand the generation of men's sexual violences. Given that it is based on Connell's (1987, 1995) conception of power relations it is compatible with the analysis underlying the remainder of the study. Using that model of sexual violences, we were able to confirm the major themes that need to be addressed in treatment and preventative work with men and boys. It was also relevant to the second major topic of this chapter, developing strategies that may go some way towards reducing the levels of sexual violence perpetrated upon service users by welfare workers.

Those strategies do not claim to eradicate sexual violences in welfare settings totally: we know some perpetrators are far too determined for any situation to be completely safe. Moreover, women sex offenders do exist (in relatively small numbers) and they will need to be dealt with separately. Even so, we can suggest that the strategies we advocated for men workers should offer more hope than the Hunt Report (1994) is able to provide in its bleak assessment of the situation. Some of our strategies are controversial and we hope the discussion in this chapter will stimulate further constructive debate.

Much of what we have said about the generation of sexual violences and the prevention of them is also applicable to other forms of violence perpetrated by men, in particular physical violences. In Chapter 7 we noted that there is considerable debate about the causation of men's physical violences, especially the relative weight that should be given to issues of social stress on the one hand and issues of patriarchal power relations on the other hand.

Although no definitive answer regarding this debate is possible, we did conclude in Chapter 7 that the operation of hegemonic forms of masculinity had a central, although not necessarily exclusive, role in the generation of men's physical violences. In Chapter 7, we already saw that there was an important overlap between men's sexual and physical violences with regard to the importance of "choice" in the generation of both. We can conclude that with care we may apply many of our conclusions about men's sexual violences to their physical violences as well.

Our strategies for limiting men's sexual violences in welfare systems should also limit their physical violences. However, it is likely that physical violence in welfare systems is not quite so gender-specific as sexual violence in terms of perpetrators. So agencies will have to give considerable attention to finding ways of limiting women's physical violence in those systems. That, however, is not the subject of this study.

In this chapter we also noted how dominant power relations structured many of the services available (or not available) to various categories of service user. There were clearly gaps in provision which men as welfare workers and as users could address within their anti-oppressive activity at all the levels we have considered, and deploying all the strategies for change that we have explored throughout this study.

Finally, we used a practice example to understand how women and men, welfare workers and service users, could collaborate in a democratic and empowering fashion to have an impact on welfare structures and raise awareness about sexual abuse at the community level. In the course of that discussion, we found a situation where men were working

with women and displaying ways of relating to other people far removed from those associated with dominant forms of masculinity. This
confirmed the possibility, via individual work and groupwork, of helping men explore the repertoire of masculinities that each possesses so
they can deploy them in more constructive ways.

In the final chapter we bring together the themes of this chapter and
the preceding one to delineate the framework for men's practice that we
have been building up throughout this study.

Chapter 9
Men and social welfare

In the course of this study we have identified numerous issues across the whole range of the welfare services that are particularly appropriate for men to address. Indeed, as we saw in Chapter 1, men have a duty to address them. Men involved with social welfare have a particular responsibility to challenge oppressive attitudes, behaviours, practices, patterns of provision or structures where that oppression emanates from relations of power associated with hegemonic forms of masculinity.

In this final chapter, I do not intend to compile a record of the many examples of oppression that men should challenge, for the list is endless. As we have said before, there is no shortage of opportunities for practice. We have catalogued many of them in each chapter of this book. However, there will be far more we have not mentioned.

My aim in this chapter is, instead, to begin the process of designing a framework within which men can engage in that form of anti-oppressive practice. Most of the components of the framework we have already encountered in earlier chapters. Hopefully this framework will stimulate a debate that will lead to further refinement of our ideas about this subject. Having designed the framework, in the second half of this chapter I want to summarize the difficulties of men engaging in this form of anti-oppressive activity.

A framework for men's practice

Critiquing the stereotype

In Chapter 2 we started to critique a very stereotypical model of men, women and social welfare.

In that stereotypical model, men working for welfare agencies were said to congregate in those sectors of welfare organizations most associated with social control. Women by contrast were said to be concentrated in the caring functions of welfare systems and in the lower echelons of welfare organizations. As for service users, the engagement of men and boys with social welfare was similarly supposed to occur in sectors mainly concerned with social control: for example, child protection, criminal justice. On the other hand, the engagement of women and girls with welfare was alleged to take place within the more caring elements of welfare systems: for example, as young women in the care system and as informal carers being supported by welfare services to look after vulnerable adults and children.

In Chapters 2 to 6 we saw that this stereotypical model is indeed valid in many respects. However, it does over-simplify the picture in a considerable number of ways. In the course of the study we added complexity to this picture in terms of: the patterns of oppression that operate outside and within social welfare agencies; the role of men as carers within social welfare systems; the confusion and overlap between controlling and caring functions that characterizes most areas of social welfare.

Connell's analysis of power and anti-oppressive practice

In the preceding chapters we have shown that men involved with social welfare systems do have a major role to play in countering oppressions which, we concluded, are engendered by power relations associated with the operation of hegemonic forms of masculinity (Connell 1987, 1995).

As we have seen, we cannot explain the dominant structures associated with hegemonic masculinities purely in terms of patriarchal relations, important though they are. Many other axes of domination are also involved, of which some of the most vital relate to issues of sexual identity, "race", age, disability and class. Men who attempt to work against the complex and shifting structures of power related to hegemonic masculinity in the social welfare system have to resist all forms of domination, including that of men over women. This is consonant with the concept of anti-oppressive practice (AOP) which has gained wide currency in many fields of social welfare over recent years, although it is under considerable pressure from the social policies of the government in Britain. AOP provides the best basis for a framework within which men can challenge the relations of power associated with hegemonic masculinity.

Those power relations structure the forms of domination that permeate our society. Logically one would expect our social welfare system to alleviate the social problems that are the negative outcomes of these forms of domination. In some respects it does. However, frequently that is not the case. On the contrary, this study has demonstrated that social welfare agencies often compound those patterns of domination. This is because the oppressive power relations that structure our society also tend to structure the systems of social welfare that operate within the terms of that society. One additional outcome of this state of affairs is that, to an extent, the people who work in social welfare agencies are subject to the same forms of domination as those who use their services.

Men as welfare workers and service users

When we talk above about "men who are involved with social welfare" countering patterns of oppression, we are referring to men who work in social welfare agencies and men who are users of them. We are also referring to patterns of oppression that occur outside and inside welfare systems.

In many cases men who are workers will identify, in the course of their duties, oppressions bearing down on service users, oppressions from within the workings of society or from within welfare agencies themselves. There are many opportunities for workers and users who are men to address issues of oppression together, sometimes building on the common experience they share as men.

In recent years user groups working for change from outside of agencies have developed rapidly (Beresford & Croft 1993): men who are users can form such groups themselves or in alliance with women, depending on the issues and situation.

Moreover, there is a growing awareness of the advantages of welfare workers and users forming alliances and seeking change to establish structures and services that are enabling to them all (Beresford & Croft

1993). Men as workers and men as users can develop this approach when addressing issues where both have a common agenda in relation to oppressions either inside or outside welfare agencies. Such collaboration itself can be anti-oppressive when it is a process that challenges the power differentials dividing workers from users.

Seeking change in welfare organizations

In Chapter 7 we provided a set of approaches that might offer strategies to either men users or welfare workers who are trying to create change within organizations: for instance, networking in its many forms including support networks; use of media; exploiting the contradictions in power structures that always exist in large bureaucracies; positive reframing of objectives to enlist the widest range of potential allies; using systems perspectives to understand power flows inside organizations and between them; data collection/research; use of strategic interventions.

In previous chapters we have noted that seeking change in agencies, and in those systems that operate above agencies, is a central and essential part of the practice perspective that this study advocates. It has to be tackled in a highly concerted and organized manner, which is what the approaches listed above are meant to assist.

This applies to all agencies but it is particularly essential in those agencies where services are very narrowly prescribed by resource shortages and governmental policies. For instance, we have in mind the statutory social services. In such agencies, much initial anti-oppressive effort by men may need to be devoted to their agency structures and policies in order to carve out more space for anti-oppressive practice. Lack of resources should never be an excuse for avoiding such practice. It is always possible even in the most statutory and constrained situations (Barber 1991, Fook 1993). However, it will be limited by lack of resources and policy restrictions.

In this study we have seen that men have to engage in anti-oppressive activity at different levels of potential change ranging from the individual to the societal. We consider those levels below. At all of them, alliances between workers and users can be a major asset.

Later in this chapter we will summarize some of the problems that can occur when men who are welfare workers and service users seek to collaborate. Even so, many issues are best dealt with in this way because of the potential strength of such alliances.

Developing mutuality, commonality, reciprocity

What may often aid this process is the fact that the boundary between workers and users is a social construction that can sometimes be dissolved quite appropriately. When this boundary is relaxed, considerable areas of commonality between men can be revealed and they can work in a reciprocal fashion, even though power differentials between workers and users will frequently remain due to structural factors. Some commentators, especially in the disability movement, have emphasized that reciprocity of service is an important practice principle that assists service users to develop their sense of self-esteem.

In Chapter 7 we recommended a number of theoretical and practice-based approaches that workers and users could draw upon to encourage mutuality and use of commonalities in work between staff and users: for instance, feminist groupwork (Butler & Wintram 1991), self-directed groupwork (Mullender & Ward 1991), Rogerian counselling (Mearns & Thorne 1988), radical casework (Fook 1993), community-oriented collaboration (Barber 1991), user-centred models (Beresford & Croft 1993).

Men and masculinities: opening up men's options

Those areas of commonality may be ones that are very practical and impersonal. However, sometimes they may be much more personal: issues such as sexuality, emotion, violence, relationships, friendship, power. Where men as users or workers can come together and address these kinds of personal issues, they are already engaging in AOP because men's normal reluctance to do this is part of the process whereby structures of oppression are created. Dominant forms of heterosexuality also seem to be central to that process and many men appear to identify with them (Hearn 1992, Kimmel 1994, Connell 1995). Those dominant forms are characterized by the need to control, to exercise power over others, to fear emotions other than anger, to avoid closeness in relations, to objectify human beings. Thus, any attempt to promote alternatives to these qualities strikes at the heart of men's oppressiveness: for instance, alternatives such as a willingness to acknowledge dependency on others, expression of the full range of emotions, a willingness to make oneself vulnerable and share control in close relationships (Herek 1987).

In Chapter 8 we saw how some gay men manage to incorporate aspects of dominant forms of heterosexual masculinity while at the same time subverting them. This creativity in transforming different forms of masculinity indicates that all men might be able to apply the same degree of creativity to the range of masculinities available to them. In that chapter we also suggested that each man probably has a large repertoire of potential masculinities open to him but often is not able to access them due to the constraints of the dominant forms, noted above (Applegate & Kaye 1993, Hearn & Collinson 1994, Connell 1995).

In a sense, working with men may be partly about helping them get in touch with their multiple masculinities to see which ones they would really like to use in particular situations. We noted that for various reasons some men may be able to access alternative, more benign forms of masculinity with greater ease than others: perhaps because they have had particular experiences or because they have been placed in particular situations.

Expanding men's caring functions in the family

Throughout this study we have seen situations where men have demonstrated some of those qualities that are not associated with dominant forms of masculinity: lone fathers; gay carers of friends or partners who are ill; men who are informal carers of adults; non-abusing fathers of abused children; partners of women who are survivors of child sexual abuse. Part of men's AOP practice is to seek to provide services that will support men in such situations. For we saw that in many cases these activities were not well supported by welfare services, perhaps because men in those roles do not conform to the sexist and heterosexist assumptions that underlie the provision of those services and that have their origins in the oppressive structures of the welfare agencies.

It is important for men workers to assist the process by which more men share the care of children in the home and the care of adult relatives. However, this has to be done in ways that ensure dependants are looked after safely. For we also saw that men's sexual violences could be directed against those most dependent upon them. This can be achieved by working with men in a preventative way using the themes developed in Chapters 7 and 8 and which we summarize below once again.

Men working with men in family centres is a good site for this sort of activity in relation to child care. In view of what we said in Chapter 8 about the limitations that it may be necessary to impose on men workers dealing with very young children in certain day care settings, perhaps in some cases men who are workers there should concentrate their efforts on the vital task of engaging with fathers.

There will be numerous opportunities for doing this kind of work in all settings: workers must be creative in persuading their agencies to allow them space and resources. That entails having an impact on the way the agency operates by using the kinds of strategies we listed earlier in this chapter.

Supporting women's independence

Encouraging men to play a more responsible role in the families where they live is one side of the picture, and an important one. In Chapter 4 we saw that the other side of the picture is the situation of women. Men as workers and users of welfare services should be active in supporting action that seeks to change policies, procedures and resource allocations so that women can have the freedom of independent, equal incomes and the liberty to decide how far they work in the home or outside.

Changes in housing, employment, social security and child care policies would also enable women to freely choose whether or not they wanted to live with a particular man. At present many women are forced to remain with abusive men because the supports and structures that would enable them to be independent do not exist. Such changes in themselves would play a major part in reducing woman and child abuse. The capacity of women to be independent if they choose to be so might also act as an inducement for men to change their behaviour in a positive way. As Lynne Segal says (1990), men's current resistance to change may often be attributed to the simple fact that it is not in their interests to change. If women had the material capacity to end unsatisfying or abusive relationships with men, some of the latter might then have cause to reassess whether it is worth creating change in their lives. Men engaged in the AOP activity that is the object of this study should work for changes in this sphere and support their women colleagues who are already engaged in this struggle.

Halting men's violences: the priority for men in social welfare

In this study we touched on most of the major issues in the social welfare field that should be addressed within this form of men's AOP activity and some of them are mentioned above. However, we deliberately concentrated on the subject of halting men's violences for a number of reasons: first, the sheer enormity of the problem that is one of the greatest our society faces; secondly, the centrality of this issue (particularly sexual violence) to the process by which relations of domination associated with hegemonic masculinity permeate society.

For the same reasons, the halting of these violences must be the priority task for men involved with social welfare. We saw that engagement of men users in child protection services was sometimes problematic (Ch. 3). We suggested that for various reasons, agencies and welfare workers might sometimes collude with men's resistance to engagement. Consequently, greater determination in pursuing men's engagement might be required rather than new strategies, although we indicated some ways in which this could be facilitated, including the increased involvement of men workers in such cases.

We also emphasized the need to support non-abusing parents (often mothers) more effectively. Although it is important to assess whether non-abusing parents can protect their children, we concluded that at the moment many non-abusing parents are set up to fail by being subject to a negative form of scrutiny rather than positive support.

One result of all these suggestions about how to approach women and men in child protection work would probably be the need for more resources. In services such as statutory social work, current resources are very limited. Earlier, we noted that the scope for men's anti-oppressive practice might be particularly constrained in this sector by that lack of resources. We now see that there is even more justification for men in those agencies giving a high priority to securing enhanced services by making anti-oppressive changes in agency structures.

For instance, in the field of child protection it would seem sensible to use the societal size of violence to children as an argument for gaining resources. Men in agencies might find forging links with campaigns such as Zero Tolerance (Ch. 7) or PACSA (Ch. 8) a useful strategy. This should be done in alliance with women colleagues if the latter feel it is appropriate.

Returning to a wider view of men's violences and social welfare, we saw that these violences are widespread in society and appear to be quite common within welfare agencies themselves, although we desperately need more research in the field of adult care and more research generally from within Britain.

Men's responsibility for violence is most clearly seen in the area of sexual violence where men appear to constitute the vast majority of perpetrators in terms of abuse to adults and children. Moreover, on the basis of prevalence data presented in this study, that sexual violence is extremely common. However, it is not only common: it is also extensive. Both genders are sexually assaulted by men. As well as gender, issues of age, sexuality and disability all seem to be factors involved in the process by which men's sexual violences are generated.

For these reasons we have focused on sexual violences in this study. We developed a model to explain the generation of men's sexual violences, based again on Connell's analysis of power relations (1987, 1995).

Using that model we sought to find ways by which sexual violences committed by men welfare workers could be effectively reduced. Previous efforts to reduce it seemed rather limited in their impact because they had not adopted any coherent model by which to explain the phenomenon. Our model confirmed that it is unlikely any method could be devised by which abusers might be targeted before being caught, so the implication is that measures have to be taken that apply to all men staff. These measures involve men working on their own masculinities (see below) and making changes in oppressive agency structures. In addition, other strategies were advocated that included training and the adaptation of men's behaviour when working with children.

Adaptation of men's behaviour was suggested to protect children from sexual abuse and to protect workers from misinterpretation by children of their actions. The adaptations would often be relatively small but in extreme situations might entail consideration of exclusion of men from particular types of work or particular tasks. The variation in level of adaptation would depend on the potential dangers to the child in each specific situation. Guidelines were suggested to assist in assessment of this potential danger. Other additional recommendations were made.

Finally, it was tentatively suggested that staff and agencies dealing with adult care should also start to consider some of these issues pending further research. One commentator at least (Holt 1994) is suggesting that we may need to think of statutory protective services being developed for adults that would focus on abuse outside and inside welfare systems. Provided the inadequacies of the current child protection services were not replicated in adult services, this suggestion would seem worth considering.

We have seen that up to a point our conclusions about men's sexual violences can also be applied to some of their other violences, including their physical violences. We know, for instance, that choice is a crucial issue in the processes by which men's sexual and physical violences are generated.

Because of the emphasis that we place on choice in the generation of men's violences, we acknowledge that working with men and boys to prevent such violences is extremely useful: it may help them to choose not to be violent. Men have a vital role to play in that work. It can take several forms. First, work with men or boys who are already abusers. Secondly, work with men and boys focused on preventing violences in the future. Thirdly, even when men are working with men or boys on issues where the focus is not primarily preventative, they should always have in mind that this work can still be given a secondary preventative function.

Drawing on our empirical data about men's violences (Chs 3 and 5) and on our theoretical model of sexual violence (Ch. 8), we have identified six themes that need to be addressed in any focused work with men or boys. These are applicable to both sexual and physical violence: assisting men and boys to acknowledge their own capacity for acting oppressively; making explicit the links between men's oppressive acts and the structural oppressions that permeate society; countering societal attitudes that reinforce men's oppressions (myths about women, "real men", violence, control, racism, heterosexism); recognizing how peer group activities reinforce men's tendency to oppress; devising strategies to avoid situations where oppressive behaviour is most likely; helping men look at their own masculinity and to reconsider the forms of masculinity they will use in various aspects of their lives.

Levels of men's practice

The activity described in the last paragraph is an example of men working at an individual or group level. In fact men's anti-oppressive action in social welfare needs to be progressed on a series of different but interlinked levels: work with oneself; one-to-one work; groupwork with men; creating change at agency, local or community levels; change also at societal levels. In the course of this study we have at different points considered all these forms of intervention. Different issues need to be addressed at different levels. The overall project requires a multidimensional response by men. Depending upon his individual situation, each man will be in a position to address some issues better than others and to work at some levels more than others. However, it is important that as far as possible men's networking with men and women should include activities that are occurring at different levels. For as we have said, work at each level impacts on the others: co-ordination is therefore at a premium.

Summary

We can summarize anti-oppressive activity by men involved with social welfare as follows. Its objectives include halting men's violences and promoting more positive, creative ways in which men can relate to other human beings. In addition, men who are workers and service users should work for changes at the levels of policy, procedure and practice that result in the empowerment of those users and workers who are oppressed by structures associated with hegemonic masculinity.

In challenging these structures we have to remember that dynamics of domination based on "race", age, disability, class, sexual identity and gender are all involved and need to be addressed as appropriate.

This then is our framework in which men may seek to carry forward their efforts to challenge those dimensions of power related to hegemonic masculinities. Having set out this framework, I finally want to address some of the dilemmas that men will meet in pursuing these goals.

Problems of men working for change

Other services must not gbe adversely affected by development of services for men

In developing services for men, those services must not be established at the expense of services to women or other groups of people. If substitution of services does occur, that process only replicates the patterns of domination that we are, ironically, seeking to change. Services for men must use additional, rather than existing, resources and the allocation of these should be an objective of men working within an AOP framework.

The problem of collusion

As we said at the very beginning of this chapter, the commonalities between men can be a great source of creativity and energy for positive change. Consequently in many men's groups engaged in AOP, developing commonalities between members and facilitators based on their shared experience as men can be a valuable strategy. However, the line between on the one hand emphasizing the commonalities between men and on the other hand men colluding about oppressive attitudes and behaviours is a very thin one. For some of our main commonalities

214

as men may of course be our sexism, our homophobia or our racism. Collusion on the part of men acting as facilitators is an ever-present threat when men work with men and takes many forms, ranging from open reinforcement of oppression through to failing to challenge oppressive remarks. Collusion quickly undermines all AOP efforts.

In our study we stressed that men must take major steps to guard against collusion: it is not enough to hope for the best, or to think you will not do it, or to dismiss it as a "one-off" or unimportant. The appropriate steps to take will vary from situation to situation and there is a wide range to choose from.

For instance, working on one's own oppressive behaviour should perhaps take place in the context of using a men's group or co-counsellor to check out one's ideas and feelings.

Safeguards to monitor men's practice can be built into the framework of activities such as one-to-one work and groupwork with boys or men. Moreover, these checks are strategies that constitute good practice in general and should be incorporated when doing this kind of work anyway. The sorts of safeguards I am suggesting would be some combination of the following and would be determined depending upon circumstances: using a female co-worker; having a consultation team to monitor the work; videotaping and reviewing of sessions; use of live supervision. Where consultation teams or live supervision are used, the personnel involved should if possible be predominantly women, well versed in the relevant issues.

Where a project, either statutory or voluntary, focuses on work with men from an AOP point of view, structures should be created whereby women well versed in issues of oppression have some management oversight of it. For instance, a project working with men who engage in woman abuse might invite the local Women's Aid group to have some control in its running – and that control would have to be meaningful rather than token.

In some situations the idea of alliance-building or establishing commonalities between men workers and users can only be developed within certain limits. For instance, in working with non-sex offenders on the general links between masculinity and crime in a probation setting one would have to fully acknowledge the considerable power differentials between workers and users as well as the necessary boundaries. Even then, a degree of mutuality between workers and users is still possible and beneficial within those boundaries. Barber (1991) demonstrates how this kind of limited work can be done on an individual basis with "involuntary" users.

However, there are specific situations where men working with men ought to use all safeguards possible to limit the risks of collusion and should therefore wholly abandon strategies based on commonalities and collaborative engagement. This is particularly the case when men are working with sex offenders to put a halt to their offending.

Of course there probably will be many commonalities between therapists and sex offenders: that is the conclusion we have to draw from the evidence in previous chapters. It is vital to treat those commonalities with extreme care because sex offenders may well use them as a means of diverting attention from their responsibility for their crimes. We know from practice that sex offenders will re-interpret whatever they can as reassurance that the abuse they perpetrated was normal or harmless (Morrison et al. 1994). In this context, recourse to mutuality as a therapeutic tool is simply dangerous. Sex offenders must be confronted with their responsibility for choosing to sexually assault another person. Issues of men's mutuality will only distract from that purpose. At a much later point, after confrontative work has been completed, more collaborative engagement with offenders may be possible, perhaps with different therapists, to carry further forward the ongoing task of assisting men to reassess their masculinities. However, that collaborative work could only occur when there was some real assurance that offenders were controlling their offending.

For the same reasons, we should be very careful about how far mutuality is appropriate in work between facilitators (either welfare workers or ex-service users) and groups of men who use physical and emotional violence against partners; or indeed in individual work with these men. Establishing commonalities with them may partly depend upon the stage the abusive men are at: how many changes they have already made in their behaviour and how far they have travelled emotionally. Even so, facilitators must be very wary lest they inadvertently collude with and reinforce abusive attitudes.

I want to briefly mention one further issue about collusion. In work between men (whether workers or users) there is often a dilemma about whether to challenge another man about his oppressive behaviour (for instance his use of language) or to keep quiet, thereby colluding with him. In Chapter 7 we pointed out that oppressive behaviour should always be challenged but that the term "challenge" embraces a wide range of strategies. If you challenge someone else, you should choose whichever strategy is likely to have the most positive result in that particular situation: simply alienating someone cannot usually be counted as a positive result.

What lies behind all my concerns about collusion is a central problem about working with men within an AOP context. For, where one is challenging the oppressions of men in work with men, some anti-oppressive processes may in certain situations be counter-productive: they may "let men off the hook" in taking responsibility for themselves. Women working with women according to feminist principles are usually not in quite the same position. Having said this, I do believe mutuality and commonality can in the majority of cases be positive strategies in work between men, provided the safeguards around collusion are observed in the ways suggested.

The problem of abuse

There is another, even more important, reason why the same sorts of safeguards mentioned above (videotaping, use of female co-worker, use of female consultation team) are strategies that men should adopt in certain forms of work. For they can be useful in protecting users whose situations make them vulnerable to sexual or other forms of abuse at the hands of therapists or welfare workers, especially men. We discussed this risk earlier in the chapter when we mentioned some strategies that could be used to limit risk, such as adapting men's behaviour with children. Using the safeguards being discussed in this section and the previous section should be seen as further ways of protecting children. Men who are workers should note that all these measures also protect staff members in situations where children may misinterpret workers' actions as being abusive.

When AOP is oppressive: a paradox

This final point encompasses the previous three and extends beyond them. In the study we saw ways in which work with men and boys to counter oppressions associated with hegemonic masculinity can, paradoxically, sometimes result in a reinforcement of those oppressions. This is a reflection of the pervasive quality of those structures of domination that we are trying to dismantle. However, this does not, of course, invalidate the need for men to work anti-oppressively in this way. It does mean that as men we always have to think carefully about the results of our actions. To borrow some ideas from systems theory, we must not allow our solutions to become problems themselves, thereby creating "more of the same". We have already mentioned the negative effects of work with men draining resources away from services for women; men therapists colluding with men's oppressions; and creating situations where male users might be abused by male workers. These are all examples of apparent AOP having oppressive outcomes. There are many other ways in which the same difficulty can arise and I mention one more of them now.

Men's annexation of women's AOP work

Men active in the field of social welfare must guard against annexing and colonizing anti-oppressive work being done by women. That occurs only too frequently and we provided examples of such annexation in Chapters 7 and 8. This applies to men as workers and as users. We need to think very carefully about the rules by which men engaged on anti-sexist and AOP activity should relate to women engaged in the same kinds of project. Many women involved in struggles against the domination of men believe it is vital that men should also engage in this struggle: but that does not mean it has to be on exactly the same ground.

There are many complex issues here that we have explored in Chapters 7 and 8. At the risk of over-simplifying, we may conclude that men can relate to women engaged in the same sort of struggle in three ways that overlap:

(a) Men can work separately. This is often the most appropriate strategy in view of what has been said above. However, it is important to ensure that men's actions do complement women's and do not undermine them. Having women involved in oversight or management of men's work can be one way of ensuring this.

(b) Men can actively support women's efforts. This can be carried out at all levels of engagement. For instance, it can occur within an individual relationship. In groups this is also possible where women are clearly in charge and men have an explicitly ancillary role.

(c) Women and men working together. This may often be the most difficult model to operate largely because of familiar oppressive dynamics which can reassert themselves in mixed group settings. It is probably most likely to succeed where: the men actively try to express themselves via non-dominant forms of masculinity; the women and men involved are very aware of potential difficulties; men are in a minority; the group has access to consultation services that are themselves based on clear anti-sexist and AOP principles. Elsewhere I have written about the problems that can occur in mixed gender groups engaged in anti-sexist and AOP practice (Pringle 1990, 1993d).

I have spent some time considering all these issues because it is important to be honest about how very difficult it is to have men engaging in the kind of activities advocated in this study.

Difficult though it is, men must make the effort. We cannot go on abrogating responsibility for ourselves individually or collectively any longer. This study takes a few steps in helping men, as welfare workers and as service users, think about how to accept that responsibility within the field of social welfare. I know it leaves many questions unanswered and many areas relatively unexplored. Partly that is a function of space. But it is also a function of the fact that as a man I certainly lack many of the answers. I look forward to the debates that may result from this book. However, I hope those debates give us more answers and not merely more questions. For we are talking about peoples' lives and their pain.

Bibliography

Abbott, P. & C. Wallace 1990. *An introduction to sociology: feminist perspectives.* London: Routledge.

Ahmad, B. 1990. *Black perspectives in social work.* Birmingham, England: Venture Press.

Ahmed, S. 1994. Anti-racist social work: a black perspective. In *Practising social work*, C. Hanvey & T. Philpot (eds), 119–33. London: Routledge.

Ahmed, S., J. Cheetham, J. Small 1986. *Social work with black children and their families.* London: Batsford.

Andersen, T. 1991. Reflections on reflecting with families. See McNamee & Gergen (1992), 54–68.

Andrews, B. 1994. Family violence in a social context: factors relating to male abuse of children. See Archer (1994), 195–209.

Applegate, J. S. & L. W. Kaye 1993. Male elder caregivers. In *Doing "women's work": men in non-traditional occupations*, C. L. Williams (ed.), 152–67. Los Angeles: Sage.

Arber, S. & N. Gilbert 1989. Men: the forgotten carers. *Sociology* **23**(1), 111–18.

Archer, J. 1994. Power and male violence. See Archer (1994), 310–31.

— (ed.) 1994. *Male violence.* London: Routledge.

Armstrong, L. 1991. Surviving the incest industry. *Trouble and Strife* **21**, 29–32.

Baldock, J. 1993. Old age. See Dallos & McLaughlin (1993), 123–53.

Baldock, J. & C. Ungerson 1991. What d'ya want if you don't want money. In *Women's issues in social policy*, M. McLean & D. Groves (eds), 136–58. London: Routledge.

Baldwin, S. & J. Twigg 1991. Women and community care – reflections on a debate. In *Women's issues in social policy*, M. McLean & D. Groves (eds), 117–35. London: Routledge.

Barber, J. G. 1991. *Beyond casework.* London: Macmillan.

Barker, R. W. 1994. *Lone fathers and masculinities.* Aldershot, England: Avebury.

Barn, R. 1993. *Black children in the public care system.* London: Batsford.

Barnes, M., R. Bowl, M. Fisher 1990. *Sectioned: social services and the 1983 Mental Health Act.* London: Routledge.

Barnes, M. & N. M. Maple 1992. *Women and mental health: challenging the stereotypes.* Birmingham, England: Venture Press.

Bateson, G. 1972. *Steps to an ecology of the mind.* New York: Ballantine.

Begum, N. 1992. Disabled women and the feminist agenda. *Feminist Review* **40**, 70–84.

Benedict, M. I., S. Zuravin, D. Brandt, H. Abbey 1994. Types and frequency of child maltreatment by family foster care providers in an urban population. *Child Abuse and Neglect* **18**, 577–85.

Benstead, J., A. Brown, C. Forbes, R. Wall 1994. Men working with men in groups: masculinity and crime. *Groupwork* **7**, 37–49.

Beresford, P. & S. Croft 1993. *Citizen involvement.* London: Macmillan.

Bernard, C. 1994. Social work with mothers whose children have been sexually abused. See Lupton & Gillespie (1994), 96–122.

Berridge, D. 1994. Foster and residential care reassessed: a research perspective. *Children and Society* **8**, 132–50.

Bhatti-Sinclair, K. 1994. Asian women and violence from male partners. See Lupton & Gillespie (1994), 75–95.

Blachford, G. 1981. Male dominance and the gay world. In *The making of the modern homosexual*, K. Plummer (ed.), 184–210. London: Hutchinson.

Bly, R. 1991. *Iron John: a book about men.* Shaftesbury, England: Element Books.

Bor, R. & J. Elford 1994. *The family and HIV.* London: Cassell.

Bogle, M. T. 1988. Brixton Black Women's Centre: organising on child sexual abuse. *Feminist Review* **28**, 132–35.

Bowl, R. 1985. *Changing the nature of masculinity – a task for social work?* Norwich, England: University of East Anglia.

Brake, M. & C. Hale 1992. *Public order and private lives: the politics of law and order.* London: Routledge.

Briere, J., K. Smiljanich, D. Henschel 1994. Sexual fantasies, gender, and molestation history. *Child Abuse and Neglect* **18**, 131–137.

Brod, H. 1987. A case for men's studies. In *Changing men: new directions on research on men and masculinities*, M. S. Kimmel (ed.), 263–77. Los Angeles: Sage.

— 1990. Pornography and the alienation of male sexuality. See Hearn & Morgan (1990), 124–39.

Brook, E. & A. Davis (eds) 1985. *Women, the family and social work.* London: Tavistock.

Brown, A. 1994. Hammersmith and Fulham play it safe 91/93 HIV service. *Working with Men* **1**, 10–11.

Brown, A. & B. Caddick (eds) 1993. *Groupwork with offenders.* London: Whiting & Birch.

Brown, H. & A. Craft 1989. *Thinking the unthinkable: papers on sexual abuse and people with learning difficulties.* London: FPA.

Brown, H. & V. Turk 1992. Defining sexual abuse as it affects adults with learning disabilities. *Mental Handicap* **20**, 44–55.

— 1994. Sexual abuse in adulthood: ongoing risks for people with learning disabilities. *Child Abuse Review* **3**, 26–35.

Brown, H. C. 1992. Lesbians, the state and social work practice. See Langan & Day (1992), 201–19.

Brownmiller, S. 1975. *Against our will: men, women and rape.* New York: Bantam Books.

Bryan, A. 1992. Working with black single mothers: myths and reality. See Langan & Day (1992), 169–85.

Burrell, G. & J. Hearn 1989. The sexuality of organisation. In *The sexuality of organisation*, J. Hearn, D. L. Sheppard, P. Tancred-Sheriff, G. Burrell (eds), 1–28. London: Sage.

Butler, S. & C. Wintram 1991. *Feminist groupwork.* London: Sage.

Campbell, A. 1993. *Out of control: men, women and aggression.* London: Pandora.

Campbell, A. & S. Muncer 1994. See Archer (1994), 332–51.

Campbell, B. 1993. *Goliath: Britain's dangerous places.* London: Methuen.

— 1994. Universal failure. *Community Care* (13 October), 24.

Canaan, J. E. & C. Griffin 1990. The new men's studies: part of the problem or part of the solution? See Hearn & Morgan (1990), 206–14.

Cannan, C. 1992. *Changing families changing welfare.* Hemel Hempstead, England: Harvester Wheatsheaf.

Carlen, P. & J. Wardhaugh 1991. Locking up our daughters. In *Social work and social welfare year book 3*, P. Carter, T. Jeffs, M. K. Smith (eds), 1–16. Milton Keynes, England: Open University Press.

Carrigan, T., R. Connell, J. Lee 1985. Towards a new sociology of masculinity. *Theory and Society* **14**, 551–603.

Carter, P. 1993. The problem of men: a reply to Keith Pringle, CSP issue 36. *Critical Social Policy* **38**, 100–5.

Carter, P., A. Everitt, A. Hudson 1992. Malestream training? Women, feminism and social work education. See Langan & Day (1992), 112–28.

Carter, P. & T. Jeffs 1992. The hidden curriculum: sexuality in professional education. See Carter, Jeffs, Smith (1992), 231–44.

Carter, P., T. Jeffs, M. K. Smith (eds) 1992. *Changing social work and welfare.* MIlton Keynes, England: Open University Press.

Cashman, H. 1993. *Christianity and child sexual abuse.* London: SPCK.

Cashmore, E. & E. McLaughlin 1991. Out of order? See Cashmore & McLaughlin (1991), 10–41.

— (eds) 1991. *Out of order? Policing black people.* London: Routledge.

Cecchin, G. 1987. Hypothesizing, circularity and neutrality revisited: an invitation to curiosity. *Family Process* **26**, 404–14.

Chandler, T. 1993. Working with fathers in a family centre. *Working with Men*, 4, 11–13.

Channer, Y. & N. Parton 1990. Racism, cultural relativism and child protection. See Violence Against Children Study Group (1990), 105–20.

Chigwada, R. 1991. The policing of black women. See Cashmore & McLaughlin (1991), 134–50.

Chodorow, N. 1978. *The reproduction of mothering: psychoanalysis and the sociology of gender*. London: University of California.

Christian, H. 1994. *The making of anti-sexist men*. London: Routledge.

Clarke, J. (ed.) 1993. *A crisis in care? Challenges to social work*. London: Sage.

Clatterbaugh, K. 1990. *Contemporary perspectives on masculinity: men, women, and politics in modern society*. Boulder, CA: Westview Press.

Cochrane, A. 1993a. Challenges from the centre. See Clarke (1993), 69–103.

— 1993b. The problem of poverty. See Dallos & McLaughlin (1993), 189–226.

Cohen, P. 1993. Conviction not comfort. *Community Care* (16 September), 14–15.

Connell, R. W. 1987. *Gender and power: society, the person and sexual politics*. Cambridge: Polity.

— 1995. *Masculinities*. Cambridge: Polity.

Cornwall, A. 1994. Gendered identities and gender ambiguities among travestis in Salvador, Brazil. See Cornwall & Lindisfarne (1994), 111–32.

Cornwall, A. & N. Lindisfarne 1994. Introduction. See Cornwall & Lindisfarne (1994), 1–10.

— (eds) 1994. *Dislocating masculinity: comparative ethnographies*. London: Routledge.

Coulshed, V. 1991. *Social work practice: an introduction*. London: Macmillan.

Cowburn, M. 1993. Groupwork programme for male sex offenders: establishing principles for practice. In *Groupwork with offenders*, A. Brown & B. Caddick (eds), 218–30. London: Whiting & Birch.

Cox, P. 1993. Professional survival – a double jeopardy: some implications for training, education and practice. See Ferguson, Gilligan, Torode (1993), 134–40.

Dallos, R. & Boswell, D. 1993. Mental Health. See Dallos & McLaughlin (1993), 83–92.

Dallos, R. & E. Mclaughlin (eds) 1993. *Social problems and the family*. London: Sage.

Darton, K., J. Gorman, L. Sayce 1994. *Eve fights back: the success of MIND's stress on women campaign*. London: MIND.

Davis, A., S. Llewelyn, G. Parry 1985. Women and mental health: towards an understanding. See Brook & Davis (1985), 70–91.

Davis, E., L. Kidd, K. Pringle 1987. *Child sexual abuse training programme for foster parents with teenage placements*. Newcastle upon Tyne, England: Barnardos.

De'Ath, E. 1989. Families and children. In *Child care research, policy and practice*, B. Kahan (ed.), 30–54. London: Hodder & Stoughton.

Dell, P. F. 1989. Violence and the systemic view: the problem of power. *Family Process* **28**, 1–14.

Dennis, N. 1993. *Rising crime and the dismembered family*. London: Institute for Economic Affairs.

Dennis, N. & G. Erdos 1992. *Families without fatherhood*. London: Institute for Economic Affairs.

de Shazer, S. 1991. *Putting difference to work*. New York: Norton.

Dingwall, R. 1989. Some problems about predicting child abuse and neglect. In *Child abuse: professional practice and public policy*, O. Stevenson (ed.), 28–53. Hemel Hempstead, England: Harvester Wheatsheaf.

Dobash, R. E. & R. P. Dobash 1984. The nature and antecedents of violent events. *The British Journal of Criminology* **24**, 269–88.

— 1992. *Women, violence and social change*. London: Routledge.

Dominelli, L. 1988. *Anti-racist social work*. London: Macmillan.

— 1991. *Gender, sex offenders and probation practice*. Norwich, England: Novata Press.

Dominelli, L. & E. McLeod 1989. *Feminist social work*. London: Macmillan.

Driver, E. & A. Droisen (eds) 1989. *Child sexual abuse: feminist perspectives*. London: Macmillan.

Edwards, T. 1990. Beyond sex and gender: masculinity, homosexuality and social theory. See Hearn & Morgan (1990), 110–23.

— 1994. *Erotics and politics: gay male sexuality, masculinity and feminism*. London: Routledge.

Eichenbaum, L. & S. Orbach 1982. *Outside in, inside out*. London: Penguin.

Eley, R. 1989. Women in management in social services departments. In *Women and social services departments*, C. Hallett (ed.), 155–87. Hemel Hempstead, England: Harvester Wheatsheaf.

Elliott, M. (ed.) 1993. *Female sexual abuse of children: the ultimate taboo*. Harlow, England: Longman.

Ennew, J. 1986. *The sexual exploitation of children*. Cambridge: Polity.

Entwistle, P. 1993. Counselling in male infertility. *Working with Men* **3**, 8–11.

Erooga, M. 1994. Where the professional meets the personal. See Morrison, Erooga, Beckett (1994), 203–20.

Fagan, J. A., D. K. Stewart, K. V. Hansen 1983. Violent men or violent husbands? Background factors and situational correlates. In *The dark side of families*, D. Finkelhor, R. J. Gelles, G. T. Hotaling, M. A. Straus (eds), 49–67. Los Angeles and London: Sage.

Fanshel, D. 1990. *Foster children in life course perspective*. New York: Columbia University Press.

Farrell, W. 1994. *The myth of male power*. London: Fourth Estate.

Ferguson, H. 1990. Rethinking child protection practices: a case for history. See Violence Against Children Study Group (1990), 121–42.

— 1992. Cleveland in history: the abused child and child protection, 1880–1914. In *In the name of the child: health and welfare, 1880–1940*, R. Cooter (ed.), 146–73. London: Routledge.

Ferguson, H., R. Gilligan, R. Torode (eds) 1993. *Surviving childhood adversity*. Dublin: Social Studies Press.

Fernando, S. 1989. *Race and culture in psychiatry*. London: Croom Helm.

Finch, J. 1990. The politics of community care in Britain. In *Gender and caring:*

work and welfare in Britain and Scandinavia, C. Ungerson (ed.), 34–58. Hemel Hempstead, England: Harvester Wheatsheaf.

Finch, J. & D. Groves 1985. Old girl, old boy: gender divisions in social work with the elderly. See Brook & Davis (1985), 92–111.

Finkelhor, D. (ed.) 1984. *Child sexual abuse: new theory and research.* Los Angeles: Sage.

— 1991. The scope of the problem. In *Intervening in child sexual abuse*, K. Murray & D.A. Gough (eds), 9–17. Edinburgh: Scottish Academic Press.

— 1992. What do we know about child sexual abuse? Issues for policy and research. Paper presented at "Surviving Childhood Adversity" conference, Trinity College, Dublin, Republic of Ireland.

Finkelhor, D., S. Araji, L. Baron, A. Browne, S. D. Peters, G. E. Wyatt 1986. *A sourcebook on child sexual abuse.* Los Angeles: Sage.

Finkelhor, D., G. Hotaling, I. A. Lewis, C. Smith 1990. Sexual abuse in a national survey of adult men and women: prevalence, characteristics and risk factors. *Child Abuse and Neglect* 14, 19–28.

Finkelhor, D., L. M. Williams, N. Burns 1988. *Nursery crimes: sexual abuse in day care.* Los Angeles: Sage.

Fisher, D. 1994. Adult sex offenders: who are they? Why and how do they do it? See Morrison, Erooga, Beckett (1994), 1–24.

Foley, M. 1994. Professionalising the response to rape. See Lupton & Gillespie (1994), 39–54.

Foley, R. 1993. Zero Tolerance. *Trouble and Strife* 27, 16–20.

Fook, J. 1993. *Radical casework: a theory of practice.* Sydney: Allen & Unwin.

Foreman, S. & R. Dallos 1993. Domestic violence. See Dallos & McLaughlin (1993), 7–46.

Frenken, J. & B. Van Stolk 1990. Incest victims: inadequate help by professionals. *Child Abuse and Neglect,* 14, 253–63.

Frosh, S. 1988. No man's land?: the role of men working with sexually abused children. *British Journal of Guidance and Counselling* 16, 1–10.

Frost, N. & M. Stein 1989. *The politics of child welfare.* Hemel Hempstead, England: Harvester Wheatsheaf.

Furniss, T. 1991. *The multi-professional handbook of child sexual abuse: integrated management, therapy and legal intervention.* London: Routledge.

Gelles, R. J. 1994. Through a sociological lens: social structure and family violence. See Gelles & Loseke (1994), 31–46.

Gelles, R. J. & D. R. Loseke 1994. *Current controversies on family violence.* Los Angeles: Sage.

Gelsthorpe, L. 1990. Feminist methodologies in criminology: a new approach or old wine in new bottles? See Gelsthorpe & Morris (1990), 89–106.

Gelsthorpe, L. & A. Morris (eds) 1990. *Feminist perspectives in criminology.* Milton Keynes, England: Open University Press.

Gergen, K. J. & J. Kaye 1992. Beyond narrative in the negotiation of therapeutic meaning. See McNamee & Gergen (1992), 166–86.

Gilbert, N. 1994. Examining the facts: advocacy research overstates the incidence of date and acquaintance rape. See Gelles & Loseke (1994), 120–32.

Gilbert, P. 1994. Male violence: towards an integration. See Archer (1994), 352–89.

Gillespie, T. 1994. Under pressure: rape crisis centres, multi-agency work and strategies for survival. See Lupton & Gillespie (1994), 15–38.

Gilroy, P. 1987. *There ain't no black in the Union Jack*. London: Hutchinson.

— 1992. The end of anti-racism. In *"Race", culture & difference*, J. Donald & A. Rattansi (eds), 49–61. London: Sage.

Glaser, D. & S. Frosh 1993. *Child sexual abuse*, 2nd edn. London: Macmillan.

Glasgow, D., L. Horne, R. Calam, A. Cox 1994. Evidence, incidence, gender and age in sexual abuse of children: towards a developmental analysis of child sexual abuse. *Child Abuse Review* **3**, 196–210.

Glasgow Women's Support Project/*Glasgow Evening Times* 1990. *Violence against women survey*. Glasgow Women's Support Project.

Goldner, V. 1985. Feminism and family therapy. *Family Process* **24**, 31–47.

Golombok, S., A. Spencer, M. Rutter 1983. Children in lesbian and single parent households: psychosexual and psychiatric appraisal. *Journal of Child Psychology and psychiatry* **24**, 551–72.

Gough, J. 1989. Theories of sexual identity and the masculinization of gay men. In *Coming on strong: gay politics and culture*, S. Shepherd & M. Wallis (eds), 119–36. London: Unwin Hyman.

Gough, J. & M. Macnair 1985. *Gay liberation in the eighties*. London: Pluto.

Graham, H. 1983. Caring: a labour of love. In *A labour of love: women, work and caring*, J. Finch & D. Groves (eds), 13–30. London: Routledge & Kegan Paul.

— 1993a. Caring for children in poverty. See Ferguson, Gilligan, Torode (1993), 65–75.

— 1993b. Social divisions in caring. *Women's Studies International Forum* **16**, 461–70.

Gray, S., M. Higgs, K. Pringle 1995. Services for people who have been sexually abused. In *Researching women's health: methods and process*, L. Mckie (ed.). London: Mark Allen Publishing.

Green, G. 1994. Social support and HIV. See Bor & Elford (1994), 79–97.

Green, R. 1986. Lesbian mothers and their children: a comparison with solo parent heterosexual mothers and their children. *Archives of Sexual Behaviour* **15**(12), 168–84.

Gregory, J. & S. Lees 1994. In search of gender justice: sexual assault and the criminal justice system. *Feminist Review* **48**, 80–93.

Grimwood, C. & R. Popplestone 1993. *Women, management and care*. London: Macmillan.

Haley, J. 1976. *Problem-solving therapy*. New York: Harper Colophon.

— 1986. *Uncommon therapy: the psychiatric techniques of Milton H. Erickson, M.D.*, 2nd edn. New York: Norton.

Hallett, C. 1989. The gendered world of the social services department. In *Women and social services departments*, C. Hallett (ed.), 1–43. Hemel Hempstead, England: Harvester Wheatsheaf.

Hanks, H. & J. Saradjian 1991. Women who abuse children sexually: characteristics of sexual abuse of children by women. *Human Systems: the Journal of Systemic Consultation and Management* **2**, 247–62.

Hanmer, J. 1990. Men, power and the exploitation of women. See Hearn & Morgan (1990), 21–42.

Hanmer, J. & M. Maynard (eds) 1987. *Women, violence and social control.* London: Macmillan.

Hanmer, J. & D. Statham 1988. *Women and social work: towards a woman-centred practice.* London: Macmillan.

Harlow, E., J. Hearn, W. Parkin 1992. Sexuality and social work organisations. See Carter, Jeffs, Smith (1992), 131–43.

Harris, T. 1993. Surviving childhood adversity: what can we learn from naturalistic studies? See Ferguson, Gilligan, Torode (1993), 93–107.

Hart, G., R. Fitzpatrick, J. McLean, J. Dawson, M. Boulton 1994. Gay men, social support and HIV disease: a study of social integration in the gay community. See Bor & Elford (1994), 110–17.

Hazlehurst, M. 1993. Breaking in . . . breaking out. *Working with Men* **2**, 14–15.
— 1994. Men in social work. *Working with Men* **1**, 6.

Hearn, J. 1982. Notes on patriarchy, professionalization, and the semi-professions. *Sociology* **16**, 184–202.
— 1987. *The gender of oppression. Men, masculinity and the critique of Marxism.* Brighton, England: Wheatsheaf.
— 1990. "Child abuse" and men's violence. See Violence Against Children Study Group (1990), 63–85.
— 1992. The personal, the political, the theoretical: the case of men's sexualities and sexual violences. In *Between men and feminism*, D. Porter (ed.), 161–81. London: Routledge.

Hearn, J. & D. Collinson 1994. Theorizing unities and differences between men and between masculinities. In *Theorizing masculinities*, H. Brod & M. Kaufman (eds), 97–118. Los Angeles: Sage.

Hearn, J. & D. Morgan (eds) 1990. *Men, masculinities and social theory.* London: Unwin Hyman.

Hearn, J. & W. Parkin 1987. *"Sex" at "work": the power and paradox of organisation sexuality.* Brighton, England: Wheatsheaf.

Hekman, S. J. 1990. *Gender and knowledge: elements of a postmodern feminism.* Cambridge, England: Polity.

Helm, M., K. Pringle, R. Taylor (eds) 1993. *Surviving sexual abuse.* Barkingside, England: Barnardos.

Henderson, J. 1993. Surviving. Unpublished paper, MIND.
— 1994. Reflecting oppression: symmetrical experiences of social work students and service users. *Social Work Education* **13**, 16–25.

Hennessy, E., S. Martin, P. Moss, E. Melhuish 1992. *Children and day care: lessons from research.* London: Paul Chapman Publishing.

Herek, G. M. 1987. On heterosexual masculinity: some psychical consequences of the social construction of gender and sexuality. In *Changing men:*

new directions in research on men and masculinity, M. S. Kimmel (ed.), 68–82. Los Angeles: Sage.

HMSO 1988a. *Report of the inquiry into child abuse in Cleveland 1987*. London: HMSO.

— 1988b. *Protecting children: a guide for social workers undertaking a comprehensive assessment*. London: HMSO.

— 1989a. *Caring for people. Community Care in the next decade*. London: HMSO.

— 1989b. *Children Act 1989*. London: HMSO.

— 1989c. *Working together under the Children Act 1989: a guide to arrangements for inter-agency co-operation for the protection of children from abuse*. London: HMSO.

— 1992. *Choosing with care: the report of the committee of inquiry into the selection, development, and management of staff in children's homes*. London: HMSO.

— 1993. *Adoption: the future*. London: HMSO.

Hoffman, L. 1992. A reflexive stance for family therapy. See McNamee & Gergen (1992), 7–24.

Holt, C. 1992. *Developing effective work with men within family centres*. Mimeograph. Barnardos, in press.

Holt, M. 1993. Elder sexual abuse in Britain: preliminary findings. *Journal of Elder Abuse and Neglect* **5**, 63–71.

— 1994. Personal communication.

Home Office 1992. *Memorandum of good practice on video recorded interviews with child witnesses for criminal proceedings*. London: HMSO.

hooks, b. 1992. Men in feminist struggle – the necessary movement. In *Women respond to the men's movement: a feminist collection*, K. L. Hagan (ed.), 111–18. San Francisco, CA: Pandora.

Hooper, C. 1992. *Mothers surviving child sexual abuse*. London: Routledge.

— 1994. Do families need fathers? The impact of divorce on children. See Mullender & Morley (1994), 86–101.

Hudson, A. 1992. The child sexual abuse industry and gender relations in social work. See Langan & Day (1992), 129–48.

Hudson, A., L. Ayensu, C. Oadley, M. Patocchi 1994. Practising feminist approaches. In *Practising social work*, C. Hanvey & T. Philpot (eds), 93–105. London: Routledge

Hughes, B. & M. Mtezuka 1992. Social work and older women: where have older women gone? See Langan & Day (1992), 220–41.

Hugman, R. 1991. *Power in the caring professions*. London: Macmillan.

Humphries, M. 1992. A gay man's reflections on the men's movement. In *Between men and feminism*, D. Porter (ed.), 140–60. London: Routledge.

Hunt, P. 1994. *Report of the independent inquiry into multiple abuse in nursery classes in Newcastle upon Tyne*. Newcastle upon Tyne: City Council of Newcastle upon Tyne.

Ivory, M. 1993. Opposing video views. *Community Care* (2 September), 6.

Jefferson, T. 1991. Discrimination, disadvantage and police work. See Cashmore & McLaughlin (1991), 166–88.

Jeffreys, S. 1990. *Anticlimax: a feminist perspective on the sexual revolution.* London: The Women's Press.

Jones, G. 1989. Women in social care: the invisible army. In *Women and social services departments,* C. Hallett (ed.), 132–54. Hemel Hempstead, England: Harvester Wheatsheaf.

Jones, L., K. Pringle, M. A. Zaccheo 1988. Can young people change the care system? *Social Work Today* **19**(51), 14–15.

Kelly, L. 1987. The continuum of sexual violence. See Hanmer & Maynard (1987), 46–60.

— 1988. *Surviving sexual violence.* Cambridge: Polity.

— 1991. Unspeakable acts: women who abuse. *Trouble and Strife* **21**, 13–20.

— 1992. The connections between disability and child abuse: a review of the research evidence. *Child Abuse Review* **1**, 157–67.

— 1993. Talking about a revolution. See Clarke (1993), 131–6.

Kelly, L., L. Regan, S. Burton 1991. *An exploratory study of the prevalence of sexual abuse in a sample of 16–21 year olds.* London: Polytechnic of North London.

Kennedy, M., & L. Kelly (eds) 1992. Special issue on abuse and children with disabilities. *Child Abuse Review* **1**(3).

Kidd, L. & Pringle, K. 1988. The politics of child sexual abuse. *Social Work Today* **20**(3), 14–15.

Kimmel, M. S. 1994. Masculinity as homophobia: fear, shame, and silence in the construction of gender identity. In *Theorizing Masculinities,* H. Brod & M. Kaufman (eds), 119–41. Los Angeles: Sage.

Kirkwood, C. 1993. *Leaving abusive partners: from the scars of survival to the wisdom for change.* London: Sage.

Kirwan, M. 1994. Gender and social work: will Dip.S.W. make a difference? *British Journal of Social Work* **24**, 137–55.

Koss, M. P. & S. L. Cook 1994. Facing the facts: date and acquaintance rape are significant problems for women. See Gelles & Loseke (1994), 104–19.

Kurz, D. 1994. Physical assaults by husbands: a major social problem. See Gelles & Loseke (1994), 88–104.

La Fontaine, J. 1990. *Child sexual abuse.* Cambridge: Polity.

Landau, H. & G. Nathan 1983. Discrimination in the criminal justice system. *British Journal of Criminology* **23**, 128–49.

Langan, M. 1992. Who cares? Women in the mixed economy of care. See Langan & Day (1992), 67–91.

— 1993a. New directions in social work. See Clarke (1993), 149–63.

— 1993b. The rise and fall of social work. See Clarke (1993), 47–68.

Langan, M. & L. Day (eds) 1992. *Women, oppression and social work: issues in anti-discriminatory practice.* London: Routledge.

Langan, M. & P. Lee (eds) 1989. *Radical social work today.* London: Unwin Hyman.

Laws, S. 1994. Un-valued families. *Trouble and Strife* **28**, 5–11.

Lax, W. D. 1992. Postmodern thinking in a clinical practice. See McNamee &

Gergen (1992), 69–85.

Lees, J. & T. Lloyd 1994. *Working with men who batter their partners: an introductory text.* London: Working with Men/The B Team.

Levinson, D. 1989. *Family violence in cross-cultural perspective.* Los Angeles: Sage.

Liddle, A. M. 1993. Gender, desire and child sexual abuse: accounting for the male majority. *Theory, Culture and Society* **10**, 103–26.

Littlewood, R. & M. Lipsedge 1989. *Aliens and alienists: ethnic minorities and psychiatry.* London: Unwin Hyman.

Lupton, C. 1992. Feminism, managerialism and performance measurement. See Langan & Day (1992), 92–111.

— 1994. The British refuge movement: the survival of an ideal. See Lupton & Gillespie (1994), 55–74.

Lupton, C. & T. Gillespie (eds) 1994. *Working with violence.* London: Macmillan.

McBeath, G. B. & S. A. Webb 1990–1. Child protection language as professional ideology in social work. *Social Work and Social Services Review* **2**, 122–45.

McCann, K. & E. Wadsworth 1994. The role of informal carers in supporting gay men who have HIV-related illness: what do they do and what are their needs? See Bor & Elford (1994), 118–28.

McCollum, H., L. Kelly, J. Radford 1994. Wars against women. *Trouble and Strife* **28**, 12–18.

McFadden, E. J. 1984. *Preventing abuse in foster care.* Michigan: Eastern Michigan University.

McFadden, E. J. & P. Ryan 1991. Maltreatment in family foster homes: dynamics and dimensions. *Child and Youth Services* **15**, 209–31.

MacKinnon, L. K. & D. Miller 1987. The new epistemology and the Milan approach: feminist and sociopolitical considerations. *Journal of Marital and Family Therapy* **13**, 139–55.

MacLeod, M. & E. Saraga 1988. Challenging the orthodoxy: towards a feminist theory and practice. *Feminist Review* **28**, 16–55.

— 1991. Clearing a path through the undergrowth: a feminist reading of recent literature on child sexual abuse. In *Social work and social welfare yearbook 3*, P. Carter, T. Jeffs, M. K. Smith (eds), 30–45. Milton Keynes, England: Open University Press.

McMullen, R. J. U. 1990. *Male rape.* London: Gay Men's Press.

McNamee, S. & K. J. Gergen (eds) 1992. *Therapy as social construction.* London: Sage.

McNay, M. 1992. Social work and power relations: towards a framework for an integrated practice. See Langan & Day (1992), 48–66.

Maiuro, R. D., T. S. Cohn, P. P. Vitaliano, B. C. Wanger, J. B. Zegree 1988. Anger, hostility and depression in domestically violent versus generally assaultive men and nonviolent control subjects. *Journal of Consulting and Clinical Psychology* **56**, 17–23.

Margolin, L. 1991. Child sexual abuse by non-related caregivers. *Child Abuse and Neglect* **15**, 213–21.

— 1993. In their parent's absence: sexual abuse in child care. *Violence Update* (May), 1–8.

Mason, B. & E. Mason 1990. Masculinity and family work. See Perelberg & Miller (1990), 209–17.

Matthews, J. K. 1993. Working with female sexual abusers. See Elliott (1993), 61–78.

Matthews, J. K., R. Mathews, K. Speltz 1991. Female sexual offenders: a typology. In *Family sexual abuse: frontline research and evaluation*, M. Q. Patton (ed.), 119–219. Los Angeles: Sage.

May, C. 1992. Individual care? Power and subjectivity in therapeutic relationships. *Sociology* **26**, 589–602.

Mearns, D. & B. Thorne 1988. *Person-centred counselling in action*. London: Sage.

Metcalfe, A. & M. Humphries (eds) 1985. *The sexuality of men*. London: Pluto.

Middleton, P. 1992. *The inward gaze*. London: Routledge.

Millar, J. 1994. State, family and personal responsibility: the changing balance for lone mothers in the United Kingdom. *Feminist Review* **48**, 24–39.

Milner, J. 1993. Avoiding violent men: the gendered nature of child protection policy and practice. See Ferguson, Gilligan, Torode (1993), 179–90.

Minuchin, S. 1974. *Families and family therapy*. London: Tavistock.

Mooney, J. 1993. *The hidden figure: domestic violence in North London*. Centre for Criminology, Middlesex University.

Morgan, D. 1987. Masculinity and violence. See Hanmer & Maynard (1987), 180–92.

— 1992. *Discovering men*. London: Routledge.

Morris, J. 1991. *Pride against prejudice: transforming attitudes to disability*. London: The Women's Press.

— 1993. Gender and disability. See Swain, Finkelstein, French, Oliver (1993), 85–93.

Morrison, T., M. Erooga, R.C. Beckett (eds) 1994. *Sexual offending against children: assessment and treatment of male abusers*. London: Routledge.

Mullender, A. & R. Morley (eds) 1994. *Children living with domestic violence: putting men's abuse of women on the child care agenda*. London: Whiting & Birch.

Mullender, A. & D. Ward 1991. *Self-directed groupwork: users take action for empowerment*. London: Whiting & Birch.

Murphy K. 1993. Groupwork on men and offending. *Working with Men* **1**, 7–11.

Murray, C. 1990. *The emerging British underclass*. London: Institute for Economic Affairs.

National Association of Young People In Care (NAYPIC) 1990. *Abuse in the care system*. London: NAYPIC.

Nicholson, L. (ed.) 1990. *Feminism/postmodernism*. London: Routledge.

Nunno, M. & N. Reindfleisch, 1991. The abuse of children in out of home care. *Children and Society* **5**, 295–305.

O'Brien, M. 1990. The place of men in a gender-sensitive therapy. See Perelberg & Miller (1990), 195–209.

O'Callaghan, D. & B. Print 1994. See Morrison, Erooga, Beckett (1994), 178–202.

O'Hara, M. 1993. Child protection in the context of domestic violence. See Ferguson, Gilligan, Torode (1993), 126–33.

O'Neill, S. 1990. *Men and social work: is there an anti-sexist practice?* Masters degree in social work thesis, University of Sussex.

Ogg, J. & Munn-Giddings 1993. Researching elder abuse. *Ageing and Society* **13**, 389–413.

Oliver, M. 1990. *The politics of disablement.* London: Macmillan.

Oliver, M. & C. Barnes 1993. Discrimination, disability, and welfare: from needs to rights. See Swain, Finkelstein, French, Oliver (1993), 267–77.

Orme, J. 1994. Violent women. See Lupton & Gillespie (1994), 170–89.

Orme, J. & B. Glastonbury 1993. *Care management: tasks and workloads.* London: Macmillan.

Pahl, J. 1985. Part I: violent husbands and abused wives: a longitudinal study. In *Private violence and public policy: the needs of battered women and the response of the public services*, J. Pahl (ed.), 23–94. London: Routledge & Kegan Paul.

Palazzoli, M. S., G. Cecchin, G. Prata, L. Boscolo 1978. *Paradox and counter-paradox.* New York: Jason Aronson.

Papp, P. 1983. *The process of change.* New York: Guildford Press.

Parker, G. 1990. *With due care and attention: a review of the literature on informal care*, 2nd edn. London: Family Policy Studies Centre.

— 1993. A four-way stretch? The politics of disability and caring. See Swain, Finkelstein, French, Oliver (1993), 249–56.

Parkin, W. 1989. Private experiences in the public domain: sexuality and residential care organizations. In *The sexuality of organization*, J. Hearn, D. L. Sheppard, P. Tancred-Sheriff, G. Burrell (eds), 110–25. London: Sage.

Parton, C. 1990. Women, gender. oppression and child abuse. See Violence Against Children Study Group (1990), 41–62.

Parton, C. & N. Parton 1989. Child protection, the law and dangerousness. In *Child abuse: public policy and professional practice*, O. Stevenson (ed.), 54–73. Hemel Hempstead, England: Harvester Wheatsheaf.

Parton, N. 1985. *The politics of child abuse.* London: Macmillan.

— 1990. Taking child abuse seriously. See Violence Against Children Study Group (1990), 7–24.

— 1991. *Governing the family: child care, child protection and the state.* London: Macmillan.

Patterson, C. J. 1992. Children of lesbian and gay parents. *Child Development* **63**, 1025–42.

Penhale, B. 1993. The abuse of elderly people: considerations for practice.

British Journal of Social Work **23**, 95–111.

Perelberg, R. J. & A. C. Miller (eds) 1990. *Gender and power in families.* London: Routledge.

Perrott, S. 1994. Working with men who abuse women and children. See Lupton & Gillespie (1994), 135–52.

Peterson, R. F., S. M. Basta, T. A. Dykstra 1993. Mothers of molested children: some comparisons of personality characteristics. *Child Abuse and Neglect* **17**, 409–18.

Petruchenia, J. & R. Thorpe (eds), 1990. *Social change and social welfare practice.* Sydney, Australia: Hale & Iremonger.

Phillips, A. 1993. *The trouble with boys: parenting the men of the future.* London: Pandora.

Pillemer, K. 1994. The abused offspring are dependent: abuse is caused by the deviance and dependence of abusive caregivers. See Gelles & Loseke (1994), 237–50.

Pitts, J. 1990. *Working with young offenders.* London: Macmillan.

Plummer, K. 1981. *The making of the modern homosexual.* London: Hutchinson.

Pollard, P. 1994. Sexual violence against women: characteristics of typical perpetrators. See Archer (1994), 170–94.

Popplestone, R. 1980. Top jobs for women: are the cards stacked against them? *Social Work Today* **12**(4), 12–15.

Price, P. 1994. Personal communication.

Pringle, K. 1990. *Managing to survive.* Barkingside: Barnardos.

— 1991. A new, clear family? *Social Work Today* **22**(42), 20.

— 1992. Child sexual abuse perpetrated by welfare personnel and the problem of men. *Critical Social Policy* **36**, 4–19.

— 1993a. Gender issues in child sexual abuse committed by foster carers: a case study for the welfare services? See Ferguson, Gilligan, Torode (1993), 245–56.

— 1993b. Child sexual abuse committed by welfare personnel: British and European perspectives. Paper presented at Fourth European Conference on Child Abuse and Neglect, Padova, Italy.

— 1993c. Feminist perspectives on the way forward. See Helm, Pringle, Taylor (1993), 85–91.

— 1993d. Danger! Men at (social) work: the role of the male social worker in cases of sexual abuse. See Helm, Pringle, Taylor (1993), 22–6.

— 1994a. Is there a future for men in families? Paper presented at Zero Tolerance Debate, City Chambers, Edinburgh, Scotland. Zero Tolerance Trust, in press.

— 1994b. Review of Barker's *Lone fathers and masculinities. Youth and Policy* **46**, 75–8.

— 1994c. The problem of men revisited. *Working with Men* **2**, 5–8.

Public Eye 1992. *Sex in the forbidden zone.* London: Diverse Productions for British Broadcasting Corporation.

Ramazanoglu, C. 1987. Sex and violence in academic life or you can keep a good woman down. See Hanmer & Maynard (1987), 61–74.

— (ed.) 1993. *Up against Foucault: explorations of some tensions between Foucault and feminism.* London: Routledge.

Ramazanoglu, C. & J. Holland 1993. Women's sexuality and men's appropriation of desire. See Ramazanoglu (1993), 239–64.

Raynor, P., D. Smith, M. Vanstone 1994. *Effective probation practice.* London: Macmillan.

Rhead, A. 1994. The Crown vs the child. *Community Care* (11 August), 16.

Rice, M. 1990. Challenging orthodoxies in feminist theory: a black feminist critique. See Gelsthorpe & Morris (1990), 57–69.

Rickford, F. 1992. Fostering with pride. *Social Work Today* **28** (May), 12–13.

Roberts, H. (ed.) 1981. *Doing feminist research.* London: Routledge & Kegan Paul.

Rojek, C., G. Peacock, S. Collins, 1988. *Social work and received ideas.* London: Routledge.

Rosenthal, J. A., J. K. Motz, D. A. Edmonson, V. Groze 1991. A descriptive study of abuse and neglect in out-of-home placement. *Child Abuse and Neglect* **15**, 249–60.

Rouf, K. 1990. My self in echoes. My voice in song. In *Listening to children: the professional response to hearing the abused child*, A. Bannister, K. Barrett, E. Shearer (eds), 1–18. Harlow, England: Longman.

Russell, J. 1993. *Out of bounds: sexual exploitation in counselling and therapy.* London: Sage.

Rutter, P. 1990. *Sex in the forbidden zone.* London: Unwin Hyman.

Ruxton, S. 1991. *"What's he doing at the family centre?": the dilemmas of men who care for children.* MA dissertation, Polytechnic of North London.

— 1994. Men – too dangerous to work with children? *Working with Men* **1**, 16–20.

Ryan, G. & S. Lane (eds) 1991. *Juvenile sexual offending – causes, consequences and corrections.* Lexington, MA: Lexington Books.

Ryan, P., E. J. McFadden, P. Wienceck 1988. Case work services in preventing abuse in family foster care. Paper presented at National Symposium on Child Victimization, Anaheim, CA, United States.

Salond, I. 1994. The Zero Tolerance Campaign. *Working with Men* **1**, 8–9.

Salter, A. C. 1988. *Treatment of sexual offenders and their victims.* Los Angeles: Sage

Sands, R. S. & K. Nuccio 1992. Postmodern feminist theory and social work. *Social Work* **37**, 489–94.

Saraga, E. 1993. The abuse of children. See Dallos & McLaughlin (1993), 47–82.

Satir, V. 1964. *Conjoint family therapy.* Palo Alto, CA: Science and Behaviour Books.

Saunders, D. G. 1994. Child custody decisions in families experiencing woman abuse. *Social Work* **39**, 51–9.

Sawicki, J. 1991. *Disciplining Foucault: feminism, power and the body.* New York: Routledge, Chapman & Hall.

Scott, S. M. 1993. The time for revelations has passed. See Helm, Pringle, Taylor (1993), 20–1.

Scraton, P. 1990. Scientific knowledge or masculine discourses? Challenging patriarchy in criminology. See Gelsthorpe & Morris (1990), 10–25.

Segal, L. 1990. *Slow motion: changing masculinities, changing men.* London: Virago Press.

Seidler, V. J. 1991. *Recreating sexual politics: men, feminism and politics.* London: Routledge.

— 1994. *Unreasonable men: masculinity and social theory.* London: Routledge.

Shepherd, S. & M. Wallis (eds) 1989. *Coming on strong: gay politics and culture.* London: Unwin Hyman.

Shotter, J. 1993. *Conversational realities: constructing life through language.* London: Sage.

Smart, D. 1993. A chance for gay people. See Clarke (1993), 107–9.

Smith, G. 1994. Parent, partner, protector: conflicting role demands for mothers of sexually abused children. See Morrison, Erooga, Beckett (1994), 178–202.

Sobsey, D. 1994. Sexual abuse of individuals with intellectual disability. In *Practice issues in sexuality and learning disabilities*, A. Craft (ed.), 93–115. London: Routledge.

Spender, D. 1985. *Man made language*, 2nd edn. London: Routledge & Kegan Paul.

Stafford-Clark, D. & A. C. Smith 1978. *Psychiatry for students*, 5th edn. London: Allen & Unwin.

Stanko, E. 1987. Typical violence, normal precautions: men, women and interpersonal violence in England, Wales, Scotland and the USA. See Hanmer & Maynard (1987), 122–34.

— 1990. *Everyday violence: how women and men experience sexual and physical danger.* London: Pandora.

Stanley, L. (ed.) 1990. *Feminist praxis: theory and epistemology in feminist sociology.* London: Routledge.

Stanley, L. & S. Wise 1983. *Breaking out: feminist consciousness and feminist research.* London: Routledge & Kegan Paul.

Steier, F. (ed.) 1991. *Research and reflexivity.* London: Sage.

Stein, M. 1993. The abuses and uses of residential child care. See Ferguson, Gilligan, Torode (1993), 234–44.

Steinmetz, S. K. 1977–8. The battered husband syndrome. *Victimology* 2(3/4), 499–509.

— 1994. The abused elderly are dependent: abuse is caused by the perception of stress associated with providing care. See Gelles & Loseke (1994), 222–36.

Straus, M. A. 1994. Physical assaults by wives: a major problem. See Gelles & Loseke (1994), 67–87.

Swain, J., V. Finkelstein, S. French, M. Oliver (eds) 1993. *Disabling barriers – enabling environments.* London: Sage.

Swigonski, M. E. 1994. The logic of feminist standpoint theory for social work research. *Social Work* **39**, 387–93.

Taylor, C. 1994. Is gender inequality in social work management relevant to social work students? *British Journal of Social Work* **24**, 157–72.

Taylor, G. 1993. Challenges from the margins. See Clarke (1993), 105–49.

Thomas, C. 1993. De-constructing concepts of care. *Sociology* **27**, 649–69.

Thompson, N. 1993. *Anti-discriminatory practice*. London: Macmillan.

Thorpe, D. 1994. *Evaluating child protection*. Milton Keynes, England: Open University Press.

Tift, L. 1993. *Battering of women: the failure of intervention and the case for prevention*. Boulder, CO: Westview Press.

Tong, R. 1989. *Feminist thought: a comprehensive introduction*. London: Routledge.

Turnbull, J. 1994. Personal communication.

Ungerson, C. 1987. *Policy is personal: sex, gender and informal care*. London: Tavistock.

— 1990. The language of care: crossing the boundaries. In *Gender and caring: work and welfare in Britain and Scandinavia*, C. Ungerson (ed.), 8–33. Hemel Hempstead, England: Harvester Wheatsheaf.

Ussher, J. 1991. *Women's madness: misogyny or mental illness?* Hemel Hempstead, England: Harvester Wheatsheaf.

Violence Against Children Study Group (eds) 1990. *Taking child abuse seriously: contemporary issues in child protection theory and practice*. London: Unwin Hyman.

Walker, M. A. 1988. The court disposal of young males, by race in London in 1983. *British Journal of Criminology* **28**, 441–51.

Waller, B. & M. Lindsay 1990. The abuse of power. *Community Care* (21 June), 20–2.

Walmsley, J. 1993. "Talking to top people": some issues relating to citizenship of people with learning difficulties. See Swain, Finkelstein, French, Oliver (1993), 257–66.

Walters, M. 1990. A feminist perspective in family therapy. See Perelberg & Miller (1990), 13–33.

Waterhouse, L., J. Carnie, R. Dobash 1993. The abuser under the microscope. *Community Care* (24 June), 24.

Wattam, C. 1992. *Making a case in child protection*. Harlow, England: Longman.

Watzlawick, P., J. Weakland, R. Fisch 1974. *Change: principles of problem formation and problem resolution*. New York: Norton.

Weeks, J. 1985. *Sexuality and its discontents: meanings, myths and modern sexualities*. London: Routledge & Kegan Paul.

— 1989. *Sex, politics and society: the regulation of sexuality since 1800*, 2nd edn. Harlow, England: Longman.

Westcott, H. 1994. In shot. (Inside supplement) *Community Care* (30 June), 7.

White, M. & D. Epston 1990. *Narrative means to therapeutic ends*. New York: Norton.

Will, D. 1989. Feminism, child sexual abuse, and the (long overdue) demise of systems mysticism. *Context* **9**, 12–15.

Williams, C. 1994. A fragile protection. *Community Care* (27 October), 22–3.

Williams, F. 1989. *Social policy: a critical introduction*. Cambridge: Polity.

— 1992a. "The family": changes, challenges and contradictions. See Carter, Jeffs, Smith (1992), 14–25.

— 1992b. Women with learning difficulties are women too. See Langan & Day (1992), 149–68.

Williams, P. 1993. Mind over matter: testicular cancer and men. *Working with Men* **3**, 6–8.

Wilson, M. 1993. *Crossing the boundary: black women survive incest*. London: Virago Press.

Working with Men 1993. Peer education and young men. *Working with Men* **2**, 10–11.

Wyre, R. & A. Swift 1987. *Women, men and rape*. Oxford, England: Perry Publishers.

Index

INDEX

244